To students, teachers, and lovers of Shakespeare

[THE SOURCEBOOKS SHAKESPEARE]

Othello

ADVISORY EDITORS
DAVID BEVINGTON, BARBARA GAINES, AND PETER HOLLAND

SERIES EDITORS
MARIE MACAISA AND DOMINIQUE RACCAH

William Shakespeare

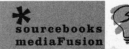

An Imprint of Sourcebooks Inc.®
Naperville, Illinois

Published by Sourcebooks, Inc.
P.O. Box 4410, Naperville, Illinois 60567-4410
(630) 961-3900
Fax: (630) 961-2168
www.sourcebooks.com

Library of Congress Cataloging-in-Publication Data

Shakespeare, William, 1564-1616.
  Othello / William Shakespeare ; Marie Macaisa, editor.
      p. cm.
  ISBN 1-4022-0645-3 -- ISBN 1-4022-0102-8 1. Othello (Fictitious character)--Drama. 2. Interracial marriage--Drama. 3. Venice (Italy)--Drama. 4. Jealousy--Drama. 5. Muslims--Drama. I. Macaisa, Marie. II. Title.

PR2829.A2M33 2005
822.3'3--dc22

                                    2005023285

Printed and bound in the United States of America.
              LB 10 9 8 7 6 5 4 3 2 1

Contents

On the CD

The audio selections bring Shakespeare's words to life, showing you different ways in which speeches have been interpreted by some of the greatest
Shakespeareans of all time.

1. What is the reason for this terrible summons? 1.1.84–1.1.125
   Peter Yapp as Brabantio, John McAndrew as Roderigo,
   Anton Lesser as Iago

2. Most potent, grave, and reverend signiors 1.3.86–1.3.104
   Paul Robeson as Othello

3. Most potent, grave, and reverend signiors 1.3.86–1.3.104
   John Kani as Othello

4. (BONUS) Most potent, grave, and reverend signoirs
   F. Scott Fitzgerald (ca. 1940)

5. Her father loved me, oft invited me 1.3.142–1.3.185
   Hugh Quarshie as Othello

6. Her father loved me, oft invited me 1.3.142–1.3.185
   John Kani as Othello

7. (BONUS) Her father loved me, oft invited me
   Edwin Booth as Othello (1890)

8. Thus do I ever make my fool my purse 1.3.387–1.3.408
   Anton Lesser as Iago

9. Thus do I ever make my fool my purse 1.3.387–1.3.408
   Jose Ferrer as Iago

10. O my fair warrior! 2.1.190–2.1.225
    Hugh Quarshie as Othello, Emma Fielding as Desdemona

11. O my fair warrior! 2.1.190–2.1.225
    Paul Robeson as Othello, Uta Hagen as Desdemona

12. Good name in man and woman, dear my lord 3.3.176–3.3.216
    Hugh Quarshie as Othello, Anton Lesser as Iago

13. Good name in man and woman, dear my lord 3.3.176–3.3.216
    Paul Robeson as Othello, Jose Ferrer as Iago

14. I am glad I have found this napkin 3.3.324–3.3.367
    Patience Tomlinson as Emilia, Anton Lesser as Iago

15. I am glad I have found this napkin 3.3.324–3.3.367
    Dorothy Gould as Emilia, Richard Haddon Haines as Iago
16. Lie with her? 4.1.38–4.1.54
    Hugh Quarshie as Othello, Anton Lesser as Iago
17. Lie with her? 4.1.38–4.1.54
    Paul Robeson as Othello, Jose Ferrer as Iago
18. Now, if this suit lay in Bianca's power 4.1.121–4.1.168
    Anton Lesser as Iago, Roger May as Cassio, Hugh Quarshie as Othello,
    Allison Pettit as Bianca
19. My mother had a maid called Barbary 4.3.28–4.3.60
    Emma Fielding as Desdemona, Patience Tomlinson as Emilia
20. Dost thou in conscience think—tell me, Emilia 4.3.64–4.3.110
    Uta Hagen as Desdemona, Edith King as Emilia
21. Dost thou in conscience think—tell me, Emilia 4.3.64–4.3.110
    Joanna Weinberg as Desdemona, Dorothy Gould as Emilia
22. It is the cause 5.2.1–5.2.22
    Paul Scofield as Othello
23. It is the cause 5.2.1–5.2.22
    Hugh Quarshie as Othello
24. Thou art rash as fire, to say that she was false 5.2.159–5.2.197
    Patience Tomlinson as Emilia, Hugh Quarshie as Othello
25. Thou art rash as fire, to say that she was false 5.2.160–5.2.196
    Dorothy Gould as Emilia, John Kani as Othello
26. Soft you, a word or two before you go 5.2.387–5.2.409
    Paul Robeson as Othello
27. Soft you, a word or two before you go 5.2.387–5.2.409
    John Kani as Othello
28. Speaking Shakespeare
    Andrew Wade with Bill McCallum

Note from the Series Editors

For many of us, our first and only encounter with Shakespeare was in school. We may recall that experience as a struggle, working through dense texts, filled with unfamiliar words. However, those of us who were fortunate enough to have seen a play performed may have altogether different memories. It may be of an interesting scene or an unusual character, but it is most likely a speech. Often, just hearing part of one instantly transports us to that time and place. "Friends, Romans, countrymen, lend me your ears," "But, soft! What light through yonder window breaks?," "To sleep, perchance to dream," "Tomorrow, and tomorrow, and tomorrow."

The Sourcebooks Shakespeare series is our attempt to use the power of performance to help you experience the play. On these pages, you will see photographs from various productions, on film and on stage, historical and contemporary, known worldwide or in your community. You may even learn of some popular actors' surprising Shakespearean performances. You will see set drawings, costume designs, and scene edits, all reproduced from original notes. Finally, on the enclosed audio CD, you will hear scenes from the play as performed by some of the most accomplished Shakespeareans of our times. Often, we include multiple interpretations of the same scene, showing you the remarkable richness of the text. Hear the great Paul Robeson in a 1944 recording reciting Othello's speech to the Senate. Compare that to a private recording made by Edwin Booth in 1890. Listen to a modern version made in 2000. The performers are using the same words but creating different Othellos.

As you read the text of the play, you can consult explanatory notes for definitions of unfamiliar words and phrases or words whose meanings have changed. These notes appear on the left pages, next to the text of the play. The audio, photographs, and other production artifacts augment the notes, and they too are indexed to the appropriate lines. You can use the pictures to see how others have staged a particular scene and get ideas on costumes, scenery, and blocking. As for the audio, each track represents a particular interpretation of a scene. Sometimes, a passage that's difficult to comprehend opens up when you hear it out loud. Furthermore, when you hear more than one version, you gain a keener understanding of the characters and the larger themes. Was Emilia a victim of domestic violence? Was Mercutio in love with Romeo? Was Hamlet depressed or suicidal? The actors made their choices and so can you. You may even come up with your own interpretation.

The text of the play, the definitions, the production notes, the audio—all of these go together, and they are here for your enjoyment. The audio, being excerpts of performances, is meant to entertain. When you see a passage with an associated clip, you can read along as you hear the actors perform the scenes for you. Or, you can sit back, close your eyes, and listen, and then go back and reread the text with a new perspective. Finally, since the text is actually a script, you may find yourself reciting the lines out loud and doing your own performance!

You will undoubtedly notice that some of the audio does not exactly match the text. Also, there are photographs of and references to scenes that aren't in your edition. There are many reasons for this, but foremost among them is the fact that Shakespeare scholarship continues to move forward and the prescribed ways of dealing with and interpreting text are always changing. Thus a play that was edited and published in 1944 will be different from one published in 2005. It may also surprise you to know that there frequently isn't one definitive early edition of each play. *Othello*, for example, appeared in four editions before 1642. The first quarto, published in 1622, was believed to have been a scribal transcript of his full, working draft of the play—his "foul papers." The first quarto, published in 1623, was thought to have been printed from a scribal transcript of his "fair copy" of the play. Finally, artists have their own interpretation of the play and they too cut and change lines and scenes according to their vision. Bianca's role was cut from the play in the eighteenth and nineteenth centuries, and the "willow scene," once thought of simply as an opportunity for a pathetic song from Desdemona, is now played to bring out the friendship between Desdemona and Emilia.

The ways in which *Othello* has been presented have varied considerably through the years. We've included essays in the book to give you glimpses into the range of the productions, showing you how other artists have approached the play and providing examples of just what changes were made and how. Janet Suzman's essay on her seminal production in 1987 in South Africa during apartheid is a compelling artistic and political state-ment. Lois Potter, in her essay, "In Production," steps back to provide an overview of how the play has been performed through the years, discussing its early history when mostly white actors played Othello to Paul Robeson's breakthrough portrayal to more recent productions: Raul Julia in 1979, Ben Kingsley in 1985, and Patrick Stewart in the so-called "photo-negative" version in 1997. Douglas Lanier's "It is the Green-eyed Monster" presents an intriguing look at how the play has been appropriated, twisted, and adopted by popular culture. He explores three key motifs in the play: Black self-representation, Black-White relations, and Relationships and Jealousy. Finally, for the actor in you (or for those of you who want to look behind the curtain), we have two essays that you may find intriguing. Andrew Wade, voice coach of the Royal Shakespeare Company for thirteen years, shares his point of view on how to understand the text and speak it; you will also hear him working with actors on the audio CD so that you too can learn the art of speaking Shakespeare. "The Cast Speaks" is actually from an interview we conducted: we talked to each member of a cast performing *Othello* (in this case, Actors From The London Stage) and asked about their characters and relationships. We found it fascinating to hear what they had to say on various topics: whether Emilia was abused, why Desdemona is not racist, Othello's willingness to be manipulated by Iago. The characters come to life in a way that's different from reading the book or watching a performance.

One last note: we are frequently asked why we didn't include the whole play, either in audio or video. While we enjoy the plays and are avid theatergoers, we are trying to do something more with the audio (and the production notes and essays) than just presenting them to you. In fact, our goal is to provide you tools that will enable you to explore the play on your own, from many different directions. Our hope is that the different pieces of audio, the voices of the actors, old production photos and notes, all these will engage you and illuminate the play in various ways so that you can construct your own understanding and create your own production, as it were.

Though the productions we have referenced and the audio clips we have included are but a miniscule sample of the play's history, we hope they encourage you to further delve into the works of Shakespeare. New editions of the play come out yearly, movie adaptations are regularly being produced, there are hundreds of theater groups in the U.S. alone, and performances could be going on right in your backyard. We echo the words of noted writer and poet Robert Graves, who said, "The remarkable thing about Shakespeare is that he is really very good—in spite of all the people who say he is very good."

We welcome you now to The Sourcebooks Shakespeare edition of *Othello*.

Dominique Raccah and Marie Macaisa
Series Editors

In Production:

Lois Potter

The stage history of *Othello* is full of stories of audiences reacting in a way that we now associate only with the final moments of a football game: not only were they left in tears, they are said to have shouted warnings to the characters, or shot the hero, or attacked the villain. They saw the play in terms of hero, heroine, and villain, not of black man, white woman, and white villain. This is one respect in which it has changed in the last fifty years.

In the seventeenth and eighteenth centuries, great acting was about the expression of great emotions. Othello's role was dominated by love and jealousy (a complex emotion made up of fear and hatred), and thus allowed the actor to express more emotions than almost any other part in the theatrical repertoire. The play depended on Othello for its success, while Desdemona's role was never considered a major one. Iago seems not to have become a major character until the nineteenth century.

POETIC TO POIGNANT — OTHELLO IN THE 19TH CENTURY

The greatest Othello of the Romantic period, Edmund Kean (1787–1833), played both Othello and Iago but disliked playing the latter—apparently, because he did not want to be identified with a totally loathsome character. When Kean played his (heavily cut) Othello, the audience experienced the role as a series of infinitely melancholy events that he made them share with him. His greatest moment was the "now forever farewell" speech, in which his voice gave a sense of infinite loneliness. The focus was on the tragedy of this long-suffering man, who was to lose the source of all his happiness through the vilest treachery. Careful cutting of the text meant that the audience did not see him strike Desdemona or fall into a fit, nor did they hear any obscenities, either from him or from Iago. The play's effect was mainly poetic.

The greatest American nineteenth-century actor, Edwin Booth (1833–93), toured the country many times as both Othello and Iago, also playing both parts in England and on the European continent. Booth, who insisted in a letter that "my idea of Othello is not animal but poetic," was frequently contrasted with the Italian actor Salvini, who was applauded for throwing Iago to the floor and carrying a struggling Desdemona to her deathbed. Booth embraced Desdemona only "with delicacy" and promised the English actress Ellen Terry that he would always keep his robe in his hand when he touched her, so as to avoid marking her with his makeup. His Othello was light-skinned. Kean is supposed to have originated the "tawny" makeup, but the evidence is inconclusive; he may have adopted it because black makeup made his facial expression, an important part of his performance, hard to see in the large, candle-lit theaters. In Booth's case, given the racially charged situation in the United States, it was probably important to look like someone from the exotic East rather than from an American plantation. (Booth's brother, John Wilkes Booth, also an actor, is most famous as the assassin of Abraham Lincoln.)

However, a black American actor, of whom Booth probably never heard, had also played the part in the nineteenth century and toured perhaps even

Edmund Kean, Ira Aldridge, Tommaso Salvini

more widely. Ira Aldridge (1807–1867) seems never to have played Othello in the United States, although companies of black actors did exist in some of the northern states. Unable to achieve major roles at major theaters in England, he was much more successful on tour; he won honors and distinctions in Germany, eastern Europe, Scandinavia, and especially Russia, where liberal intellectuals, deeply involved in the contemporary debate over emancipating the serfs and aware of the abolition debate in the United States, found his performances profoundly moving. Aldridge played a still more heavily cut text than Kean's, since he gave most of his performances with a cast of local actors performing in their own language and relying on visual cues from him to tell them when to speak. It is evident that much of the enthusiasm that audiences felt for him came precisely from the fact that they heard what he said as the expression of his own feelings rather than Othello's. He is said to have thought of returning to the United States at the end of the Civil War, but died on tour in Poland before he could carry out his plan. His daughter, however, was to meet the next great black actor, Paul Robeson, when he was preparing to play Othello in 1930, and to help him with the work on his diction and blank verse rhythms that he felt was needed before he could confront an English audience.

CONFRONTING RACE

Robeson was already a famous singer, film actor, and musical comedy performer (in the English production of *Showboat*) when he first took on the role; he played it in England because it was still considered too risky for a black man to play it in the United States. The young Peggy Ashcroft, who was his Desdemona, received hate mail, something that had not happened to white actresses who played opposite Aldridge. The production was poor, as was the Iago, but Ashcroft went on to have a great career, while American directors almost immediately began trying to find a way to have Robeson play Othello in his own country.

It was only with the coming of World War II, the integration of the U. S. Army, and a more internationalist attitude, that it finally became possible to depict a black performer in a role where he would kiss and later kill a white woman. The two actors who played opposite Robeson, José Ferrer as Iago and Uta Hagen as Desdemona, went on themselves to be famous (although one effect of the production was the breakup of their marriage). The production started in two small theaters in university towns, but in the following year moved to Broadway and then to a national tour, refusing to play except to integrated audiences. Given that there was often a gasp when Robeson's Othello first kissed Uta Hagen's Desdemona, there was no way that Robeson could play the hero as anything other than a noble, gentle, and rather distant figure. But his personal charisma and beautiful voice, along with the same sense of identification with the role that had struck Aldridge's audiences, made the performance memorable.

Portrait of Paul Robeson as Othello, Carl Van Vechten Estate

To focus exclusively on race in a discussion of this play's history is, in many ways, unfair to the many fine white actors who have played Othello, not to mention the many fine Iagos. Some of these can be seen on video: Lawrence Olivier's powerful Othello (directed by John Dexter, adapted for video by Stuart Burge) plays opposite a deliberately pallid, scaled-down Iago from Frank Finlay; Anthony Hopkins, in the widely-distributed BBC Shakespeare series (directed by Jonathan Miller), is brought down by a small, giggling psychopath (Bob Hoskins). But there is no doubt that Robeson, like Aldridge before him, made Othello the center of the play, at a time when Iago was beginning to steal it from him. Audiences were finding Othello's emotionalism embarrassing. More encouragingly, perhaps, they were no longer prepared to believe that a man who murdered his wife on suspicion alone deserved to be seen as a tragic figure rather than a criminal. When a black actor played the part, it became easier to see him as a victim of prejudice (from Brabantio, Roderigo, and Iago) and cultural misunderstanding (from and towards Desdemona). The same effect could have been achieved, of course, by a white actor made up to look black, but this kind of impersonation, like the playing of Shylock by non-Jewish actors, began to seem insulting in the 1960s. First in the United States, then in the rest of the English-speaking world, it became more or less understood that no white actor should play Othello. The actor could be Puerto Rican, like Raul Julia (1940–1992), who first played it in Central Park in 1979, or could have an Indian father, like Ben Kingsley at Stratford, England, in 1985–1986, even if he did not look particularly different from the rest of the cast.

Janet Suzman's 1990 production in Johannesburg, South Africa, restored the shock effect to the play by emphasizing the background of apartheid and overtly expressed racism that was still part of people's lives. The Iago (Richard Haddon Haines) was modeled on a white supremacist leader and

Joanna Weinberg as Desdemona and John Kani as Othello in The Market Theater production, directed by Janet Suzman, 1987
Photo by Ruphin Coudyzer

his vicious performance, which involved threatening his wife with a knife, spitting, and mimicking Othello's supposedly monkey-like behavior, was intensified by the fact that he towered over the small, frail-looking African John Kani. There was really no hope for this hero from the beginning, in spite of the bravely honest Desdemona (Joanna Weinberg). His bewildered wretchedness at the end was almost unbearable, as was the recognition of Emilia (Dorothy Gould) that the tragedy was her fault. The racist background, in which Emilia shared, also made more poignant her choice to tell Othello the truth instead of protecting Iago.

In 1997, Patrick Stewart, a white actor whose success on television guaranteed him an audience for any theatrical role he chose, found a way to play Othello: directed by Jude Kelly, he starred in a "photo-negative" production where the rest of the cast was black (apart from the Cypriots, who were mainly mixed race or Hispanic). No lines were changed to accommodate this reversal, a fact that bothered some spectators but not others. The production emphasized the age difference between Othello and Desdemona (a charming,

Franchelle Stewart Dorn as Emilia, Ron Canada as Iago, Patrice Johnson as Desdemona, and Patrick Stewart as Othello in The Shakespeare Theatre's 1997-1998 production directed by Jude Kelly
Photo by Carol Rosegg

Othello on Stage: A Personal Note

Even though many Othellos have been famous before they ever played the part, and thus walked on stage to an audience that was already expecting something great, the play is so powerful that it can make an effect without such advantages. Some of the productions that have most moved me include an outdoor one in California, where the audience, mostly unfamiliar with the play, could hardly believe that anyone could be so evil as Iago; there were gasps and nervous laughs throughout, and absolute horror at the end. After a production by the students in the Professional Theatre Training Program at the University of Delaware, the colleagues and students I talked to wished they had not seen the tragedy at all, because it left them feeling so wretched, yet they agreed that it had been a beautiful experience. With the ethereal beauty of Desdemona's song lingering in my head, I remembered her words, as quoted by Othello in Act 1: the effect of his story, he says, was such that "She wished she had not heard it." At the same time, he goes on, she also said that "she wished/ That heaven had made her such a man."

and very young, Patrice Johnson) more than their racial difference. Stewart's mysterious, dreamy Othello, with a tragic past from which he hoped Desdemona would rescue him, was totally, even comically, besotted with her. Both female directors emphasized the brutality of Iago toward Emilia, which was so public as to make one wonder how the other characters could continue to tolerate and trust him. The answer, in each case, seemed to lie in the social setting. What apartheid was for Suzman, the military environment was for Kelly. Her Iago, Ron Canada, was a fat, lazy sergeant type, never happier than when writing things down in his notebook and barking out orders. The director's vision of the play contrasted the warmth of Cyprus (Venus' island) with the cold and rain of Venice, as well as emphasizing the oppression of the Cypriots by the militaristic Venetians. Iago was their representative, just as, in Suzman's production, he represented the full hideousness of apartheid.

FROM RACE TO SEX

A less heavily cut text made it possible to bring out a greater complexity in all the characters, not merely the hero. Desdemona, seen in the nineteenth century mainly as a timid and rather boring vision of sexless purity, benefited from a greater freedom to express her sexuality in the fact that she "did love the Moor to live with him". Restoring more of the text, so that the audience heard Iago's obscene language and saw the full extent of Othello's brutality toward her, also brought out, by contrast, her goodness and courage. For instance, Trevor Nunn's Royal Shakespeare Theatre Company production of 1989 depicted a vital, playful Desdemona (Imogen Stubbs) who could never have imagined herself dying at the hands of her husband (the opera singer Willard White). This production, like many other recent ones, also developed the relationship between Desdemona and Emilia (Zoe Wanamaker). The "willow scene," once thought of simply as an opportunity for a pathetic song from Desdemona, is now played to bring out the friendship between two women, originally separated by class, or difference in age, or by Emilia's feelings of guilt over an affair with Othello in her past, or by her revulsion at the mixed marriage or envy of its happiness. Almost too late, the two women finally achieve an understanding in their mutual unhappiness, an understanding that finally leads to Emilia's courageous and suicidal defiance of her husband. Even Bianca (whose role was cut from the play in the eighteenth and nineteenth centuries) has been reevaluated, seen not as a tart but a spirited woman who understands Cassio better than the great lady whom he idealizes. And of course the restoration of Bianca to the play affects the characterization of Cassio, no longer just an innocent victim of Iago but an ambitious young officer who has trouble fitting his sexual appetite into his career plans. Trevor Nunn's late nineteenth-century setting lent itself to a psychologically subtle reading of all the characters, particularly Ian McKellen's brilliant study of Iago's repressed sexuality.

FROM RACE TO RELIGION?

Othello was once a play about a passionate lover who is deceived into murdering the woman he loves. It is now a play about a black man who marries, and later murders, a white woman. The explosiveness of this subject matter is the result of history, which has intersected with the play to an alarming extent. Until recently, there was a tendency to assume that any production that made Othello a brown north African Moor instead of a black subequatorial African was being racist in ignoring the importance of the specific type of racial conflict that exists in North America. Given the extent of religious conflict in the twenty-first century and the increasing visibility of the Arab world, I should guess that in future productions the balance may tip in the other direction and religion may play as great a role in the tragedy as race.

Janet Suzman

The year is 1987, the place Johannesburg. In only three years time Nelson Mandela will walk out of prison after twenty-seven years, but we weren't to know that at the time; to us it looked as if apartheid would continue to wreak its havoc until the crack of doom. The governing regime appeared unassailable, in spite of worldwide boycotts.

Us? We were the people who were involved in founding The Market Theatre in 1976—formerly a Victorian meat market and then transformed into a magical quasi-Globe in downtown Johannesburg, where apartheid was entirely banished and its absurdities and cruelties roundly mocked from the stage. When you live in a free country you take the theater for granted, but you can't imagine how exciting going to the theater can be in a police state—how exhilarating it is to mingle for a few talkative hours with like-minded people, to feel deliciously subversive watching plays that satirize the life outside—rule-bound and cruelly policed. Freedom of thought, richness of language, uncensored celebration of the human comedy—these become precious if you're not allowed them in the outside world. (That's not to say The Market didn't frequently have to answer to a Censorship Board when some individual complained that he was being corrupted and depraved.)

Memories are short and history moves on. I am so happy that apartheid is over, but perhaps a quick reminder to those who are too young to remember: the system of apartheid was based on separating the black and white races—and every shade in between—by law; laws made specifically by whites for the protection of the white minority. It was a system of discrimination based solely on a racist agenda. Acts of Parliament were passed to make bigotry legal. Can you imagine? It was against this context that we sought to mount a production of *Othello*.

PROTEST PLAY

In *Othello* the idea of "erring from nature" is raised several times whenever the marriage of Desdemona and Othello is mentioned. The doctrinaire Afrikaner Calvinist view was that Nature itself abhors miscegenation, and that since, in the natural world, like only propagates with like, the same natural embargo must prevail with human beings. In other words, they chose to see the human race as being made up of different species. This is the same viciously skewed argument that informed Nazi policies in the last World War—that certain peoples were "sub-human" and therefore had to be exterminated. The Afrikaner Nationalist view was that they must merely be separated at every level of social intercourse.

> *OTHELLO*
> And yet, how nature erring from itself,—
>
> *IAGO*
> Ay, there's the point. As, to be bold with you—
> Not to affect many proposèd matches
> Of her own clime, complexion, and degree,
> Whereto we see in all things nature tends—
> Foh! One may smell in such a will most rank,
> Foul disproportion, thoughts unnatural.
>
> 3.3.257–263

Othello, tussling with the alien notion that his beloved wife might be betraying him, fears that Desdemona's nature—loyal, honest, transparent—might have become its own opposite—disloyal, dishonest, opaque—i.e., erring from itself. Read again Iago's reply to this agonized lament, and you will read, in essence, a manifesto expressing the essential elements of Grand Apartheid. (Grand was applied to the overall concept of this vicious policy, Petty to the daily enforcement of its rules). Basically, Iago says this: "If you don't marry someone of your own kind—a rule which all of the natural world obeys—it is a willful, disgusting aberration that goes against the natural order."

Now perhaps you will begin to understand why I so much wanted to direct this great play in the South African context of the time. Shakespeare, entirely unaware of apartheid, has nevertheless imagined the sort of mindset that brought it into being. Someone once said that Shakespeare's plays, "like iron filings to a magnet, seem to attract whatever crisis is in the air." Again and again a play of his will hit a political/historical nail right on the head. To a South African eye, Iago seemed unmistakeably to represent the white enforcers intent on trashing the transgressing marriage of a black man and a white woman. Desdemona had not affected a match "of her own clime, complexion, and degree" and just deserts would surely follow, the subtext being that if they didn't he'd make them. The metaphor of the play, as we read it, was sound. (Although, strictly speaking, there is no subtext in Shakespeare: the clues to character and motivation being perfectly visible to the naked eye if you search thoroughly. The great scholar and teacher John Barton says that in Shakespeare, text *is* character.)

Because of the prevailing international cultural boycott, it was necessary to obtain permission from the Cultural Desk of the African National Congress in-exile to mount this play, which we did, on the grounds that we saw *Othello* as a protest play. Since Shakespeare has always been used subversively in societies where freedom of expression was restricted, we succeeded in getting the requisite nod to proceed.

CHARACTERS IN A RACIST SOCIETY
Armchair Liberal

Once you start to see this play through the prism of racist South Africa, it is astonishing how the characters emerge as a familiar cross-section of society. Brabantio is the all-too familiar armchair liberal, flaunting his openminded credentials by inviting the black general to dinner, but heaven forbid he should marry his daughter. His insulting language when he finds out that his child has gone betrays the prejudice sitting just beneath the skin:

> corrupted: 1.3.68
> for nature so preposterously to err: 1.3.70
> foul thief: 1.2.75
> Damned as thou art: 1.2.76
> sooty bosom: 1.2.83
> such a thing as thou, to fear not to delight: 1.2.84
> foul charms: 1.2.86
> an abuser of the world, a practiser of arts inhibited: 1.2.91–92

and then this outburst:

> ... and she, in spite of nature,
> Of years, of country, credit, every thing,
> To fall in love with what she feared to look on!
> It is a judgment maimed and most imperfect
> That will confess perfection so could err
> Against all rules of nature and must be driven
> To find out practices of cunning hell...

1.3.107–113

So you see, Iago's "thoughts unnatural" have found a higher advocacy.

Bigots

Iago and Roderigo, from the start, are the out-and-out bigots. It is absolutely shocking to hear Roderigo call Othello "the thick lips" (1.1.66). Iago uses "gross" twice in describing Othello, and begins his nasty game of invoking animals to denigrate him:

> you'll have your daughter covered with a
> Barbary horse; you'll have your nephews neigh to you;

1.1.118–119

He calls Othello "an old black ram" and most famously conjures this image:

> ...your daughter and the Moor are now
> making the beast with two backs

1.1.122–123

Donkeys, goats, and monkeys enter his malicious menagerie; he is foully insulting. South Africa once abounded with those openly racist types, their brutality protected by the prevailing laws sanctioning discrimination. They simply conduct themselves more covertly now, as they do in most countries where racist behavior is not legal. Leopards don't change their spots.

Perpetrator

If you search for the reason why Iago trashes the marriage, you will search in vain for an overridingly watertight one. He offers up several for your consideration: he's jealous of Cassio's advancement; he's suspicious that the Moor has had a fling with his wife Emilia; he despises Othello because he's black, or because he's credulous; he's disgusted with Desdemona for breaking the rules of white Venice. Put all these into the stewing-pot of Iago's character and they'll bubble away merrily, but do they measure up to the snarling rapaciousness of Iago's revenge? I think not.

There are two more revealing insights into his singular mind: of Cassio he says: "He hath a daily beauty in his life / Which makes me ugly." Think about what that tells us about Iago's character. And this is the final word from Iago in the play:

> Demand me nothing. What you know, you know.
> From this time forth, I never will speak word.
>
> 5.2.347–348

This is a flat refusal to explain or excuse himself. Now look at the beginning of the play and you might say that he places his being beyond rational explanation: "I am not what I am" (1.1.66). In the Bible, Jehova is described by the mighty enigma of "I am what I am"—what diametric opposite is Shakespeare suggesting here for his creation of Iago? The perpetrators of apartheid likewise never seemed bothered to excuse that abominable era in history. These resonant quotes should keep you discussing the mysteries of human behavior for hours. Othello calls Iago a demi-devil; is evil explicable, even to itself?

Richard Haddon Haines as Iago
Photo by Ruphin Coudyzer

CHARACTERS IN THE PLAY

Iago

The actor who played Iago was a friendly bear of a man with a huge talent, Richard Haddon Haines, and I can hardly bear to tell you that he died of a brain tumor barely two years after this production, having just played a fine King Lear for the Royal Shakespeare Company. A tragic waste. Richard knew well the threat of uniformed power in South Africa, and how its public face took pains to appear reliable. Othello sees Iago as a wholly trustworthy officer, he is described as "honest" about eighteen times in the play. His bedside manner, so to speak, is impeccable. (Shakespeare is fascinated, in all of his plays, with the idea of appearance and reality.) Only in his soliloquies, when he shares his wickedness with the audience, does gleeful malevolence seep through the armor of this sober ensign. Iago can be funny. Evil can be alluring, dangerous stuff.

Cassio

Cassio's sheer decency shows itself at every point; even more wonder that Othello's judgment goes so badly awry in condemning him solely on the evidence of Iago's plausible storytelling. (What an actor! No, what a dissembler— actors always try to be truthful; liars try to cover it up, and the trick is to sail as close to the truth as possible. Iago is a consummate con man.) Desdemona and Cassio are obviously out of the same social drawer, and feel easy with each other. Cassio is secretly and entirely honorably in love with Desdemona, rather like a schoolboy crush. Perceiving their fondness and friendliness, which plays right into his hands, Iago skews an innocent friendship into something it isn't. The slightest shift of viewpoint and comfortable familiarity becomes threatening intimacy. Jealousy, with its glaring green eyes, is spawned. It is significant that at the end, wise Lodovico acknowledges Cassio's qualities by appointing him ruler of Cyprus in Othello's place. (5.2.381)

Emilia

Emilia is often seen as the first feminist in literature. She seems to view her life with a certain clear-eyed reality, though she cannot do much about it. I always saw her as an abused wife; I can't imagine Iago not hurting her when he feels like it. Her speech to Desdemona in 4.3.89–108 bears that out. She is too obedient to be entirely sure of herself. She brings her husband the stolen handker-

chief as he has asked, but fear informs the giving. Her journey in the play hur-
tles towards a fatal self-awareness by the end. She dies telling the truth, she
dies for telling the truth, and she knows what she is doing, which to me denotes
a figure growing in tragic stature. Neither Desdemona nor Othello reach self-
knowledge with the same fierce flame which, once lit, burns in her. I don't
want to overly push the point, but South Africa had its full share of those brave
enough to defy authority and be punished for fighting for a fairer world. In a
great drama, the courage to stand up and shout out is given words.

Desdemona

Desdemona too has enormous courage. She defies her father, she presents a
fine case to the Senate to accompany her husband to war-torn Cyprus, she
outrides a storm at sea. We watch her bearing the ensuing humiliations as the
drama unfolds with an unswerving steadiness of heart, as if waiting patiently

Dorothy Gould as Emilia and Joanna Weinberg as Desdemona
Photo by Ruphin Coudyzer

for yet another storm to pass. It hardly needs saying that she has not an ounce of her father's prejudice in her. "I saw Othello's visage in his mind" (1.3.269) has to be the ultimate reply to all those fools who cannot see beyond the color of a person's skin. Look, too, at the exquisite couplet that ends Act 4; only a supremely decent human being could find such generosity after being so hellishly used. Finally, with her dying breath she blames herself and excuses her husband. She finds, to my mind, an exquisite, almost oriental, fatalism. She holds herself ready to accept whatever comes her way and find good in it since it stems from the man she loves. But she can fight too, as she does for her life at the end—too late. It makes for good drama to wish so fervently that she'd fought before it was too late.

Othello

The sight of white actors blacking up is always faintly ludicrous to my eyes. Even the great Laurence Olivier I could not wholly believe in, though much seduced by his glamorous gleam and those unfurling pink palms. Olivier was a sophisticate, a worldly man, which Othello is not; by reputation a master on the battlefield, the strategies of the bedchamber quite defeat him. John Kani, on the other hand, was the real thing—a black African giving the impression of being at home in white society but most emphatically not of it. He speaks a magnificently vivid, colloquial English, but he dreams in Xhosa, his mother tongue. During those apartheid years, he surely despised the society that ruled his life, but he worked within its margins with authority and grace, biding his time. He kept his home life, his tribal affiliations—all those things nearest to his heart—entirely out of sight, yet, like the superb professional he is, worked hard on his public commitments.

I think John was the first black Othello who was a true exotic, the "wheeling stranger of here and everywhere," the man whose previous life is a mystery. More importantly, unlike previous great Othellos of American extraction, whose native tongue was English, John sounded foreign. In blank verse, the vowels need to be generous; they are like conduits that rush the feelings onwards eventually to pour into the open sea of meaning. The consonants are the sluice gates, controlling the flow, giving measure and smoothness to the speaking. The Xhosa accent in English tends to compress the diphthongs (beds for birds, eth for earth, stet for state, etc.) and in blank verse they need their full stretch. It took a huge effort to adjust his speaking

John Kani as Othello
Photo by Ruphin Coudyzer

habits and make the poetry live as vividly and movingly as John did. I salute him. I salute the whole cast in fact, because there were many youngsters who had never spoken blank verse before, not the least, luminous Desdemona and fiery Bianca, but after a few intense days of immersion in the structures that inform the speaking of it, they all came to inhabit the verse with great naturalness. No one need ever be in awe of Shakespeare—trust the verse and the sense will inevitably emerge. It's worth remembering that Shakespeare wrote for actors, not academics.

A FINAL WORD

I am sure that one of the legacies of this particular production of *Othello*, born in oppression, is that after John Kani it is no longer possible for a white actor to take the role without an uncomfortable feeling of usurpation. The same would go for Aaron in *Titus Andronicus*. Times have changed. I am not in the least an advocate of documentary casting—for instance, that only a Jewish actor should play Shylock and so on; however, for Othello, blackness starts with the right skin color. All other dramatic roles require a purely imaginative assumption. One other point—whereas a white actor would need to preserve a certain old-fashioned operatic distance between himself and the woman he suffers the pangs of hell for, a black actor need have no fear of leaving smudges on his Desdemona. Passion can have its moment in a play that pivots on physical enthrallment. If white people slammed out of the theater in disgust at the moments of tenderness between husband and wife, then that was more revealing of their closed minds than our unforced enactment of marital love. Likewise, if young black people from Soweto queued up in the hundreds to see this play, then that too revealed how much the tragic humiliation of a black man by a white thug spoke volumes to them in lives cursed by apartheid. Now that South Africa is bathed in the sunlight of democracy, it might be interesting to see how the shadows might fall if the situation was reversed—a white Othello holding office in a black state. Or would that be too contrived?

"It is the Green-eyed Monster":

Othello AND POP CULTURE

Douglas Lanier

Throughout much of the nineteenth and twentieth centuries *Othello* has been closely associated in the popular imagination with questions of racial identity, not with tragically misguided romantic passion. *Othello* has long been a vehicle in Anglo-American popular culture for addressing the vexed cultural status of black men in white society. Accordingly, the play has, on the one hand, perpetuated racist stereotypes and, on the other, garnered empathy for a noble black man brought low by prejudice and the demands of divided identity. Because Othello is Shakespeare's most prominent black character and yet has repeatedly been drafted into service for racist purposes, black actors and artists have often been interested in finding ways of reclaiming Othello as a figure for the dignity of black identity and culture.

BLACKFACE AND MINSTREL SHOWS

The 1840s were to see a complementary development in popular culture: the rise of the blackface minstrel Othello. Developing in the early 1800s and extending throughout the nineteenth century into the early twentieth, minstrel shows offered a mélange of musical numbers, comic banter, parodies of contemporary culture and farcical skits performed by white (and, in a few cases, black) musicians in burnt cork makeup and "plantation" dialect. Undeniably racist in their humor, such shows typically used stereotypical black characters to poke fun at social pretensions and mainstream "proper" culture, of which Shakespeare was a prime example. As the most famous blackface play in the classical theatrical repertory, Shakespeare's *Othello* was an irresistible target for minstrel lampoon. Minstrel performer T. D. Rice, the original "Jim Crow," produced a parody of *Othello* in 1844 (he billed it as a "burlesque opera" and modeled it after a British burlesque produced ten years earlier), the first of a long line of minstrel Othellos. In these parody versions of Shakespeare's play, with titles like "Desdemonum" and "Da's De Money," Othello's blackness is emphasized, imagined through the racist stereotypes of the minstrel show. In these plays Othello speaks with a thick plantation or West Indian accent, crudely pursues women or money (or both), lapses into jealousy with little motivation, and mangles the plot of Shakespeare's play by falling into slapstick brawls or minstrel songs. This version of Othello provided definitive evidence of his unrefined, uncivilizable nature, though, it should be added, these working-class burlesques often were ambivalent about being the value of conforming to standards of bourgeois "polite" behavior. From its American origins, minstrel Shakespeare was to become an international phenomenon in the nineteenth century whose popularity and effects would last well into the twentieth. Minstrelsy was thereby to become a powerful filter through which Shakespeare's Moor was perceived.

It is important to recognize that nearly all performances of the character of Othello up to the 1940s were in blackface, particularly in the United States. It was not until the 1940s, with Paul Robeson's Broadway performance, that the color barrier was definitively broken and the role was opened up to black actors.

BLACK SELF-REPRESENTATION AND RACIAL DIGNITY

Because it is the "classical" play most closely associated with the practice of blackface performance, *Othello* remains a lightning rod for issues of black self-representation on the stage and film. It is interesting, then, to note that in some popular works addressed to black audiences that the opportunity for a black man to play Othello carries symbolic resonance. In *Paradise in Harlem* (1939, Joseph Seiden), a so-called "race" film produced for predominantly African American audiences, the protagonist Lem's aspiration to play Othello is the centerpiece of his noble lifelong struggle against racism; tellingly, as the film opens he is stuck performing in a minstrel show. The film ends with a triumphal performance of the final scene of *Othello* with Lem as the Moor, the first film portrayal of Othello by a black actor. Interestingly Lem's performance of the murder of Desdemona slowly morphs into a musical number in which the black audience enthusiastically celebrates, and Othello's confession and suicide are silently excised. More recently, *True Identity* (1991, Charles Lane), written as a star vehicle for British comic Lenny

Henry, also features a struggling black actor, Miles Pope, who dreams of playing Othello. The twist is that when Miles becomes pursued by a hit man, he resorts to disguise as a white man—complete with whiteface makeup—to elude danger, in the process sending up white mannerisms and privilege, in effect reversing the racial polarity of minstrel show blackface. His performance of Othello at film's end becomes the means for him to expose the plot against him and thus to regain his true identity as a black man. In both films, these actors view Othello as a role through which they can assert racial dignity and cultural power.

BLACK-WHITE RELATIONS

Othello's close association with issues of racial identity and black-white relations also regularly surfaces in popular culture adaptations and references. This association can be played for comedy, as in "Lamont as Othello," an episode of the African American TV series *Sanford and Son* (broadcast September 14, 1973), in which irascible Fred Sanford (played by veteran black comic Redd Foxx) catches his son Lamont choking a white woman as they rehearse a scene from *Othello*. Fred's comic reaction—he thinks Lamont is really murdering her—uses *Othello* to lampoon the racist assumption that black young men are at bottom brutish, lusty louts, an assumption which Shakespeare's play has been used to exemplify. More often, however, popular adaptations of *Othello* make contemporary challenges of black identity the stuff of modern tragedy. Indeed, several recent adaptations of *Othello* have made subtle forms of racism in contemporary society their central concern. The American film *O* (2001, Tim Blake Nelson) recasts Othello as Odin, a black basketball star for a Southern prep school; the British TV film *Othello* (2002, Geoffrey Sax) depicts Othello as a black police captain who is elevated to his position as a way of quelling tensions during a racially-charged police scandal. Both films use *Othello* to demonstrate how, despite their outward success, these black professionals continue to find themselves plagued by inner doubt and subtle, rather than direct, forms of racism. This focus also found voice in journalism. Shakespeare's play was a ubiquitous touchstone in the media frenzy surrounding the 1995 trial of O. J. Simpson for the murders of Nicole Brown Simpson and Ronald Goldman, where a cross-racial marriage riven by jealousy and the precipitous fall of a black celebrity lionized by white society became the shaky foundation upon which all manner of comparisons between O. J. and Othello were erected. The comparison between the two even became the basis for the play *OJ / Othello* at the 1998 Edinburgh Fringe Festival. References to *Othello*, as well as several other Shakespeare plays, also made cameo appearances in Clarence Thomas's confirmation for the U.S. Supreme Court. It is striking that the critical issue that so exercised nineteenth-century critics, the enigma of Iago's motive for malignity, hardly registers in most pop culture, though Phil Willmott's play *Iago* (1992) and the heavy metal band Thorne's concept album *Iago* (1998) are interesting exceptions. Equally unexplored is Desdemona's plight: in most pop songs, she has become a mere type of the beautiful or long-suffering girlfriend, though a handful of writers have sought to reexamine her character from a feminist perspective, as in Paula Vogel's play *Desdemona: A Play About a Handkerchief* (in which Desdemona is gleefully, unapologetically promiscuous), Ann Marie MacDonald's play *Goodnight Desdemona (Goodmorning Juliet)*, and Louise Plummer's young adult novel *The Unlikely Romance of Kate Bjorkman*.

RELATIONSHIPS AND JEALOUSY

Certainly *Othello* has served as the touchstone for many popular tales of jealousy that do not directly engage the issue of race. Examples include the period melodrama *Les enfants du paradis* (1945, Marcel Carné), the western *Jubal* (1956, Delmer Daves), the horror film *The Flesh and Blood Show* (1974, Pete Walker), the police thriller *Internal Affairs* (1990, Michael Figgis), and the Mexican dance drama *Huapango* (2004, Ivan Lipkies). "Sergeant Iago," an episode of *Gomer Pyle,* broadcast on February 16, 1968, treats this theme less seriously, making Iago's generation of jealousy the stuff of sitcom romance rather than tragedy.

A fascinating theme closely linked with *Othello* addresses a different sort of vexed divided identity: that of the actor. *Othello* figures prominently in a series of stories on stage and screen that involve an actor playing the Moor who comes to murder or abuse women in his "real" life, compulsively prompted by the part he plays. Two of the earliest examples of this plotline can be found in Pordes-Milo's melodrama *Scirocco* and August Blom's silent short *Desdemona* (1911). In Blom's film, an actor who learns of his costar's affair with a gentleman takes his revenge upon her as he and she enact the final scene of *Othello*. (Remarkably, in Blom's film it is not the actor but the gentleman whom the audience blames.) Myriad variations were to follow, especially on film: *A Modern Othello* (1917), *Carnival* (1921, remade as a talkie in 1931), *Men are not Gods* (1937), and *Anna's Sin* (1955) all feature elements of this plotline. There are even comic versions. "Homicidal Ham," an episode of the TV series *Cheers* (broadcast October 27, 1983), turns on Diane Chambers' fears that her costar in an amateur production of *Othello*, a recently released criminal, is a homicidal maniac bent on murdering her in mid-performance. *A Double Life* (1947, George Cukor), an artful *film noir* for which Ronald Colman won an Oscar for best actor, offers an especially well-crafted variation on this theme. When he gets the part of Othello, Anthony John, a Broadway actor, finds that the Moor's suspicions and jealous rage invade his mind, fueling his anger against his ex-wife Brita, with whom he maintains a romantically ambiguous relationship, and against Pat Kroll, a seedy waitress at the Venice Café with whom he has begun an affair. When Kroll innocently tells him to "put out the light," John is compelled to murder her and later, convinced that Brita is attracted to Bill Friend, a reporter, John attempts to strangle him as well. The film is exceptionally skillful in portraying John's helpless descent into guilt, paranoia, and self-loathing, all of which converges on the film's climax, a performance of the final scene of *Othello* in which John nearly strangles Brita, confesses his guilt in character as Othello, and stabs himself in earnest onstage. In this version of *Othello*, the Moor comes to symbolize the "dark" unconscious of John's otherwise debonair demeanor, a "blackness" uncontrollably brought to the surface just by uttering Shakespeare's words.

This theme is by no means spent. Two recent films use *Othello* to explore the fluid line between acting and reality, but they develop the theme in novel ways. Roysten Abel's 2003 film *In Othello* (from his stage play) concerns an English-speaking troupe in New Delhi who, as they mount a cross-cultural production of *Othello*, find themselves riven by jealousy, professional rivalry, and ethnic tension, all of which bears striking resemblance to the details of Shakespeare's plays. Abel's film demonstrates the long cultural reach of *Othello*'s association with this metatheatrical theme. Richard Eyre's *Stage Beauty* (2004, from Jeffrey Hatcher's play) uses the final scene of *Othello* to consider the divided nature of the cross-dressed stage in the early Restoration. The film chronicles the downfall of Ned Kynaston, a man who specializes in women's parts, as he is challenged by his imitator, the actress Maria. Their rivalry turns on their competing depictions of Desdemona's

death, both of which suffer from artificiality. At the film's climax, by push-
ing the final scene of *Othello* from a stylized spectacle to a seemingly real
murder, Kynaston coaxes a realistic, Method-style performance from Maria
and so resolves the problem of woman's divided identity on the stage. The
film comedy *I Will Avenge You, Iago!*, currently in post-production, offers yet
another contemporary variation on this perennial storyline. In all these
works, race is hardly at issue; rather, all testify to the newly problematic
nature of the theater in an age of cinema, even as they celebrate—albeit per-
versely—the overwhelming power of Shakespeare's language and characters, a power akin, they suggest, to the perverse power of Iago.

OTHELLO IN MUSIC—FROM OPERA TO HIP-HOP

Many have sought to popularize Shakespeare by transposing his work into
musical forms. In this, *Othello* has been no exception, though the play has not
been as popular a subject for music than some of Shakespeare's other works,
perhaps because the sensitive racial issues in the play defy easy musical
adaptation. Though Gioachino Rossini's operatic *Otello* (1816) was popular
throughout the nineteenth century, it was eclipsed in popularity when
Guiseppe Verdi's *Otello* premiered in 1887; both have become staples of the
operatic repertoire. Verdi's version epitomizes a romantic conception of the
play, emphasizing Othello's intense, finally tragic love for Desdemona rather
than his racial victimization by Iago. Indeed, in his remarks on the opera
librettist Arriga Boito speaks of Otello and Iago as deracialized personifica-
tions of elemental passion: "...Otello is Jealousy and Iago Envy." When jazz
became a craze in mid-twentieth century America and Europe, it seemed to
offer a new vehicle for adapting Shakespeare to popular musical form, one
perhaps especially amenable to *Othello* because jazz was, at least initially,
identified as "black" music. The film *Paradise in Harlem*, which melds the
final scene of *Othello* with gospel and jazz music, illustrates the possibility of
such a hybrid, as does Duke Ellington's *Such Sweet Thunder*, a 1957 jazz
suite based on Shakespearean characters which gives Othello special promi-
nence. Tellingly enough, both adaptations were produced by black artists. A
fully-fledged jazzed-up *Othello* did finally appear in the form of the film *All
Night Long* (1962, Basil Dearden). It tells the tale of ambitious drummer
Johnny Cousin, who, on an effort to advance his career, poisons the marriage
between black band leader Aurelius Rex (clearly modeled on Ellington) and

his white wife Delia Lane, a singer. Especially deft is the Iago figure's use of an edited tape recording to incriminate Cass, the sax player with Rex's band who has been rehearsing privately with Delia. But for all the film's clever modernization and cameos by real jazz stars such as Charles Mingus, Johnny Dankworth, and Dave Brubeck, it arrived after jazz had moved from swing, a widely popular musical style, to bop and after, a coterie art. What is more, rather surprisingly *All Night Long* reveals little interest in the changing racial politics of the moment, in the jazz world or elsewhere. No one bats an eye at Rex and Delia's interracial marriage, and Cousin betrays Rex to advance his own flagging career, not because Rex is black.

By the mid-sixties, popular taste had moved in the direction of rock and roll (yet another "black" musical form), and the success of rock operas such as *Tommy* and *Jesus Christ Superstar* in the late sixties prompted the emergence of Shakespearean rock opera. *Othello* provided the basis for *Catch My Soul* (1969, lyrics and book by Jack Good, music by Ray Pohlman and Emil Dean Zoghby), a rock opera that reconceived Othello as the charismatic leader of a hippie religious commune undone by a demonic Iago. Patrick McGoohan's film version of *Catch My Soul* (1973) featured Richie Havens, the popular black folk singer, in the role of Othello, presenting him as a clearly Christ-like martyr dressed in a white robe who kills Desdemona and himself in a village church. Although the independent film is rather crudely made, its engagement with contradictions and conflicts within sixties counterculture make it a fascinating historical document. A number of other attempts have been made to recraft *Othello* in musical terms, among them the Canadian country-and-western musical *Cruel Tears* (1975), a German adaptation *Othello: Die Rock-oper* (1994, Hans von Chelius and Stefan Maro) and Mirta de la Torre Mulhare's *O.T.* (2001). Though the Reduced Shakespeare Company's *The Complete Works of Wllm Shkspr (Abridged)* (1994) wickedly lampooned the prospect of adapting *Othello* to hip-hop, the currently popular "black" musical idiom, it has not prevented that possibility from being explored: the student ensemble HWS-Rembiko presented *The Tragedy of Othella, the Hip Hop Diva of Venice Beach* at the Edinburgh Fringe Festival in 2003.

A FINAL WORD

Despite gains in the status of peoples of color in the past half-century and the extraordinary prevalence of black music in popular culture, *Othello* continues to reside in the long shadow of Anglo-American society's jaundiced attitudes toward black men, a fact amply demonstrated by the speed and ease with which Othello became a popular paradigm for discussing O. J. Simpson at the height of that *cause celebre*. As is so often the case with popular cultural appropriations of Shakespeare, *Othello*'s afterlife has been profoundly ambivalent, at once a means for perpetuating outmoded stereotypes and yet a vehicle for progressive representations of black identity and culture. But the firm association of *Othello* with questions of race has also worked to mute the play's potential in popular culture for engaging other, equally important themes, most notably questions of religious difference and marital abuse.

Dramatis Personae

DUKE OF VENICE

BRABANTIO, a senator

Other Senators

GRATIANO, brother to Brabantio

LODOVICO, kinsman to Brabantio

OTHELLO, a noble Moor in the service of the Venetian state

CASSIO, his lieutenant

IAGO, his ancient

RODERIGO, a Venetian gentleman

MONTANO, Othello's predecessor in the government of Cyprus

Clown, servant to Othello

DESDEMONA, daughter to Brabantio and wife to Othello

EMILIA, wife to Iago

BIANCA, mistress to Cassio

Sailor, Messenger, Herald, Officers, Gentlemen, Musicians, and Attendants

[Othello

Act 1

Scene: "Brabantio appears above, at a window": Set rendering of "Brabantio's House" from the 1951 staging by Orson Welles at St. James Theatre

Rare Book and Special Collections Library, University of Illinois at Urbana-Champaign

1: **tush:** interjection suggesting mild contempt

3: **as if the strings were thine:** as if the money were Iago's own

4: **'sblood:** a contraction of "God's Blood" used as an impolite curse word

10: **off-capped:** took off his cap (i.e., bowed in deference)

13: **bombast circumstance:** stuffy, inflated discourse

14: **epithets :** expressions, phrases

16: **nonsuits:** rejects a suit

16: **certes:** certainly

19: **forsooth:** In truth (here used with a suggestion of contempt)

21: **A fellow...fair wife:** editors debate this line; Cassio is unmarried in the rest of the play

24: **theoric:** theory (instead of practice)

25: **togèd:** wearing a toga or gown

25: **consuls:** senator

Act 1, Scene 1]

[Enter RODERIGO and IAGO]

RODERIGO
  Tush! Never tell me. I take it much unkindly
  That thou, Iago, who hast had my purse
  As if the strings were thine, shouldst know of this.

IAGO
  'Sblood, but you will not hear me.
  If ever I did dream of such a matter,   5
  Abhor me.

RODERIGO
  Thou told'st me thou didst hold him in thy hate.

IAGO
  Despise me if I do not. Three great ones of the city,
  In personal suit to make me his lieutenant,
  Off-capped to him, and, by the faith of man,   10
  I know my price; I am worth no worse a place.
  But he, as loving his own pride and purposes,
  Evades them, with a bombast circumstance
  Horribly stuffed with epithets of war.
  And, in conclusion,   15
  Nonsuits my mediators, for "Certes," says he,
  "I have already chose my officer."
  And what was he?
  Forsooth, a great arithmetician,
  One Michael Cassio, a Florentine,   20
  A fellow almost damned in a fair wife,
  That never set a squadron in the field,
  Nor the division of a battle knows
  More than a spinster, unless the bookish theoric,
  Wherein the togèd consuls can propose   25

30: **beleed:** placed on the lee (i.e., in a position unfavorable to the wind)

31: **counter-caster:** arithmetician (i.e., Cassio)

33: **ancient:** ensign or standard-bearer

36–38: **Preferment...to the first:** Promotions are granted by favoritism and not by seniority (the traditional way)

39: **affined:** bound to, required

46: **knee-crooking:** courtseying

49: **provender:** dry animal feed

49: **cashiered:** sold off; dismissed

51: **trimmed...duty:** maintaining the outward appearance of being dutiful

As masterly as he. Mere prattle, without practice,
Is all his soldiership. But he, sir, had the election,
And I, of whom his eyes had seen the proof
At Rhodes, at Cyprus, and on other grounds
Christian and heathen, must be beeled and calmed   30
By debitor and creditor. This counter-caster,
He, in good time, must his lieutenant be,
And I — God bless the mark! — his Moorship's ancient.

RODERIGO
By heaven, I rather would have been his hangman.

IAGO
But, there's no remedy. 'Tis the curse of service.   35
Preferment goes by letter and affection,
And not by old gradation, where each second
Stood heir to the first. Now, sir, be judge yourself,
Whether I, in any just term, am affined
To love the Moor.   40

RODERIGO
                    I would not follow him then.

IAGO
O, sir, content you.
I follow him to serve my turn upon him.
We cannot all be masters, nor all masters
Cannot be truly followed. You shall mark   45
Many a duteous and knee-crooking knave,
That, doting on his own obsequious bondage,
Wears out his time, much like his master's ass,
For nought but provender and when he's old, cashiered.
Whip me such honest knaves. Others there are   50
Who, trimmed in forms and visages of duty,
Keep yet their hearts attending on themselves,
And, throwing but shows of service on their lords,
Do well thrive by them; and when they have lined their coats,
Do themselves homage. These fellows have some soul,   55

Costume rendering for Roderigo from the 1951 staging by Orson Welles at St. James Theatre

Rare Book and Special Collections Library, University of Illinois at Urbana-Champaign

59: In following...myself: Iago is following the Moor in self-interest

61: peculiar: private

61–64: For when...extern: For when my behavior actually reflects my inner feelings

67: thicklips: a derogatory reference to Othello

77: timorous accent: fearful tone

And such a one do I profess myself. For, sir,
It is as sure as you are Roderigo,
Were I the Moor, I would not be Iago.
In following him, I follow but myself.
Heaven is my judge, not I, for love and duty,   60
But seeming so, for my peculiar end.
For when my outward action doth demonstrate
The native act and figure of my heart
In compliment extern, 'tis not long after
But I will wear my heart upon my sleeve   65
For daws to peck at. I am not what I am.

RODERIGO
What a full fortune does the thicklips owe
If he can carry't thus!

IAGO
                    Call up her father.
Rouse him, make after him, poison his delight,   70
Proclaim him in the streets. Incense her kinsmen,
And, though he in a fertile climate dwell,
Plague him with flies. Though that his joy be joy,
Yet throw such changes of vexation on't
As it may lose some colour.   75

RODERIGO
Here is her father's house; I'll call aloud.

IAGO
Do, with like timorous accent and dire yell
As when, by night and negligence, the fire
Is spied in populous cities.

RODERIGO
What, ho, Brabantio! Signior Brabantio, ho!   80

IAGO
Awake! What, ho, Brabantio! Thieves, thieves, thieves!
Look to your house, your daughter, and your bags!
Thieves! Thieves!

track 1

84–125:
Peter Yapp as Brabantio, John McAndrew as Roderigo,
Anton Lesser as Iago

89: **'zounds:** an exclamation indicating surprise or heavy stress
(abbrev. for "God's wounds")

91: **an old black ram:** i.e., Othello

92: **tupping :** fornicating with

92: **white ewe:** i.e., Desdemona

93: **snorting:** snoring

[BRABANTIO appears above, at a window]

BRABANTIO
What is the reason of this terrible summons?
What is the matter there?

RODERIGO
Signior, is all your family within?

IAGO
Are your doors locked?

BRABANTIO
                     Why, wherefore ask you this?

IAGO
'Zounds, sir, you're robbed. For shame, put on your gown.
Your heart is burst; you have lost half your soul.   90
Even now, very now, an old black ram
Is tupping your white ewe. Arise, arise!
Awake the snorting citizens with the bell,
Or else the devil will make a grandsire of you.
Arise, I say!   95

BRABANTIO
                     What, have you lost your wits?

RODERIGO
Most reverend signior, do you know my voice?

BRABANTIO
Not I; what are you?

RODERIGO
My name is Roderigo.

BRABANTIO
                     The worser welcome.   100
I have charged thee not to haunt about my doors.

track 1

84–125:
Peter Yapp as Brabantio, John McAndrew as Roderigo,
Anton Lesser as Iago

104: **distempering draughts:** alcohol

113: **grange:** a solitary farm house

116: **if:** even if

119: **Barbary horse:** a horse from Northern Africa (i.e., Othello)

120: **coursers:** race horses

120: **gennets:** small Spanish horses

120: **germans:** kin, family

121: **profane:** disrespectful

123: **making the beast with two backs:** engaging in sexual intercourse

In honest plainness, thou hast heard me say
My daughter is not for thee, and now, in madness,
Being full of supper and distempering draughts,
Upon malicious bravery, dost thou come   105
To start my quiet.

RODERIGO
Sir, sir, sir, —

BRABANTIO
                          But thou must needs be sure
My spirit and my place have in them power
To make this bitter to thee.   110

RODERIGO
                          Patience, good sir.

BRABANTIO
What tell'st thou me of robbing? This is Venice;
My house is not a grange.

RODERIGO
                          Most grave Brabantio,
In simple and pure soul I come to you.   115

IAGO
'Zounds, sir, you are one of those that will not serve God if the
devil bid you. Because we come to do you service and you think
we are ruffians, you'll have your daughter covered with a
Barbary horse, you'll have your nephews neigh to you, you'll
have coursers for cousins and gennets for germans.   120

BRABANTIO
What profane wretch art thou?

IAGO
I am one, sir, that comes to tell you your daughter and the Moor are now
making the beast with two backs.

track 1

84–125:
Peter Yapp as Brabantio, John McAndrew as Roderigo,
Anton Lesser as Iago

125: a senator: (said contemptuously)

130: odd-even: between midnight and 1 a.m.

143: wheeling: wandering, not settled

148: tinder: a flammable substance used to start a fire

BRABANTIO
  Thou art a villain.

IAGO
                    You are a senator.   125

BRABANTIO
  This thou shalt answer. I know thee, Roderigo.

RODERIGO
  Sir, I will answer any thing. But, I beseech you,
  If't be your pleasure and most wise consent,
  As partly I find it is, that your fair daughter,
  At this odd-even and dull watch o' the night,   130
  Transported with no worse nor better guard
  But with a knave of common hire, a gondolier,
  To the gross clasps of a lascivious Moor.
  If this be known to you and your allowance,
  We then have done you bold and saucy wrongs.   135
  But if you know not this, my manners tell me
  We have your wrong rebuke. Do not believe
  That, from the sense of all civility,
  I thus would play and trifle with your reverence.
  Your daughter, if you have not given her leave,   140
  I say again, hath made a gross revolt,
  Tying her duty, beauty, wit and fortunes
  In an extravagant and wheeling stranger
  Of here and everywhere. Straight satisfy yourself.
  If she be in her chamber or your house,   145
  Let loose on me the justice of the state
  For thus deluding you.

BRABANTIO
                    Strike on the tinder, ho!
  Give me a taper! Call up all my people! —
  This accident is not unlike my dream;   150
  Belief of it oppresses me already. —
  Light, I say! Light!

                                        [Exit above]

154: **meet:** appropriate

155–156: **produced...against:** revealed not to be supporting

157: **cheque:** rebuke

158: **cast:** dismiss

161: **fathom:** ability

167: **Sagittary:** a public building in Venice

170: **despisèd time:** remaining years when Brabantio is socially condemned (because his daughter eloped)

IAGO

> Farewell, for I must leave you.
It seems not meet, nor wholesome to my place,
To be produced — as, if I stay, I shall —   155
Against the Moor. For I do know, the state,
However this may gall him with some cheque,
Cannot with safety cast him, for he's embarked
With such loud reason to the Cyprus wars,
Which even now stand in act, that, for their souls,   160
Another of his fathom they have none
To lead their business. In which regard,
Though I do hate him as I do hell pains,
Yet, for necessity of present life,
I must show out a flag and sign of love,   165
Which is indeed but sign. That you shall surely find him,
Lead to the Sagittary the raisèd search,
And there will I be with him. So, farewell.

[Exit]
[Enter, below, BRABANTIO, with Servants and torches]

BRABANTIO

It is too true an evil. Gone she is,
And what's to come of my despisèd time   170
Is nought but bitterness. — Now, Roderigo,
Where didst thou see her? — O unhappy girl! —
With the Moor, say'st thou? — Who would be a father? —
How didst thou know 'twas she? — O she deceives me
Past thought! — What said she to you? — Get more tapers;   175
Raise all my kindred. — Are they married, think you?

RODERIGO

Truly, I think they are.

BRABANTIO

O heaven! How got she out? O treason of the blood!
Fathers, from hence trust not your daughters' minds
By what you see them act. Is there not charms   180
By which the property of youth and maidhood
May be abused? Have you not read, Roderigo,
Of some such thing?

188: **discover:** find

191: **I may command at most:** My authority allows me to demand help in most (homes)

193: **deserve your pains:** i.e., repay or reward you for your troubles

RODERIGO

          Yes, sir, I have indeed.

BRABANTIO

  Call up my brother. O, would you had had her,   185
  Some one way, some another. Do you know
  Where we may apprehend her and the Moor?

RODERIGO

  I think I can discover him, if you please,
  To get good guard and go along with me.

BRABANTIO

  Pray you, lead on. At every house I'll call;   190
  I may command at most. — Get weapons, ho!
  And raise some special officers of night. —
  On, good Roderigo; I'll deserve your pains.

                                      [Exeunt]

Set rendering of "A Street" from the 1951 staging by Orson Welles at St. James Theatre

Rare Book and Special Collections Library, University of Illinois at Urbana-Champaign

4: **to do me service:** to be useful to myself
5: **yerked:** stabbed (with a knife)
7: **prated:** bragged
8: **scurvy:** contemptible
11: **forbear:** leave alone, spare
13: **magnifico:** honorific title (referring to Brabantio)
18: **give him cable:** i.e., give him leeway, room to maneuver
20: **signiory:** rulers or governing body
21: **out-tongue:** get the better of, through talking
23: **promulgate:** publish, make known
23: **fetch:** derive, draw as a source
24: **royal siege:** i.e., great social height (Othello comes from a royal family)
25: **unbonneted:** humbly

[Enter OTHELLO, IAGO, and Attendants with torches]

IAGO

   Though in the trade of war I have slain men,
   Yet do I hold it very stuff o' the conscience
   To do no contrived murder. I lack iniquity
   Sometimes to do me service. Nine or ten times
   I had thought to have yerked him here under the ribs.   5

OTHELLO

   'Tis better as it is.

IAGO

            Nay, but he prated,
   And spoke such scurvy and provoking terms
   Against your honour
   That, with the little godliness I have,
   I did full hard forbear him. But, I pray you, sir,   10
   Are you fast married? Be assured of this,
   That the magnifico is much beloved,
   And hath in his effect a voice potential
   As double as the duke's. He will divorce you,   15
   Or put upon you what restraint and grievance
   The law, with all his might to enforce it on,
   Will give him cable.

OTHELLO

            Let him do his spite.
   My services which I have done the signiory   20
   Shall out-tongue his complaints. 'Tis yet to know, —
   Which, when I know that boasting is an honour,
   I shall promulgate — I fetch my life and being
   From men of royal siege, and my demerits
   May speak unbonneted to as proud a fortune   25

28: **unhoused:** unsettled, homeless

29: **circumscription:** restraint; confinement

30: **yond:** (short for "yonder") over there

31: **raised:** awakened and gathered (as in a raised army)

35: **Shall manifest me rightly:** Shall show me to be truthful and in the right

36: **Janus:** the Roman god of all beginnings, used here as an exclamation
(such as "By God"). Significantly, Janus is usually represented as having two faces.

41: **haste-post-haste:** very great haste/hurry

45: **heat:** importance

45: **galleys:** a flat-designed boat powered by oars

46: **sequent :** sequential, in a row

As this that I have reached. For know, Iago,
But that I love the gentle Desdemona,
I would not my unhoused free condition
Put into circumscription and confine
For the sea's worth. But look, what lights come yond?   30

IAGO

Those are the raised father and his friends.
You were best go in.

OTHELLO

          Not I; I must be found.
My parts, my title and my perfect soul
Shall manifest me rightly. Is it they?   35

IAGO

By Janus, I think no.

                    [Enter CASSIO with torches]

OTHELLO

The servants of the duke? And my lieutenant?
The goodness of the night upon you, friends!
What is the news?

CASSIO

          The duke does greet you, general,   40
And he requires your haste-post-haste appearance,
Even on the instant.

OTHELLO

          What is the matter, think you?

CASSIO

Something from Cyprus, as I may divine.
It is a business of some heat. The galleys   45
Have sent a dozen sequent messengers
This very night at one another's heels,
And many of the consuls, raised and met,
Are at the duke's already. You have been
hotly called for,   50

52: **guests:** messengers (modern texts read "quests")

55: **spend a word:** say something briefly

57: **ancient:** Cassio draws attention to Iago's lower rank, possibly angering Iago

58: **boarded a land carack:** (Iago is being vulgar) boarded = enter a boat (with sexual connotation); carack = vessel which carries cargo (he is calling Desdemona a "land carack")

67: **comes to:** comes with

When, being not at your lodging to be found,
The senate hath sent about three several guests
To search you out.

OTHELLO
          'Tis well I am found by you.
I will but spend a word here in the house   55
And go with you.

            [Exit]

CASSIO
          Ancient, what makes he here?

IAGO
Faith, he tonight hath boarded a land carack.
If it prove lawful prize, he's made for ever.

CASSIO
I do not understand.   60

IAGO
          He's married.

CASSIO
          To who?

          [Enter OTHELLO]

IAGO
Marry, to — Come, captain, will you go?

OTHELLO
          Have with you.

CASSIO
Here comes another troop to seek for you.   65
    [Enter BRABANTIO, RODERIGO, with Officers, and Torches]

IAGO
It is Brabantio. General, be advised.
He comes to bad intent.

72: **Keep up your bright swords:** Keep your swords sheathed

77: **refer me to all things of sense:** I'll appeal to things that have sense (i.e., people)

81: **wealthy curlèd darlings:** i.e., the young, handsome suitors appropriate to her class

82: **a general mock:** social ridicule

83: **guardage:** guards

83: **sooty bosom:** sooty = dark, i.e., Othello

84: **to fear, not to delight:** i.e., Desdemona should fear Othello, not take pleasure in his company

88: **motion:** sense; reason

90: **attach:** seize; arrest

92: **arts inhibited...warrant:** i.e., magical arts (inhibited = prohibited; out of warrant = illegal)

OTHELLO
          Holla! Stand there!

RODERIGO
  Signior, it is the Moor.

BRABANTIO
          Down with him, thief!   70
                                    [They draw on both sides]

IAGO
  You, Roderigo! Come, sir, I am for you.

OTHELLO
  Keep up your bright swords, for the dew will rust them.
  Good signior, you shall more command with years
  Than with your weapons.

BRABANTIO
  O, thou foul thief, where hast thou stowed my daughter?   75
  Damned as thou art, thou hast enchanted her,
  For I'll refer me to all things of sense,
  If she in chains of magic were not bound.
  Whether a maid so tender, fair and happy,
  So opposite to marriage that she shunned   80
  The wealthy curlèd darlings of our nation,
  Would ever have, t' incur a general mock,
  Run from her guardage to the sooty bosom
  Of such a thing as thou, to fear, not to delight.
  Judge me the world, if 'tis not gross in sense   85
  That thou hast practiced on her with foul charms,
  Abused her delicate youth with drugs or minerals
  That weaken motion, I'll have't disputed on.
  'Tis probable and palpable to thinking.
  I therefore apprehend and do attach thee   90
  For an abuser of the world, a practiser
  Of arts inhibited and out of warrant.
  Lay hold upon him. If he do resist,
  Subdue him at his peril.

96: **my inclining:** those who support or favor me

101: **course of direct session:** a session in court

113: **idle:** trifling, insignificant

116: **have passage free:** be allowed

OTHELLO
                    Hold your hands,   95
Both you of my inclining, and the rest.
Were it my cue to fight, I should have known it
Without a prompter. Where will you that I go
To answer this your charge?

BRABANTIO
                    To prison, till fit time   100
Of law and course of direct session
Call thee to answer.

OTHELLO
                    What if I do obey?
How may the duke be therewith satisfied,
Whose messengers are here about my side,   105
Upon some present business of the state
To bring me to him?

First Officer
                    'Tis true, most worthy signior;
The duke's in council and your noble self,
I am sure, is sent for.   110

BRABANTIO
                    How? The duke in council?
In this time of the night? Bring him away;
Mine's not an idle cause. The duke himself,
Or any of my brothers of the state,
Cannot but feel this wrong as 'twere their own,   115
For if such actions may have passage free,
Bond-slaves and pagans shall our statesmen be.

                                        [Exeunt]

Set rendering of "Council Chamber" from the 1951 staging by Orson Welles at St. James Theatre

Rare Book and Special Collections Library, University of Illinois at Urbana-Champaign

Orson Welles's sketch of "Senate" from the staging at St. James Theatre

Rare Book and Special Collections Library, University of Illinois at Urbana-Champaign

1: **composition:** agreement
2: **gives them credit:** lends them credence
3: **disproportioned:** inconsistent
4: **galleys:** oar-powered boats
7: **just:** accurate
11: **possible enough to judgment:** i.e., close enough for us to decide what to do
12: **not so secure me in the error:** i.e., not sure of the specifics

[Enter DUKE, Senators, and Officers]

DUKE OF VENICE
There is no composition in these news
That gives them credit.

First Senator
Indeed, they are disproportioned.
My letters say a hundred and seven galleys.

DUKE OF VENICE
And mine, a hundred and forty.   5

Second Senator
                    And mine, two hundred.
But though they jump not on a just account, —
As in these cases, where the aim reports,
'tis oft with difference — yet do they all confirm
A Turkish fleet, and bearing up to Cyprus.   10

DUKE OF VENICE
Nay, it is possible enough to judgment.
I do not so secure me in the error,
But the main article I do approve
In fearful sense.

Sailor
                                                        [Within]
What, ho! What, ho! What, ho!   15

First Officer
A messenger from the galleys.

                                        [Enter a Sailor]

21: **how say you:** What do you say

23: **assay:** attempt

24: **keep us in false gaze:** distract us

28: **with more facile question bear it:** more easily win it in battle

29–31: **For that it stands...dressed in:** i.e., Cyprus is not as prepared for war as Rhodes

40: **injointed:** united

DUKE OF VENICE
> Now, what's the business?

Sailor
> The Turkish preparation makes for Rhodes,
> So was I bid report here to the state
> By Signior Angelo.   20

DUKE OF VENICE
> How say you by this change?

First Senator
> This cannot be,
> By no assay of reason. 'Tis a pageant
> To keep us in false gaze. When we consider
> The importancy of Cyprus to the Turk   25
> And let ourselves again but understand
> That, as it more concerns the Turk than Rhodes,
> So may he with more facile question bear it,
> For that it stands not in such warlike brace,
> But altogether lacks the abilities   30
> That Rhodes is dressed in. If we make thought of this,
> We must not think the Turk is so unskillful
> To leave that latest which concerns him first,
> Neglecting an attempt of ease and gain,
> To wake and wage a danger profitless.   35

DUKE OF VENICE
> Nay, in all confidence, he's not for Rhodes.

First Officer
> Here is more news.

> *[Enter a Messenger]*

Messenger
> The Ottomites, reverend and gracious,
> Steering with due course towards the isle of Rhodes,
> Have there injointed them with an after fleet.   40

42: **restem:** retrace

43: **backward course:** course they followed

43: **frank appearance:** clear, obvious intention

45: **servitor:** servant

46: **free:** willing; eager

51: **post-post-haste:** great hurry

61: **flood-gate:** overwhelming (like a flood)

62: **engluts:** swallows, consumes

First Senator
  Ay, so I thought. How many, as you guess?

Messenger
  Of thirty sail. And now they do restem
  Their backward course, bearing with frank appearance
  Their purposes toward Cyprus. Signior Montano,
  Your trusty and most valiant servitor,   45
  With his free duty recommends you thus,
  And prays you to believe him.

DUKE OF VENICE
  'Tis certain, then, for Cyprus.
  Marcus Luccicos, is not he in town?

First Senator
  He's now in Florence.   50

DUKE OF VENICE
  Write from us to him, post-post-haste dispatch.

First Senator
  Here comes Brabantio and the valiant Moor.
    [Enter BRABANTIO, OTHELLO, IAGO, RODERIGO, and Officers]

DUKE OF VENICE
  Valiant Othello, we must straight employ you
  Against the general enemy Ottoman. —
  [To BRABANTIO] I did not see you. Welcome, gentle signior.   55
  We lacked your counsel and your help tonight.

BRABANTIO
  So did I yours. Good your grace, pardon me.
  Neither my place nor aught I heard of business
  Hath raised me from my bed, nor doth the general care
  Take hold on me, for my particular grief   60
  Is of so flood-gate and o'erbearing nature
  That it engluts and swallows other sorrows
  And it is still itself.

68: **abused:** deceived

69: **mountebanks:** traveling con artists

77: **proper:** own

78: **Stood in your action:** i.e., was the accused party

DUKE OF VENICE
> Why, what's the matter?

BRABANTIO
> My daughter! O, my daughter!   65

DUKE OF VENICE, *Senator*
> Dead?

BRABANTIO
> Ay, to me.
> She is abused, stol'n from me, and corrupted
> By spells and medicines bought of mountebanks.
> For nature so preposterously to err,   70
> Being not deficient, blind, or lame of sense,
> Sans witchcraft could not.

DUKE OF VENICE
> Whoe'er he be that in this foul proceeding
> Hath thus beguiled your daughter of herself
> And you of her, the bloody book of law   75
> You shall yourself read in the bitter letter
> After your own sense, yea, though our proper son
> Stood in your action.

BRABANTIO
> Humbly I thank your grace.
> Here is the man, this Moor, whom now, it seems,   80
> Your special mandate for the state-affairs
> Hath hither brought.

All
> We are very sorry for't.

DUKE OF VENICE
> *[To OTHELLO]* What, in your own part, can you say to this?

BRABANTIO
> Nothing, but this is so.   85

tracks 2-4

86–104:
Paul Robeson as Othello
John Kani as Othello
F. Scott Fitzgerald as Othello

93: **pith:** strength, force
94: **nine moons:** nine months
95: **tented field:** battlefield
97: **broil:** combat

Lines 99–101: "Yet, by your gracious patience, / I will a round unvarnished tale deliver / Of my whole course of love": The ensemble of The Shakespeare Theatre's 1997–1998 production directed by Jude Kelly
Photo: Carol Rosegg

100: **round:** plain
106: **motion:** impulses
110: **a judgment maimed:** bad judgment
114: **vouch:** declare, vow
118: **To vouch this is no proof:** i.e., To say something is true doesn't prove it is true
119: **Without...test:** without more conclusive proof

OTHELLO

    Most potent, grave, and reverend signiors,
    My very noble and approved good masters,
    That I have ta'en away this old man's daughter,
    It is most true. True, I have married her.
    The very head and front of my offending   90
    Hath this extent, no more. Rude am I in my speech,
    And little blessed with the soft phrase of peace:
    For since these arms of mine had seven years' pith,
    Till now some nine moons wasted, they have used
    Their dearest action in the tented field,   95
    And little of this great world can I speak,
    More than pertains to feats of broil and battle,
    And therefore little shall I grace my cause
    In speaking for myself. Yet, by your gracious patience,
    I will a round unvarnished tale deliver   100
    Of my whole course of love — what drugs, what charms,
    What conjuration and what mighty magic,
    For such proceeding I am charged withal,
    I won his daughter.

BRABANTIO

                A maiden never bold,   105
    Of spirit so still and quiet, that her motion
    Blushed at herself; and she, in spite of nature,
    Of years, of country, credit, every thing,
    To fall in love with what she feared to look on!
    It is a judgment maimed and most imperfect   110
    That will confess perfection so could err
    Against all rules of nature and must be driven
    To find out practices of cunning hell
    Why this should be. I therefore vouch again
    That with some mixtures powerful o'er the blood,   115
    Or with some dram conjured to this effect,
    He wrought upon her.

DUKE OF VENICE

                To vouch this is no proof,
    Without more wider and more overt test

120: **thin:** (metaphorically) easily seen through

120: **habits:** clothing, outward appearance

121: **modern seeming:** common, ordinary appearances

123: **forced courses:** i.e., by force

126: **affordeth:** results in, yields

138: **justly:** truthfully, accurately

tracks 5-7

142–185:
Hugh Quarshie as Othello
John Kani as Othello
Edwin Booth as Othello

Than these thin habits and poor likelihoods 120
Of modern seeming do prefer against him.

First Senator
But, Othello, speak.
Did you, by indirect and forced courses,
Subdue and poison this young maid's affections?
Or came it by request and such fair question 125
As soul to soul affordeth?

OTHELLO
I do beseech you,
Send for the lady to the Sagittary,
And let her speak of me before her father.
If you do find me foul in her report, 130
The trust, the office I do hold of you,
Not only take away, but let your sentence
Even fall upon my life.

DUKE OF VENICE
Fetch Desdemona hither.

OTHELLO
Ancient, conduct them; you best know the place. 135
[Exeunt IAGO and Attendants]
And, till she come, as truly as to heaven
I do confess the vices of my blood,
So justly to your grave ears I'll present
How I did thrive in this fair lady's love,
And she in mine. 140

DUKE OF VENICE
Say it, Othello.

OTHELLO
Her father loved me, oft invited me,
Still questioned me the story of my life,
From year to year: the battles, sieges, fortunes
That I have passed. 145

tracks 5-7

142–185:
Hugh Quarshie as Othello
John Kani as Othello
Edwin Booth as Othello

148: **chances:** events

150: **scapes:** escapes

150: **breach :** gap in fortifications (military term)

152: **redemption:** release

153: **portance:** conduct (possibly referring to both traveling and behavior)

154: **antres:** caves

154: **idle:** useless, infertile

158: **Anthropophagi:** cannibals

163: **She'ld:** contraction of "she would"

165: **pliant hour:** convenient time

167: **dilate:** expand upon, relate

168: **parcels:** in small increments

169: **intentively:** intently, with strong focus

I ran it through, even from my boyish days,
To the very moment that he bade me tell it.
Wherein I spake of most disastrous chances,
Of moving accidents by flood and field
Of hair-breadth scapes i' th' imminent deadly breach,   150
Of being taken by the insolent foe
And sold to slavery, of my redemption thence
And portance in my travels' history.
Wherein of antres vast and deserts idle,
Rough quarries, rocks and hills whose heads touch heaven   155
It was my hint to speak, — such was the process.
And of the Cannibals that each other eat,
The Anthropophagi and men whose heads
Do grow beneath their shoulders. This to hear
Would Desdemona seriously incline,   160
But still the house-affairs would draw her thence
Which ever as she could with haste dispatch,
She'ld come again, and with a greedy ear
Devour up my discourse. Which I observing,
Took once a pliant hour and found good means   165
To draw from her a prayer of earnest heart
That I would all my pilgrimage dilate,
Whereof by parcels she had something heard,
But not intentively. I did consent,
And often did beguile her of her tears,   170
When I did speak of some distressful stroke
That my youth suffered. My story being done,
She gave me for my pains a world of sighs.
She swore, in faith, 'twas strange, 'twas passing strange,
'Twas pitiful, 'twas wondrous pitiful.   175
She wished she had not heard it, yet she wished
That heaven had made her such a man. She thanked me
And bade me, if I had a friend that loved her,
I should but teach him how to tell my story,
And that would woo her. Upon this hint I spake.   180
She loved me for the dangers I had passed,
And I loved her that she did pity them.
This only is the witchcraft I have used.
Here comes the lady; let her witness it.

              [Enter DESDEMONA, IAGO, and Attendants]

142–185:
Hugh Quarshie as Othello
John Kani as Othello
Edwin Booth as Othello

187: **take up...at the best:** i.e., make the best of this disastrous situation
193: **light:** fall
199: **learn:** teach
208: **get:** beget

Line 209: "Come hither, Moor. / I here do give thee that with all my heart / Which, but thou hast already": Joanna Weinberg as Desdemona, John Kani as Othello, and Stuart Brown as Brabantio in The Market Theater's 1987 production directed by Janet Suzman

Photo: Ruphin Coudyzer

214: **For thy escape...tyranny:** i.e., your elopement would teach him to be much more strict
215: **hang clogs:** encumber (clogs = objects hung on animals to hinder motion or escape)

DUKE OF VENICE

    I think this tale would win my daughter too.   185

    Good Brabantio,

    Take up this mangled matter at the best.

    Men do their broken weapons rather use

    Than their bare hands.

BRABANTIO

                  I pray you, hear her speak.   190

    If she confess that she was half the wooer,

    Destruction on my head, if my bad blame

    Light on the man. — Come hither, gentle mistress:

    Do you perceive in all this noble company

    Where most you owe obedience?   195

DESDEMONA

               My noble father,

    I do perceive here a divided duty.

    To you I am bound for life and education;

    My life and education both do learn me

    How to respect you. You are the lord of duty;   200

    I am hitherto your daughter. But here's my husband,

    And so much duty as my mother showed

    To you, preferring you before her father,

    So much I challenge that I may profess

    Due to the Moor, my lord.   205

BRABANTIO

              God be with you! I have done.

    Please it your grace, on to the state affairs.

    I had rather to adopt a child than get it. —

    Come hither, Moor.

    I here do give thee that with all my heart   210

    Which, but thou hast already, with all my heart

    I would keep from thee. — For your sake, jewel,

    I am glad at soul I have no other child,

    For thy escape would teach me tyranny,

    To hang clogs on them. — I have done, my lord.   215

217: **grise:** degree, step

226: **bootless:** futile, useless

234: **are equivocal:** apply equally

240: **substitute:** delegate

240: **allowed sufficiency:** sufficient capability

241–242: **throws...you:** suggests you would ensure its safety more capably

242: **slubber:** sully, make dirty

242: **gloss:** luster, sheen

243: **stubborn:** rough, harsh

245: **flinty and steel couch:** Othello is referring to sleeping on stony, hard ground (flinty = full of hard stones; couch = bed)

246: **thrice-driven:** i.e., extremely soft

246: **agnise:** enjoy

DUKE OF VENICE
    Let me speak like yourself, and lay a sentence,
    Which, as a grise or step, may help these lovers
    Into your favour.
    When remedies are past, the griefs are ended
    By seeing the worst, which late on hopes depended.   220
    To mourn a mischief that is past and gone
    Is the next way to draw new mischief on.
    What cannot be preserved when fortune takes
    Patience, her injury a mockery makes.
    The robbed that smiles steals something from the thief;   225
    He robs himself that spends a bootless grief.

BRABANTIO
    So let the Turk of Cyprus us beguile.
    We lose it not, so long as we can smile.
    He bears the sentence well that nothing bears
    But the free comfort which from thence he hears,   230
    But he bears both the sentence and the sorrow
    That, to pay grief, must of poor patience borrow.
    These sentences, to sugar, or to gall,
    Being strong on both sides, are equivocal.
    But words are words; I never yet did hear   235
    That the bruised heart was piercèd through the ear.
    I humbly beseech you, proceed to the affairs of state.

DUKE OF VENICE
    The Turk with a most mighty preparation makes for Cyprus.
    Othello, the fortitude of the place is best known to you, and
    though we have there a substitute of most allowed sufficiency, yet   240
    opinion, a sovereign mistress of effects, throws a more safer voice
    on you. You must therefore be content to slubber the gloss of your
    new fortunes with this more stubborn and boisterous expedition.

OTHELLO
    The tyrant custom, most grave senators,
    Hath made the flinty and steel couch of war   245
    My thrice-driven bed of down. I do agnise
    A natural and prompt alacrity

251: **disposition:** arrangement, settlement

252: **reference:** appointment, assignment

252: **exhibition:** allowance, pension

253: **besort:** attendance, suitable company

259: **impatient:** angry

261: **unfolding:** explanation

261: **prosperous :** favourable

262: **charter:** privilege

263: **simpleness:** innocence

271: **consecrate:** devote

I find in hardness, and do undertake
These present wars against the Ottomites.
Most humbly therefore bending to your state,   250
I crave fit disposition for my wife,
Due reference of place and exhibition,
With such accommodation and besort
As levels with her breeding.

DUKE OF VENICE
Why, at her father's.   255

BRABANTIO
                I'll not have it so.

OTHELLO
Nor I.

DESDEMONA
                  Nor would I there reside
To put my father in impatient thoughts
By being in his eye. Most gracious duke,   260
To my unfolding, lend your prosperous ear,
And let me find a charter in your voice
T'assist my simpleness.

DUKE OF VENICE
What would you, Desdemona?

DESDEMONA
That I did love the Moor to live with him,   265
My downright violence and storm of fortunes
May trumpet to the world. My heart's subdued
Even to the very quality of my lord.
I saw Othello's visage in his mind,
And to his honour and his valiant parts   270
Did I my soul and fortunes consecrate.
So that, dear lords, if I be left behind,
A moth of peace, and he go to the war,
The rites for which I love him are bereft me,

275: **a heavy interim:** a sad interval

278: **vouch:** bear witness

280: **heat:** passion

280: **young affects:** desires of youth

281: **defunct:** is ended, dead

284: **scant:** limit, short-change

285–286: **when light-winged toys...wanton dullness:** i.e., if I am ever blinded or distracted by amorous play

288: **disports:** sports, games

289: **helm:** helmet

290: **indign:** unworthy

291: **make head:** surpass

301: **import:** concern

And I a heavy interim shall support   295
By his dear absence. Let me go with him.

OTHELLO
Let her have your voice.
Vouch with me, heaven, I therefore beg it not
To please the palate of my appetite,
Nor to comply with heat — the young affects   280
In me defunct — and proper satisfaction,
But to be free and bounteous to her mind.
And heaven defend your good souls that you think
I will your serious and great business scant
For she is with me. No, when light-winged toys   285
Of feathered Cupid seal with wanton dullness
My speculative and officed instruments,
That my disports corrupt and taint my business,
Let housewives make a skillet of my helm,
And all indign and base adversities   290
Make head against my estimation.

DUKE OF VENICE
Be it as you shall privately determine,
Either for her stay or going. Th' affair cries haste,
And speed must answer it.

First Senator
You must away tonight.   295

OTHELLO
                    With all my heart.

DUKE OF VENICE
At nine i' th' morning here we'll meet again.
Othello, leave some officer behind,
And he shall our commission bring to you
With such things else of quality and respect   300
As doth import you.

317: **in the best advantage:** in the most opportune way (advantage = opportunity)

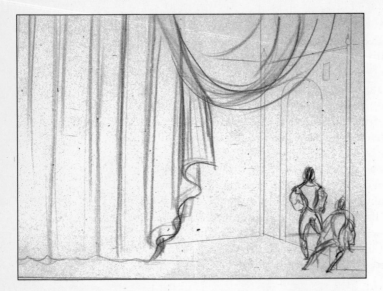

Set rendering "Outside Council Chamber" from the 1951 staging by Orson Welles at St. James Theatre

Rare Book and Special Collections Library, University of Illinois at Urbana-Champaign

OTHELLO

So please your Grace, my ancient.
A man he is of honesty and trust.
To his conveyance I assign my wife,
With what else needful your good Grace shall think   305
To be sent after me.

DUKE OF VENICE

Let it be so.
Good night to every one. *[To BRABANTIO]* And, noble signior,
If virtue no delighted beauty lack,
Your son-in-law is far more fair than black.   310

First Senator
Adieu, brave Moor, use Desdemona well.

BRABANTIO

Look to her, Moor, if thou hast eyes to see.
She has deceived her father, and may thee.
                    [Exeunt DUKE OF VENICE, Senators, Officers, &c]

OTHELLO

My life upon her faith! Honest Iago,
My Desdemona must I leave to thee.   315
I prithee, let thy wife attend on her,
And bring them after in the best advantage.
Come, Desdemona, I have but an hour
Of love, of worldly matters and direction,
To spend with thee. We must obey the time.   320
                    [Exeunt OTHELLO and DESDEMONA]

RODERIGO

Iago, —

IAGO

What say'st thou, noble heart?

RODERIGO

What will I do, think'st thou?

325: **incontinently:** immediately

332-333: **guinea hen:** disparaging euphemism for a woman

336: **fig:** disparaging euphemism for the female sex and sex organ, with an accompanying vulgar gesture

338: **hyssop:** a bushy, evergreen herb

339: **gender:** variety

341: **corrigible:** corrective

343: **poise:** balance

345: **motions:** impulses

345: **unbitted:** unbridled

346: **sect or scion:** references to grafting plants

IAGO

Why, go to bed, and sleep.

RODERIGO

I will incontinently drown myself.   325

IAGO

If thou dost, I shall never love thee after. Why, thou silly gentleman?

RODERIGO

It is silliness to live when to live is torment, and then have we a
prescription to die, when death is our physician.

IAGO

O villainous! I have looked upon the world for four times seven
years, and since I could distinguish betwixt a benefit and an   330
injury, I never found man that knew how to love himself.
Ere I would say, I would drown myself for the love of a guinea
hen; I would change my humanity with a baboon.

RODERIGO

What should I do? I confess it is my shame to be so fond, but it is not in
my virtue to amend it.   335

IAGO

Virtue! A fig! 'Tis in ourselves that we are thus or thus. Our bodies
are our gardens, to the which our wills are gardeners, so that if
we will plant nettles, or sow lettuce, set hyssop and weed up
thyme, supply it with one gender of herbs, or distract it with
many, either to have it sterile with idleness, or manured with   340
industry, why, the power and corrigible authority of this lies in our
wills. If the balance of our lives had not one scale of reason to
poise another of sensuality, the blood and baseness of our natures
would conduct us to most preposterous conclusions. But we have
reason to cool our raging motions, our carnal stings, our unbitted   345
lusts, whereof I take this that you call love to be a sect or scion.

RODERIGO

It cannot be.

350: **knit to thy deserving:** dedicated to your cause

351: **perdurable:** lasting

351–352: **stead thee:** be of use to

353: **defeat:** disfigure

353: **favour:** face, appearance

353: **usurped:** false

357: **sequestration:** rupture, divorce

359: **locusts:** sweet tasting dessert (e.g. locust fruit)

360: **coloquintida:** colocynth, a plant with a sharp tasting fruit used for medicinal purposes

360: **for youth:** because she is young

365: **erring :** wandering, homeless

365: **supersubtle:** crafty, cunning

367: **It is clean out of the way:** entirely wrong to do

368: **compassing:** achieving

370: **be fast:** be true to, devoted to

370: **depend on the issue:** pursue this course

372: **hearted:** deeply felt, from the heart

373: **conjunctive:** united

374: **cuckold:** make a cuckold of him (cuckold = a man whose wife has been unfaithful)

376: **traverse:** "March" (a military expression)

IAGO

It is merely a lust of the blood and a permission of the will. Come,
be a man. Drown thyself? Drown cats and blind puppies! I have
professed me thy friend, and I confess me knit to thy deserving   350
with cables of perdurable toughness; I could never better stead
thee than now. Put money in thy purse; follow thou the wars;
defeat thy favour with an usurped beard. I say, put money in thy
purse. It cannot be that Desdemona should long continue her love
to the Moor, — put money in thy purse, — nor he his to her. It was   355
a violent commencement in her, and thou shalt see an answerable
sequestration — put but money in thy purse. These Moors are
changeable in their wills. — Fill thy purse with money. — The
food that to him now is as luscious as locusts, shall be to him
shortly as bitter as coloquintida. She must change for youth.   360
When she is sated with his body, she will find the error of her
choice. Therefore, put money in thy purse. If thou wilt needs
damn thyself, do it a more delicate way than drowning. Make all
the money thou canst. If sanctimony and a frail vow betwixt an
erring barbarian and a supersubtle Venetian be not too hard for   365
my wits and all the tribe of hell, thou shalt enjoy her; therefore,
make money. A pox of drowning thyself! It is clean out of the way.
Seek thou rather to be hanged in compassing thy joy than to be
drowned and go without her.

RODERIGO

Wilt thou be fast to my hopes, if I depend on the issue?   370

IAGO

Thou art sure of me. Go, make money. I have told thee often, and
I retell thee again and again, I hate the Moor. My cause is hearted;
thine hath no less reason. Let us be conjunctive in our revenge
against him. If thou canst cuckold him, thou dost thyself a pleasure, me a sport. There are many events in the womb of time which   375
will be delivered. Traverse, go, provide thy money. We will have
more of this tomorrow. Adieu.

RODERIGO

Where shall we meet i' th' morning?

IAGO

At my lodging.

380: **betimes:** early in the morning

tracks 8-9

387–408:
Anton Lesser as Iago
Jose Ferrer as Iago

388: **profane:** desecrate, pollute

389: **snipe:** simpleton

392: **done my office:** fulfilled Iago's duty i.e., engaged in marital relations with Emilia

394: **surety:** certainty

394: **He holds me well:** he (Roderigo) thinks well of me

397: **plume up my will:** triumph

399: **abuse:** deceive

401: **dispose:** disposition, temper

402: **framed:** fashioned, formed

RODERIGO
I'll be with thee betimes.   380

IAGO
Go to. Farewell. Do you hear, Roderigo?

RODERIGO
What say you?

IAGO
No more of drowning, do you hear?

RODERIGO
I am changed.

IAGO
Go to. Farewell. Put money enough in your purse.   385

RODERIGO
I'll sell all my land.

[Exit RODERIGO]

IAGO
Thus do I ever make my fool my purse,
For I mine own gained knowledge should profane,
If I would time expend with such a snipe
But for my sport and profit. I hate the Moor,   390
And it is thought abroad, that 'twixt my sheets
He has done my office. I know not if 't be true,
But I, for mere suspicion in that kind,
Will do as if for surety. He holds me well,
The better shall my purpose work on him.   395
Cassio's a proper man. Let me see now.
To get his place and to plume up my will
In double knavery — How, how? Let's see. —
After some time, to abuse Othello's ears
That he is too familiar with his wife.   400
He hath a person and a smooth dispose
To be suspected, framed to make women false.

tracks 8-9

387–408:
Anton Lesser as Iago
Jose Ferrer as Iago

403: **free:** candid

403: **open:** undisguised, straightforward

404: **but:** only

405: **tenderly:** readily

407: **engendered:** begotten, conceived

The Moor is of a free and open nature,
That thinks men honest that but seem to be so,
And will as tenderly be led by th' nose   405
As asses are.
I have 't. It is engendered. Hell and night
Must bring this monstrous birth to the world's light.

[Exit]

[Othello

Act 2

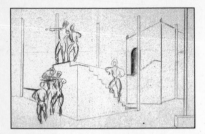

Set rendering of "Arrival at Cyprus" from the 1951 staging by Orson Welles
Rare Book and Special Collections Library, University of Illinois at Urbana-Champaign

Orson Welles's sketch of "Seawall" from the 1951 staging at St. James Theatre
Rare Book and Special Collections Library, University of Illinois at Urbana-Champaign

2: **highwrought:** with high waves
4: **descry:** discover, espy
7: **ruffianed:** raged
9: **mortise:** a wood joint (a carpentry term)
12: **chidden:** scolded, rebuked
12: **billow:** waves
14: **burning bear:** the constellation Ursa Minor
15: **ever-fixèd pole:** North Pole
14: **seems to cast...pole:** i.e., the crashing waves seem to soak all of the heavens and the earth
16: **molestation:** disturbance
17: **enchafed:** furious, angry
19: **embayed:** landlocked

Act 2, Scene 1]

[Enter MONTANO and two Gentlemen]

MONTANO
What from the cape can you discern at sea?

First Gentleman
Nothing at all. It is a highwrought flood.
I cannot, 'twixt the heaven and the main,
Descry a sail.

MONTANO
Methinks the wind hath spoke aloud at land.   5
A fuller blast ne'er shook our battlements.
If it hath ruffianed so upon the sea,
What ribs of oak, when mountains melt on them,
Can hold the mortise? What shall we hear of this?

Second Gentleman
A segregation of the Turkish fleet   10
For do but stand upon the foaming shore.
The chidden billow seems to pelt the clouds,
The wind-shaked surge, with high and monstrous mane,
seems to cast water on the burning bear,
And quench the guards of the ever-fixèd pole.   15
I never did like molestation view
On the enchafed flood.

MONTANO
If that the Turkish fleet
Be not ensheltered and embayed, they are drowned.
It is impossible they bear it out.   20
[Enter a third Gentleman]

23: **designment:** plan

24: **sufferance:** damage

28: **Veronesa:** a citizen of Verona

31: **full:** accomplished, perfect

41: **throw out our eyes:** peer out, search for

42: **main:** the main sail

42: **aerial blue:** the sky

43: **an indistinct regard:** blend together (in our sight)

46: **arrivance:** arrivals, people arriving

Third Gentleman
News, lads! Our wars are done.
The desperate tempest hath so banged the Turks
That their designment halts. A noble ship of Venice
Hath seen a grievous wreck and sufferance
On most part of their fleet.   25

MONTANO
How? Is this true?

Third Gentleman
The ship is here put in.
A Veronesa, Michael Cassio,
Lieutenant to the warlike Moor Othello,
Is come on shore, the Moor himself at sea,   30
And is in full commission here for Cyprus.

MONTANO
I am glad on't. 'Tis a worthy governor.

Third Gentleman
But this same Cassio, though he speak of comfort
Touching the Turkish loss, yet he looks sadly
And prays the Moor be safe, for they were parted   35
With foul and violent tempest.

MONTANO
Pray heavens he be,
For I have served him, and the man commands
Like a full soldier. Let's to the seaside, ho!
As well to see the vessel that's come in   40
As to throw out our eyes for brave Othello,
Even till we make the main and th' aerial blue
An indistinct regard.

Third Gentleman
Come, let's do so,
For every minute is expectancy   45
Of more arrivance.

47: **valiant:** i.e., valiant soldiers

53: **approved allowance:** proven and tested

54: **surfeited:** fed excessively

55: **Stand in bold cure:** Wait to be remedied

54–55: **Therefore...cure:** i.e., my hopes are not yet dead and may still be fulfilled

60: **shot of courtesy:** a cannon salute indicating friendship, not hostility, used by ships as they approached a foreign shore

[Enter CASSIO]

CASSIO
    Thanks you, the valiant of this warlike isle,
    That so approve the Moor! O, let the heavens
    Give him defence against the elements,
    For I have lost us him on a dangerous sea.   50

MONTANO
    Is he well shipped?

CASSIO
    His bark is stoutly timbered, his pilot
    Of very expert and approved allowance;
    Therefore my hopes, not surfeited to death,
    Stand in bold cure.   55
          [A cry within "A sail, a sail, a sail!"]
          [Enter a fourth Gentleman]

CASSIO
    What noise?

Fourth Gentleman
    The town is empty. On the brow o' th' sea
    Stand ranks of people, and they cry, "A sail!"

CASSIO
    My hopes do shape him for the governor.

          [Guns heard]

Second Gentlemen
    They do discharge their shot of courtesy;   60
    Our friends at least.

CASSIO
          I pray you, sir, go forth,
    And give us truth who 'tis that is arrived.

65: **wived:** married

68: **blazoning:** trumpeting, proclaiming

69: **vesture:** clothing (metaphorically, the human body as that in which the soul is dressed)

70: **ingener:** engineer, inventor

75: **guttered:** indented, grooved

75: **congregated sands:** wind-swept sand piles (e.g., dunes, sandbanks)

76: **ensteeped:** lying underwater

78: **mortal:** deadly

84: **se'nnight:** seven night = a week

84: **Jove:** from mythology, the supreme god, a.k.a. Jupiter, also in charge of the sky and weather

87: **quick pants:** quickening heartbeat

Second Gentleman
  I shall.

                                                                    [Exit]

MONTANO
  But, good lieutenant, is your general wived?   65

CASSIO
  Most fortunately. He hath achieved a maid
  That paragons description and wild fame,
  One that excels the quirks of blazoning pens,
  And in th' essential vesture of creation
  Does tire the ingener.   70
                              [Enter second Gentleman]
              How now! Who has put in?

Second Gentleman
  'Tis one Iago, ancient to the general.

CASSIO
  He's had most favourable and happy speed.
  Tempests themselves, high seas, and howling winds,
  The guttered rocks and congregated sands –   75
  Traitors ensteeped to clog the guiltless keel, –
  As having sense of beauty, do omit
  Their mortal natures, letting go safely by
  The divine Desdemona.

MONTANO
              What is she?   80

CASSIO
  She that I spake of, our great captain's captain,
  Left in the conduct of the bold Iago,
  Whose footing here anticipates our thoughts
  A se'nnight's speed. Great Jove, Othello guard,
  And swell his sail with thine own powerful breath,   85
  That he may bless this bay with his tall ship,
  Make love's quick pants in Desdemona's arms,

88: **extincted:** extinguished

92: **let her have your knees:** kneel to her

95: **enwheel:** surround

Lines 93–95: "Hail to thee, lady, and the grace of heaven, / Before, behind thee, and on every hand, / Enwheel thee round!": Patrice Johnson as Desdemona and Teagle F. Bougere as Cassio in The Shakespeare Theatre's 1997-1998 production directed by Jude Kelly

Photo: Carol Rosegg

Give renewed fire to our extincted spirits
And bring all Cyprus comfort!
[Enter DESDEMONA, IAGO, RODERIGO, and EMILIA]

                         O, behold,   90
The riches of the ship is come on shore!
Ye men of Cyprus, let her have your knees.
Hail to thee, lady, and the grace of heaven,
Before, behind thee, and on every hand,
Enwheel thee round!   95

DESDEMONA
                    I thank you, valiant Cassio.
What tidings can you tell me of my lord?

CASSIO
He is not yet arrived, nor know I aught
But that he's well and will be shortly here.

DESDEMONA
O, but I fear — how lost you company?   100

CASSIO
The great contention of the sea and skies
Parted our fellowship — But, hark! A sail!
                  [From within "A sail, a sail!" Guns heard]

Second Gentleman
They give their greeting to the citadel.
This likewise is a friend.

CASSIO
                    See for the news.   105
                         [Exit Gentleman]
Good ancient, you are welcome.
[To EMILIA] Welcome, mistress.
Let it not gall your patience, good Iago,
That I extend my manners. 'Tis my breeding
That gives me this bold show of courtesy.   110
[Kissing her]

Costume rendering of "Desdemona and Emilia on Arrival at Cyprus" from the 1951
staging by Orson Welles at St. James Theatre
Rare Book and Special Collections Library, University of Illinois at Urbana-Champaign

112: of her tongue she oft bestows: Iago teases that Desdemona often scolds him
(i.e., "bestows her tongue") but he also insinuates a sexual meaning to the phrase

116: list: desire, inclination

119: chides: quarrels, scolds

119: with thinking: in her mind

121: pictures out of doors: picturesque, i.e., the picture of propriety in public

124: Players in...your beds: i.e., you play at managing the household but you take
your duties in bed seriously

IAGO

    Sir, would she give you so much of her lips
    As of her tongue she oft bestows on me,
    You would have enough.

DESDEMONA

               Alas, she has no speech.

IAGO

    In faith, too much.   115
    I find it still, when I have list to sleep.
    Marry, before your ladyship, I grant,
    She puts her tongue a little in her heart
    And chides with thinking.

EMILIA

    You have little cause to say so.   120

IAGO

    Come on, come on. You are pictures out of doors,
    Bells in your parlors, wildcats in your kitchens,
    Saints in your injuries, devils being offended,
    Players in your housewifery, and housewives in your beds.

DESDEMONA

    O, fie upon thee, slanderer!   125

IAGO

    Nay, it is true, or else I am a Turk.
    You rise to play and go to bed to work.

EMILIA

    You shall not write my praise.

IAGO

    No, let me not.

DESDEMONA

    What wouldst thou write of me, if thou shouldst   130
    praise me?

134: **assay:** try, attempt
134: **one:** i.e., a messenger
136: **beguile:** deceive pleasingly

Lines 136–137: "I am not merry, but I do beguile / The thing I am by seeming otherwise": Virginia S. Burke as Emilia and Bill McCallum as Iago in the Guthrie Theater's 2003 production directed by Joe Dowling
Photo: T. Charles Erickson

140: **pate:** head
140: **birdlime:** a sticky substance used to catch birds
140: **frize:** a coarse woolen material
141: **Muse:** one of the nine Greek goddesses who served as inspiration for artists, writers and musicians
145: **black:** dark-haired
145: **witty:** clever
147: **white:** a pun on white, the opposite of black, and "wight," meaning a person, in this case, a man
147: **her blackness fit:** a pun meaning that she will find her opposite to complement her blackness (again with a sexual suggestion)
151: **folly:** desire, wantonness

IAGO
 O gentle lady, do not put me to 't,
 For I am nothing, if not critical.

DESDEMONA
 Come on, assay. — There's one gone to the harbour?

IAGO
 Ay, madam.   135

DESDEMONA
 I am not merry, but I do beguile
 The thing I am by seeming otherwise. —
 Come, how wouldst thou praise me?

IAGO
 I am about it, but indeed my invention
 Comes from my pate as birdlime does from frize.   140
 It plucks out brains and all, but my Muse labours,
 And thus she is delivered:
                If she be fair and wise, fairness and wit,
                The one's for use, the other useth it.

DESDEMONA
 Well praised! How if she be black and witty?   145

IAGO
                If she be black, and thereto have a wit,
                She'll find a white that shall her blackness fit.

DESDEMONA
 Worse and worse.

EMILIA
 How if fair and foolish?

IAGO
                She never yet was foolish that was fair;   150
                For even her folly helped her to an heir.

152: **fond:** foolish

155: **foul pranks:** sexual acts (bawdy description)

158: **vouch:** testimony

160: **tongue at will:** could control her tongue/speak eloquently

161: **gay:** ostentatiously

166: **change the cod's...tail:** exchange something of value for something of little or no value (also a sexual pun)

169: **wight:** person

171: **chronicle small beer:** record trivial matters

174: **profane:** irreverent

174: **liberal:** wanton, licentious

175: **home:** without reserve, to the point

DESDEMONA

These are old fond paradoxes to make fools laugh i' th' alehouse. What miserable praise hast thou for her that's foul and foolish?

IAGO

> *There's none so foul and foolish thereunto,*
> *But does foul pranks which fair and wise ones do.*   155

DESDEMONA

O heavy ignorance! Thou praisest the worst best. But what praise couldst thou bestow on a deserving woman indeed, one that, in the authority of her merit, did justly put on the vouch of very malice itself?

IAGO

> *She that was ever fair and never proud,*
> *Had tongue at will and yet was never loud,*   160
> *Never lacked gold and yet went never gay,*
> *Fled from her wish and yet said, "Now I may,"*
> *She that being angered, her revenge being nigh,*
> *Bade her wrong stay and her displeasure fly.*
> *She that in wisdom never was so frail*   165
> *To change the cod's head for the salmon's tail,*
> *She that could think and ne'er disclose her mind,*
> *See suitors following and not look behind,*
> *She was a wight, if ever such wights were, –*

DESDEMONA

To do what?   170

IAGO

> *To suckle fools and chronicle small beer.*

DESDEMONA

O, most lame and impotent conclusion! Do not learn of him, Emilia, though he be thy husband. How say you, Cassio? Is he not a most profane and liberal counsellor?

CASSIO

He speaks home, madam. You may relish him more in   175
the soldier than in the scholar.

179: **gyve:** bind, ensnare

181–182: **kissed your three fingers:** a gesture of courtesy

182: **play the sir:** appear to be a gentleman

184–185: **clyster-pipes:** medical tubes (e.g., for enemas)

190–225:
Hugh Quarshie as Othello, Emma Fielding as Desdemona
Paul Robeson as Othello, Uta Hagen as Desdemona

Lines 192–193: "It gives me wonder great as my content / To see you here before me": John Kani as Othello and Joanna Weinberg as Desdemona in The Market Theater's 1987 production directed by Janet Suzman
Photo: Ruphin Coudyzer

196: **bark:** ship

196: **hills of seas:** tall waves

IAGO

[*Aside*] He takes her by the palm. Ay, well said, whisper. With as
little a web as this will I ensnare as great a fly as Cassio. Ay, smile
upon her, do. I will gyve thee in thine own courtship. You say
true; 'tis so, indeed. If such tricks as these strip you out of your   180
lieutenantry, it had been better you had not kissed your three
fingers so oft, which now again you are most apt to play the sir
in. Very good; well kissed; an excellent courtesy! 'Tis so, indeed.
Yet again your fingers to your lips? Would they were clyster-
pipes for your sake!   185

[Trumpet within]

The Moor! I know his trumpet.

CASSIO

'Tis truly so.

DESDEMONA

Let's meet him and receive him.

CASSIO

Lo, where he comes!

[Enter OTHELLO and Attendants]

OTHELLO

O my fair warrior!   190

DESDEMONA

My dear Othello!

OTHELLO

It gives me wonder great as my content
To see you here before me. O my soul's joy!
If after every tempest come such calms,
May the winds blow till they have wakened death,   195
And let the labouring bark climb hills of seas
Olympus-high and duck again as low
As hell's from heaven! If it were now to die,
'Twere now to be most happy, for I fear

tracks 10-11

190–225:
Hugh Quarshie as Othello, Emma Fielding as Desdemona
Paul Robeson as Othello, Uta Hagen as Desdemona

212: **set down the pegs:** loosen the strings

221: **disembark my coffers:** remove my trunks/luggage from the ship

222: **master:** ship's captain

224: **challenge:** demand, deserve

Jimmon Cole as Roderigo and Ron Canada as Iago in The Shakespeare Theatre's
1997-1998 production directed by Jude Kelly
Photo: Carol Rosegg

My soul hath her content so absolute   200
That not another comfort like to this
Succeeds in unknown fate.

DESDEMONA
    The heavens forbid
But that our loves and comforts should increase,
Even as our days do grow!   205

OTHELLO
    Amen to that, sweet powers!
I cannot speak enough of this content.
It stops me here; it is too much of joy:
And this, and this, the greatest discords be

                                                      [Kissing her]
That e'er our hearts shall make!   210

IAGO
    [Aside] O, you are well tuned now!
But I'll set down the pegs that make this music,
As honest as I am.

OTHELLO
                    Come, let us to the castle. —
News, friends. Our wars are done, the Turks are drowned.   215
How does my old acquaintance of this isle? —
Honey, you shall be well desired in Cyprus;
I have found great love amongst them. O, my sweet,
I prattle out of fashion, and I dote
In mine own comforts. — I prithee, good Iago,   220
Go to the bay and disembark my coffers.
Bring thou the master to the citadel.
He is a good one, and his worthiness
Does challenge much respect. — Come, Desdemona. —
Once more, well met at Cyprus.   225
                    [Exeunt OTHELLO, DESDEMONA, and Attendants]

227: **be'st:** are (archaic verb tense of "to be")

229: **list me:** listen to me

233: **lay thy finger thus:** i.e., alongside the nose or possibly over the mouth (both gestures imply keeping a secret)

234: **violence:** passion, strength

235: **prating:** bragging

238: **act of sport:** sexual intercourse

239: **saiety:** excessive gratification

242: **heave the gorge:** vomit

242: **disrelish:** loathe

245: **pregnant:** clear, natural

246: **very voluble:** of quick tongue, witty

247: **conscionable:** conscientious

248: **compassing:** reach

248: **salt:** lechery

249: **hidden loose affection:** secret lasciviousness

249: **slipper:** slippery

250–251: **stamp and counterfeit advantage:** create or feign opportunity

253: **green:** young, immature

254: **pestilent:** disagreeable

256: **condition:** character, temper

IAGO

[*To attendant*] Do thou meet me presently at the harbour.
[*To Roderigo*] Come hither. If thou be'st valiant, — as they say,
base men being in love have then a nobility in their natures more
than is native to them — list me. The lieutenant tonight watches
on the court of guard. — first, I must tell thee this — Desdemona   230
is directly in love with him.

RODERIGO

With him! Why, 'tis not possible.

IAGO

Lay thy finger thus, and let thy soul be instructed. Mark me with
what violence she first loved the Moor, but for bragging and
telling her fantastical lies. To love him still for prating? Let not   235
thy discreet heart think it. Her eye must be fed, and what delight
shall she have to look on the devil? When the blood is made dull
with the act of sport there should be a game to inflame it and give
satiety a fresh appetite. Loveliness in favor, sympathy in years,
manners, and beauties, all which the Moor is defective in. Now,   240
for want of these required conveniences, her delicate tenderness
will find itself abused, begin to heave the gorge, disrelish and
abhor the Moor. Very nature will instruct her in it and compel her
to some second choice. Now, sir, this granted, — as it is a most
pregnant and unforced position — who stands so eminent in the   245
degree of this fortune as Cassio does? A knave very voluble, no
further conscionable than in putting on the mere form of civil and
humane seeming for the better compassing of his salt and most
hidden loose affection. Why, none; why, none! A slipper and subtle knave, a finder out of occasions that has an eye can stamp and   250
counterfeit advantages, though true advantage never present
itself. A devilish knave. Besides, the knave is handsome, young,
and hath all those requisites in him that folly and green minds
look after. A pestilent complete knave, and the woman hath found
him already.   255

RODERIGO

I cannot believe that in her; she's full of most blessed condition.

257: **fig's end:** an exclamation (with a bawdy undertone)

259: **paddle:** finger, toy with

262: **index:** preface

265: **mutualities:** intimacies

265: **marshal:** lead

267: **incorporate:** made one body

267: **Pish:** an interjection expressing contempt or disgust

271: **tainting:** discrediting

275: **choler:** anger (one of the four humours)

275: **haply:** perchance, by chance

278: **displanting:** removal from office

IAGO

    Blessed fig's end! The wine she drinks is made of grapes. If she
    had been blessed, she would never have loved the Moor. Blessed
    pudding! Didst thou not see her paddle with the palm of his hand?
    Didst not mark that?   260

RODERIGO

    Yes, that I did, but that was but courtesy.

IAGO

    Lechery, by this hand. An index and obscure prologue to the
    history of lust and foul thoughts. They met so near with their
    lips that their breaths embraced together. Villanous thoughts,
    Roderigo! When these mutualities so marshal the way, hard   265
    at hand comes the master and main exercise, th' incorporate
    conclusion. Pish!
    But, sir, be you ruled by me. I have brought you from Venice.
    Watch you tonight, for the command I'll lay't upon you. Cassio
    knows you not. I'll not be far from you. Do you find some occasion   270
    to anger Cassio, either by speaking too loud, or tainting his
    discipline, or from what other course you please, which the time
    shall more favourably minister.

RODERIGO

    Well.

IAGO

    Sir, he's rash and very sudden in choler and haply may strike at   275
    you. Provoke him that he may, for even out of that will I cause
    these of Cyprus to mutiny, whose qualification shall come into no
    true taste again but by the displanting of Cassio. So shall you have
    a shorter journey to your desires by the means I shall then have to
    prefer them, and the impediment most profitably removed, with-   280
    out the which there were no expectation of our prosperity.

RODERIGO

    I will do this, if I can bring it to any opportunity.

283: **warrant:** assure

288: **howbeit:** although

292: **peradventure:** perhaps

296: **hath leaped into my seat:** i.e., has had an affair with my wife

297: **inwards:** innards

303: **trash:** used twice, the first time meaning a worthless object; the second, meaning restrict movement (e.g., with the use of a choker collar or weights)

304: **putting on:** provoking

305: **on the hip:** at a disadvantage

306: **rank garb:** lustful manner

307: **with my nightcap too:** in his bed (i.e., with Emilia)

IAGO

I warrant thee. Meet me by and by at the citadel. I must fetch his
necessaries ashore. Farewell.

RODERIGO

Adieu.   285

[Exit]

IAGO

That Cassio loves her, I do well believe 't;
That she loves him, 'tis apt and of great credit.
The Moor, howbeit that I endure him not,
Is of a constant, loving, noble nature,
And I dare think he'll prove to Desdemona   290
A most dear husband. Now, I do love her too,
Not out of absolute lust — though peradventure
I stand accountant for as great a sin —
But partly led to diet my revenge,
For that I do suspect the lusty Moor   295
Hath leaped into my seat. The thought whereof
Doth, like a poisonous mineral, gnaw my inwards,
And nothing can or shall content my soul
Till I am evened with him, wife for wife.
Or failing so, yet that I put the Moor   300
At least into a jealousy so strong
That judgment cannot cure. Which thing to do,
If this poor trash of Venice, whom I trace
For his quick hunting, stand the putting on.
I'll have our Michael Cassio on the hip,   305
Abuse him to the Moor in the rank garb —
For I fear Cassio with my nightcap too —
Make the Moor thank me, love me, and reward me
For making him egregiously an ass
And practising upon his peace and quiet   310
Even to madness. 'Tis here, but yet confused.
Knavery's plain face is never seen till used.

[Exit]

2: **perdition:** destruction, ruin

Costume rendering of "Herald" from the 1951 staging by Orson Welles at St. James
Theatre

Rare Book and Special Collections Library, University of Illinois at Urbana-Champaign

Act 2, Scene 2]

[A street.]
[Enter Othello's Herald with a proclamation]

Herald
It is Othello's pleasure, our noble and valiant general, that upon
certain tidings now arrived importing the mere perdition of the
Turkish fleet, every man put himself into triumph: some to dance,
some to make bonfires, each man to what sport and revels his
addiction leads him. For, besides these beneficial news, it is the   5
celebration of his nuptial. So much was his pleasure should be
proclaimed. All offices are open, and there is full liberty of feast-
ing from this present hour of five till the bell have told eleven.
Heaven bless the isle of Cyprus and our noble general Othello!

[Exeunt]

2: **honourable stop:** i.e., the socially responsible limits of drinking

3: **outsport:** celebrate excessively (in this case, more than discretion dictates)

8: **with your earliest:** i.e., at your earliest convenience

10: **purchase:** acquisition i.e., marriage

10: **fruits are to ensue:** i.e., the marriage has yet to be consummated

Lines 9–10: "Come, my dear love. / The purchase made, the fruits are to ensue":
James Earl Jones as Othello and Julienne Marie as Desdemona in the Public
Theater's 1964 production directed by Gladys Vaughan
Photo: George E. Joseph

15: **cast:** dismissed

17: **Jove:** from mythology, the supreme god, a.k.a. Jupiter, also known for sexual
conquests

Act 2, Scene 3]

[Enter OTHELLO, DESDEMONA, CASSIO, and Attendants]

OTHELLO
Good Michael, look you to the guard tonight.
Let's teach ourselves that honourable stop
Not to outsport discretion.

CASSIO
Iago hath direction what to do,
But, notwithstanding, with my personal eye   5
Will I look to 't.

OTHELLO
                Iago is most honest.
Michael, good night. Tomorrow with your earliest
Let me have speech with you. — Come, my dear love,
The purchase made, the fruits are to ensue.   10
That profit's yet to come 'tween me and you. —
Good night.
            [Exeunt OTHELLO, DESDEMONA, and Attendants]
                            [Enter IAGO]

CASSIO
Welcome, Iago. We must to the watch.

IAGO
Not this hour, lieutenant; 'tis not yet ten o' the clock. Our general
cast us thus early for the love of his Desdemona, who let us not   15
therefore blame. He hath not yet made wanton the night with her,
and she is sport for Jove.

CASSIO
She's a most exquisite lady.

Jordan Baker as Desdemona and Avery Brooks as Othello in The Shakespeare
Theatre's 1990-1991 production directed by Harold Scott
Photo: Joan Marcus

19: **game:** i.e., sexual play

21: **sounds a parley:** calls for a conference (with an opponent)

23: **alarum:** call to arms (contrast to "love", i.e., the love-war metaphor also in line 21)

25: **stoup:** a drinking vessel

26: **without:** outside

26: **brace:** a couple

26: **gallants:** gentlemen

27: **fain:** gladly

32: **qualified:** mixed with water

IAGO
And, I'll warrant her, full of game.

CASSIO
Indeed, she's a most fresh and delicate creature.   20

IAGO
What an eye she has! Methinks it sounds a parley of provocation.

CASSIO
An inviting eye, and yet methinks right modest.

IAGO
And when she speaks, is it not an alarum to love?

CASSIO
She is indeed perfection.

IAGO
Well, happiness to their sheets! Come, lieutenant, I have a stoup   25
of wine, and here without are a brace of Cyprus gallants that
would fain have a measure to the health of black Othello.

CASSIO
Not tonight, good Iago; I have very poor and unhappy brains for
drinking. I could well wish courtesy would invent some other
custom of entertainment.   30

IAGO
O, they are our friends! But one cup; I'll drink for you.

CASSIO
I have drunk but one cup tonight, and that was craftily qualified
too, and, behold, what innovation it makes here. I am unfortunate
in the infirmity and dare not task my weakness with any more.

IAGO
What, man! 'Tis a night of revels; the gallants desire it.   35

39: **fasten:** persuade

44: **caroused:** drunk hard

45: **potations:** liquor

45: **pottle:** two-quart tankard

46: **swelling:** proud, boastful

47: **hold...distance:** i.e., scrupulous about upholding their personal integrity

52: **offend the isle:** i.e., offend the people on the island

55: **rouse:** free and copious drinking

Line 57: "Some wine, ho!": Costume rendering for Wine Carrier from the 1951 staging by Orson Welles at St. James Theatre
Rare Book and Special Collections Library, University of Illinois at Urbana-Champaign

58: **canakin:** little can

CASSIO
    Where are they?

IAGO
    Here at the door. I pray you, call them in.

CASSIO
    I'll do't, but it dislikes me.

                                                            [Exit]

IAGO
    If I can fasten but one cup upon him,
    With that which he hath drunk tonight already,   40
    He'll be as full of quarrel and offence
    As my young mistress' dog. Now, my sick fool Roderigo,
    Whom love hath turned almost the wrong side out,
    To Desdemona hath tonight caroused
    Potations pottle-deep, and he's to watch.   45
    Three lads of Cyprus, noble swelling spirits
    That hold their honours in a wary distance,
    The very elements of this warlike isle,
    Have I tonight flustered with flowing cups,
    And they watch too. Now, 'mongst this flock of drunkards,   50
    Am I to put our Cassio in some action
    That may offend the isle. — But here they come.
    If consequence do but approve my dream,
    My boat sails freely, both with wind and stream.
                    [Enter CASSIO, MONTANO, and Gentlemen]

CASSIO
    'Fore God, they have given me a rouse already.   55

MONTANO
    Good faith, a little one. Not past a pint, as I am a soldier.

IAGO
    Some wine, ho!
                                                            [Sings]

            And let me the canakin clink, clink;
            And let me the canakin clink.

66: **potting:** drinking

66: **swag-bellied:** round, beer-bellied

69: **drinks you, with facility:** outdrinks you with ease

70: **sweats not to overthrow:** effortlessly outdrinks

70: **Almain:** German

70–71: **gives...a vomit:** outdrinks (the Dutch) past the point of vomiting

75: **peer:** lord

76: **crown:** a coin (five shillings)

78: **lown:** loon (crazy)

79: **wight:** man

82: **auld:** old

> *A soldier's a man,*   60
> *A life's but a span,*
> *Why, then, let a soldier drink.*

Some wine, boys!

CASSIO
'Fore God, an excellent song.

IAGO
I learned it in England, where indeed, they are most potent in   65
potting. Your Dane, your German, and your swag-bellied Hollander
— Drink, ho! — are nothing to your English.

CASSIO
Is your Englishman so exquisite in his drinking?

IAGO
Why, he drinks you, with facility, your Dane dead drunk; he
sweats not to overthrow your Almain; he gives your Hollander a   70
vomit ere the next pottle can be filled.

CASSIO
To the health of our general!

MONTANO
I am for it, lieutenant, and I'll do you justice.

IAGO
O sweet England!

> *King Stephen was a worthy peer,*   75
> *His breeches cost him but a crown;*
> *He held them sixpence all too dear,*
> *With that he called the tailor lown.*
> *He was a wight of high renown,*
> *And thou art but of low degree.*   80
> *'Tis pride that pulls the country down;*
> *Then take thine auld cloak about thee.*

Some wine, ho!

85: **hear 't:** a contraction for "hear it"

91: **quality:** rank

93–94: **lieutenant...ancient:** note that Cassio again makes reference to his superior rank over Iago

97: **my right hand:** Cassio begins by speaking of Iago ("his right hand man"), then in his drunkenness switches to a more literal meaning

CASSIO

Why, this is a more exquisite song than the other.

IAGO

Will you hear 't again?   85

CASSIO

No, for I hold him to be unworthy of his place that does those
things. Well, God's above all, and there be souls must be saved,
and there be souls must not be saved.

IAGO

It's true, good lieutenant.

CASSIO

For mine own part, — no offence to the general, nor any man of   90
quality, — I hope to be saved.

IAGO

And so do I too, lieutenant.

CASSIO

Ay, but by your leave, not before me. The lieutenant is to be saved
before the ancient. Let's have no more of this. Let's to our affairs.
— Forgive us our sins! — Gentlemen, let's look to our business.   95
Do not think, gentlemen. I am drunk. This is my ancient; this is
my right hand, and this is my left. I am not drunk now. I can
stand well enough, and I speak well enough.

All

Excellent well.

CASSIO

Why, very well then. You must not think then that I am drunk.   100
                                                                [Exit]

MONTANO

To th' platform, masters. Come, let's set the watch.

105: **a just equinox:** of equal size, importance

108: **on:** at

108: **odd time of his infirmity:** when his defect overcomes him

112: **horologe:** clock

112: **a double set:** twice around (i.e., 24 hours)

115: **put in mind of it:** told about it

122: **second:** second in command

123: **ingraft infirmity:** deeply rooted character weakness

Set rendering for "The Brawl" from the 1951 staging by Orson Welles at St. James Theatre

Rare Book and Special Collections Library, University of Illinois at Urbana-Champaign

IAGO
  You see this fellow that is gone before?
  He is a soldier fit to stand by Caesar
  And give direction; and do but see his vice.
  'Tis to his virtue a just equinox,   105
  The one as long as th' other. 'Tis pity of him.
  I fear the trust Othello puts him in
  On some odd time of his infirmity,
  Will shake this island.

MONTANO
                    But is he often thus?   110

IAGO
  'Tis evermore the prologue to his sleep.
  He'll watch the horologe a double set,
  If drink rock not his cradle.

MONTANO
                    It were well
  The general were put in mind of it.   115
  Perhaps he sees it not, or his good nature
  Prizes the virtue that appears in Cassio
  And looks not on his evils. Is not this true?

                                    [Enter RODERIGO]

IAGO
  [*Aside to him*] How now, Roderigo!
  I pray you, after the lieutenant; go.   120
                                    [Exit RODERIGO]

MONTANO
  And 'tis great pity that the noble Moor
  Should hazard such a place as his own second
  With one of an ingraft infirmity.
  It were an honest action to say
  So to the Moor.   125

132: **twiggen:** wicker

134: **prate:** brag, speak idly

138: **mazzard:** head

Lines 137–138: "Let me go, sir, / Or I'll knock you o'er the mazzard": Neil McCarthy as Cassio in The Market Theater's 1987 production directed by Janet Suzman
Photo: Ruphin Coudyzer

IAGO
                    Not I, for this fair island.
        I do love Cassio well and would do much
        To cure him of this evil. — But, hark! What noise?
                            [Cry within: "Help! Help!"]
                        [Enter CASSIO, pursuing RODERIGO]

CASSIO
        You rogue! You rascal!

MONTANO
                    What's the matter, lieutenant?   130

CASSIO
        A knave teach me my duty!
        I'll beat the knave into a twiggen bottle.

RODERIGO
                    Beat me?

CASSIO
                    Dost thou prate, rogue?
                            [Striking RODERIGO]

MONTANO
                            Nay, good lieutenant;   135
                                    [Staying him]
        I pray you, sir, hold your hand.

CASSIO
                    Let me go, sir,
        Or I'll knock you o'er the mazzard.

MONTANO
                    Come, come, you're drunk.

CASSIO
        Drunk!   140
                                    [They fight]

141: **cry a mutiny:** rouse the neighbors with yelling

145: **Diablo:** the devil

Line 149: "'Zounds, I bleed still. I am hurt to th' death. He dies!": Sean Michael
Dooley as Citizen of Cyprus, Shawn Hamilton as Montano, Lester Purry as Othello,
Bill McCallum as Iago, and Robert O. Berdahl as Cassio in the Guthrie Theater's
2003 production directed by Joe Dowling
Photo: T. Charles Erickson

154: **whence:** what place

158: **carve for:** indulge

159: **light:** unimportant, of little value

159: **upon his motion:** as soon as he moves

161: **propriety:** proper state

IAGO

[*Aside to RODERIGO*] Away, I say. Go out, and cry a mutiny.

[*Exit RODERIGO*]

Nay, good lieutenant. — God's will, gentlemen. —
Help, ho! — Lieutenant — sir — Montano — sir —
Help, masters! — Here's a goodly watch indeed!

[*Bell rings*]

Who's that which rings the bell? — Diablo, ho!   145
The town will rise. God's will, lieutenant, hold!
You will be shamed forever.

[*Enter OTHELLO and Attendants*]

OTHELLO

What is the matter here?

MONTANO

'Zounds, I bleed still. I am hurt to th' death. He dies!

[*Attacks CASSIO*]

OTHELLO

Hold, for your lives!   150

IAGO

Hold, ho! Lieutenant — sir — Montano — gentlemen —
Have you forgot all sense of place and duty?
Hold! The general speaks to you. Hold! For shame!

OTHELLO

Why, how now, ho! From whence ariseth this?
Are we turned Turks and to ourselves do that   155
Which heaven hath forbid the Ottomites?
For Christian shame, put by this barbarous brawl.
He that stirs next to carve for his own rage
Holds his soul light; he dies upon his motion.
Silence that dreadful bell. It frights the isle   160
From her propriety. What is the matter, masters?
Honest Iago, that looks dead with grieving,
Speak, who began this? On thy love, I charge thee.

165: **like bride and groom:** i.e., like Othello and Desdemona

166: **devesting:** disrobing, undressing

167: **unwitted:** deprived of understanding

170: **peevish odds:** silly conflict

173: **you are thus forgot:** i.e., you have forgotten your manners

175: **wont:** accustomed to

178: **censure:** judgment

180: **spend your rich opinion:** compromise your reputation

182: **hurt to danger:** dangerously hurt

185: **aught:** anything

187: **Unless self-charity...vice:** unless it is wrong to care for one's own well being

191: **blood:** anger

IAGO

    I do not know. Friends all but now, even now,
    In quarter, and in terms like bride and groom   165
    Devesting them for bed. And then, but now,
    As if some planet had unwitted men,
    Swords out and tilting one at other's breast,
    In opposition bloody. I cannot speak
    Any beginning to this peevish odds,   170
    And would, in action glorious, I had lost
    Those legs that brought me to a part of it.

OTHELLO

    How comes it, Michael, you are thus forgot?

CASSIO

    I pray you, pardon me. I cannot speak.

OTHELLO

    Worthy Montano, you were wont to be civil.   175
    The gravity and stillness of your youth
    The world hath noted, and your name is great
    In mouths of wisest censure. What's the matter,
    That you unlace your reputation thus
    And spend your rich opinion for the name   180
    Of a night-brawler? Give me answer to it.

MONTANO

    Worthy Othello, I am hurt to danger.
    Your officer, Iago, can inform you,
    While I spare speech, which something now offends me,
    Of all that I do know; nor know I aught   185
    By me that's said or done amiss this night,
    Unless self-charity be sometimes a vice,
    And to defend ourselves, it be a sin
    When violence assails us.

OTHELLO

                Now, by heaven,   190
    My blood begins my safer guides to rule,

192: **collied:** blackened

193: **assays:** tries

196: **rout:** brawl

198: **Though he had...at a birth:** even if he were my own twin

204: **affined:** bound by duty of friendship

204: **leagued in office:** bound in service

216: **entreats his pause:** begs him to hold/stop

220: **then rather:** more rapidly

Line 221: "For that I heard the clink and fall of swords": Sir Derek Jacobi as Cassio and Ensemble in Stuart Burge's 1965 movie production
Courtesy: Douglas Lanier

222: **high in oath:** swearing loudly

And passion, having my best judgment collied,
Assays to lead the way. If I once stir
Or do but lift this arm, the best of you
Shall sink in my rebuke. Give me to know   195
How this foul rout began, who set it on;
And he that is approved in this offence,
Though he had twinned with me both at a birth
Shall lose me. What! In a town of war
Yet wild, the people's hearts brimful of fear,   200
To manage private and domestic quarrel
In night and on the court and guard of safety?
'Tis monstrous! Iago, who began 't?

MONTANO

If partially affined or leagued in office,
Thou dost deliver more or less than truth,   205
Thou art no soldier.

IAGO
                    Touch me not so near.
I had rather have this tongue cut from my mouth
Than it should do offence to Michael Cassio.
Yet, I persuade myself, to speak the truth   210
Shall nothing wrong him. Thus it is, general.
Montano and myself being in speech,
There comes a fellow crying out for help,
And Cassio following him with determined sword
To execute upon him. Sir, this gentleman   215
Steps in to Cassio and entreats his pause.
Myself the crying fellow did pursue,
Lest by his clamour, as it so fell out,
The town might fall in fright. He, swift of foot,
Outran my purpose. And I returned then rather   220
For that I heard the clink and fall of swords
And Cassio high in oath, which till tonight
I ne'er might say before. When I came back,
For this was brief, I found them close together,
At blow and thrust, even as again they were   225
When you yourself did part them.

232: **indignity:** insult, contemptuous injury

233: **patience:** calmness, composure

233: **pass:** ignore

Lines 236–237: "Cassio, I love thee, / But nevermore be officer of mine": Cheyenne Casebier as Desdemona, Lester Purry as Othello, and Robert O. Berdahl as Cassio in the Guthrie Theater's 2003 production directed by Joe Dowling
Photo: T. Charles Erickson

235: **mince:** soften, lessen

More of this matter cannot I report,
But men are men; the best sometimes forget.
Though Cassio did some little wrong to him,
As men in rage strike those that wish them best,   230
Yet surely Cassio, I believe, received
From him that fled some strange indignity,
Which patience could not pass.

OTHELLO
                    I know, Iago,
Thy honesty and love doth mince this matter,   235
Making it light to Cassio. Cassio, I love thee,
But never more be officer of mine.
                                        [Enter DESDEMONA, attended]
Look if my gentle love be not raised up!
I'll make thee an example.

DESDEMONA
                    What's the matter?   240

OTHELLO
All's well now, sweeting; come away to bed. —
Sir, for your hurts, myself will be your surgeon. —
Lead him off. —
                                        [MONTANO is led off]
Iago, look with care about the town
And silence those whom this vile brawl distracted. —   245
Come, Desdemona, 'tis the soldiers' life
To have their balmy slumbers waked with strife.
                                [Exeunt all but IAGO and CASSIO]

IAGO
What, are you hurt, lieutenant?

CASSIO
Ay, past all surgery.

IAGO
Marry, heaven forbid!   250

252: **immortal:** i.e., in the sense that one's reputation lives on even after one dies, a common theme in Shakespeare's sonnets

259: **recover the general:** regain his favour

259: **cast in his mood:** dismissed because of his mood (i.e., his anger)

261: **sue to him:** entreat him, beg your case to him

265: **parrot:** squawk like a parrot, babble

266: **fustian:** nonsense

273: **nothing wherefore:** no reasons why

275: **pleasance:** merriment

CASSIO

Reputation, reputation, reputation! O, I have lost my reputation! I have lost the immortal part of myself and what remains is bestial. My reputation, Iago, my reputation!

IAGO

As I am an honest man, I thought you had received some bodily wound. There is more sense in that than in reputation. Reputation is an idle and most false imposition, oft got without merit and lost without deserving. You have lost no reputation at all, unless you repute yourself such a loser. What, man, there are ways to recover the general again. You are but now cast in his mood, a punishment more in policy than in malice, even so as one would beat his offenseless dog to affright an imperious lion. Sue to him again, and he's yours.

CASSIO

I will rather sue to be despised than to deceive so good a commander with so slight, so drunken, and so indiscreet an officer. Drunk? And speak parrot? And squabble? Swagger? Swear? And discourse fustian with one's own shadow? O thou invisible spirit of wine, if thou hast no name to be known by, let us call thee devil!

IAGO

What was he that you followed with your sword? What had he done to you?

CASSIO

I know not.

IAGO

Is 't possible?

CASSIO

I remember a mass of things, but nothing distinctly; a quarrel, but nothing wherefore. O God, that men should put an enemy in their mouths to steal away their brains! That we should, with joy, pleasance revel, and applause, transform ourselves into beasts!

255

260

265

270

275

280: **moraler:** moralizer

284: **Hydra:** a creature from Greek mythology said to look like a many-headed snake; each time a head was cut off, two would grow in its place

286: **inordinate:** immoderate

291: **approved:** experienced

296: **importune:** eagerly solicit

299: **broken joint:** broken connection/friendship

300: **splinter:** bind back together (a gardening term)

300: **lay:** bet

IAGO

Why, but you are now well enough? How came you thus recovered?

CASSIO

It hath pleased the devil drunkenness to give place to the devil wrath. One unperfectness shows me another to make me frankly despise myself.

IAGO

Come, you are too severe a moraler. As the time, the place, and the   280
condition of this country stands, I could heartily wish this had not befallen, but, since it is as it is, mend it for your own good.

CASSIO

I will ask him for my place again; he shall tell me I am a drunk-ard! Had I as many mouths as Hydra, such an answer would stop them all. To be now a sensible man, by and by a fool, and   285
presently a beast! O strange! Every inordinate cup is unblessed and the ingredient is a devil.

IAGO

Come, come, good wine is a good familiar creature if it be well used. Exclaim no more against it. And, good lieutenant, I think you think I love you.   290

CASSIO

I have well approved it, sir. — I drunk!

IAGO

You or any man living may be drunk at a time, man. I'll tell you what you shall do. Our general's wife is now the general. I may say so in this respect, for that he hath devoted and given up him-self to the contemplation, mark, and denotement of her parts and   295
graces. Confess yourself freely to her. Importune her help to put you in your place again. She is of so free, so kind, so apt, so blessed a disposition, she holds it a vice in her goodness not to do more than she is requested. This broken joint between you and her hus-band entreat her to splinter, and, my fortunes against any lay   300
worth naming, this crack of your love shall grow stronger than it was before.

304: **protest:** declare (affection)

305: **betimes:** early

307: **cheque:** stop, repress

312: **probal:** probable, likely

314: **inclining:** favorably disposed

315: **framed:** formed, fashioned

315: **fruitful:** bountiful, generous

316: **free elements:** basic elements of nature

317: **win:** persuade

319: **enfettered:** chained

320: **list:** desires

322: **function:** ability

CASSIO
You advise me well.

IAGO
I protest, in the sincerity of love and honest kindness.

CASSIO
I think it freely, and betimes in the morning I will beseech the   305
virtuous Desdemona to undertake for me. I am desperate of my
fortunes if they cheque me here.

IAGO
You are in the right. Good night, lieutenant; I must to the watch.

CASSIO
Good night, honest Iago.

[Exit]

IAGO
And what's he then that says I play the villain   310
When this advice is free I give and honest,
Probal to thinking, and indeed the course
To win the Moor again? For 'tis most easy
The inclining Desdemona to subdue
In any honest suit. She's framed as fruitful   315
As the free elements. And then for her
To win the Moor — were't to renounce his baptism,
All seals and symbols of redeemèd sin —
His soul is so enfettered to her love
That she may make, unmake, do what she list,   320
Even as her appetite shall play the god
With his weak function. How am I then a villain
To counsel Cassio to this parallel course,
Directly to his good? Divinity of hell!
When devils will the blackest sins put on,   325
They do suggest at first with heavenly shows
As I do now. For whiles this honest fool
Plies Desdemona to repair his fortunes,
And she for him pleads strongly to the Moor,

331: **repeals him:** restores Cassio to his position

334: **pitch:** black tar

Lines 334–336: "So will I turn her virtue into pitch, / And out of her own goodness make the net / That shall enmesh us all": Richard Haddon Haines as Iago in The Market Theater's 1987 production directed by Janet Suzman
Photo: Ruphin Coudyzer

339: **cry:** a pack of hounds

340: **cudgelled:** beaten

340: **issue:** final result

346: **dilatory:** full of delays

348: **hast cashiered Cassio:** have gotten Cassio dismissed from office

353: **billeted:** lodged

357: **move for:** plead for

360: **jump:** exactly

362: **dull not device:** do not dampen his plot

362: **coldness:** want of zeal

I'll pour this pestilence into his ear: 330
That she repeals him for her body's lust.
And by how much she strives to do him good,
She shall undo her credit with the Moor.
So will I turn her virtue into pitch,
And out of her own goodness make the net 335
That shall enmesh them all.

[Enter RODERIGO]

How now, Roderigo!

RODERIGO

I do follow here in the chase, not like a hound that hunts, but one
that fills up the cry. My money is almost spent; I have been
tonight exceedingly well cudgelled; and I think the issue will be, 340
I shall have so much experience for my pains, and so, with no
money at all and a little more wit, return again to Venice.

IAGO

How poor are they that have not patience!
What wound did ever heal but by degrees?
Thou know'st we work by wit and not by witchcraft, 345
And wit depends on dilatory time.
Does't not go well? Cassio hath beaten thee,
And thou, by that small hurt, hast cashiered Cassio.
Though other things grow fair against the sun,
Yet fruits that blossom first will first be ripe. 350
Content thyself awhile. By the mass, 'tis morning!
Pleasure and action make the hours seem short.
Retire thee; go where thou art billeted.
Away, I say! Thou shalt know more hereafter.
Nay, get thee gone. 355

[Exit RODERIGO]

Two things are to be done.
My wife must move for Cassio to her mistress;
I'll set her on.
Myself the while to draw the Moor apart,
And bring him jump when he may Cassio find 360
Soliciting his wife. Ay, that's the way.
Dull not device by coldness and delay.

[Exit]

[Othello

Act 3

1: **masters:** the musicians

1: **content your pains:** i.e., pay for your services

3: **instruments:** musical instruments (also, pun on penis)

4: **i' th' nose:** nasally (also an allusion to syphilis, a venereal disease that also causes nasal deformity and was reputed to have first appeared in Naples)

8: **a tail:** a tale, story (also pun on penis)

Act 3, Scene 1]

[Enter CASSIO and Musicians]

CASSIO
Masters, play here. I will content your pains.
Something that's brief and bid "Good morrow, general."

[Music]
[Enter Clown]

Clown
Why masters, have your instruments been in Naples, that they
speak i' th' nose thus?

First Musician
How, sir, how?   5

Clown
Are these, I pray you, wind instruments?

First Musician
Ay, marry, are they, sir.

Clown
O, thereby hangs a tail.

First Musician
Whereby hangs a tale, sir?

Clown
Marry, sir, by many a wind instrument that I know. But, masters,   10
here's money for you; and the general so likes your music that he
desires you, for love's sake, to make no more noise with it.

First Musician
Well, sir, we will not.

21: **quillets:** clever and tricky banter

23: **favour:** indulgence (of her time)

26: **In happy time:** i.e., just in time

Set rendering of "Street" from the 1951 staging by Orson Welles at
St. James Theatre
Rare Book and Special Collections Library, University of Illinois at Urbana-Champaign

27: **abed:** to bed

30: **suit:** petition

Clown
> If you have any music that may not be heard, to 't again, but, as
> they say, to hear music the general does not greatly care.   15

First Musician
> We have none such, sir.

Clown
> Then put up your pipes in your bag, for I'll away. Go, vanish into
> air, away!
>
> > *[Exeunt Musicians]*

CASSIO
> Dost thou hear, my honest friend?

Clown
> No, I hear not your honest friend; I hear you.   20

CASSIO
> Prithee, keep up thy quillets. There's a poor piece of gold for thee. If the
> gentlewoman that attends the general's wife be stirring, tell her there's
> one Cassio entreats her a little favour of speech. Wilt thou do this?

Clown
> She is stirring, sir. If she will stir hither, I shall seem to notify unto her.

CASSIO
> Do, good my friend.   25
>
> > *[Exit Clown]*
> > *[Enter IAGO]*
>
>   In happy time, Iago.

IAGO
> You have not been abed, then?

CASSIO
> Why, no; the day had broke
> Before we parted. I have made bold, Iago,
> To send in to your wife. My suit to her   30
> Is that she will to virtuous Desdemona
> Procure me some access.

34: **a mean:** a means, a way

45: **affinity:** relations; connections

45: **wholesome:** reasonable

46: **might not but refuse:** i.e., had no choice but to refuse

47: **suitor:** petitioner

47: **likings:** inclination

56: **speak your bosom:** i.e., say what is in your heart

IAGO

           I'll send her to you presently,
And I'll devise a mean to draw the Moor
Out of the way, that your converse and business   35
May be more free.

CASSIO

I humbly thank you for 't.

                           [Exit IAGO]

           I never knew
A Florentine more kind and honest.

                  [Enter EMILIA]

EMILIA

Good morrow, good Lieutenant. I am sorry   40
For your displeasure, but all will sure be well.
The general and his wife are talking of it,
And she speaks for you stoutly. The Moor replies
That he you hurt is of great fame in Cyprus
And great affinity, and that in wholesome wisdom,   45
He might not but refuse you, but he protests he loves you
And needs no other suitor but his likings
To take the safest occasion by the front
To bring you in again.

CASSIO

           Yet, I beseech you,   50
If you think fit, or that it may be done,
Give me advantage of some brief discourse
With Desdemona alone.

EMILIA

           Pray you, come in.
I will bestow you where you shall have time   55
To speak your bosom freely.

CASSIO

I am much bound to you.

                           [Exeunt]

1: **pilot:** (of the ship that took Othello to Cyprus)

2: **do my duties:** send my compliments, do homage

3: **works:** fortifications

Lines 3–4: "That done, I will be walking on the works. / Repair there to me": Patrick Stewart as Othello and Ron Canada as Iago in The Shakespeare Theatre's 1997–1998 production directed by Jude Kelly
Photo: Carol Rosegg

4: **repair:** come

Act 3, Scene 2]

[Enter OTHELLO, IAGO, and Gentlemen]

OTHELLO
These letters give, Iago, to the pilot,
And by him do my duties to the senate.
That done, I will be walking on the works.
Repair there to me.

IAGO
                    Well, my good lord, I'll do't.   5

OTHELLO
This fortification, gentlemen, shall we see't?

Gentleman
We'll wait upon your lordship.

                                        [Exeunt]

2: **all my abilities:** i.e., all I can

3: **warrant:** declare

Lines 8-10: "Bounteous madam, / Whatever shall become of Michael Cassio, / He's never any thing but your true servant": Sir Derek Jacobi as Cassio and Maggie Smith as Desdemona in Stuart Burge's 1965 movie production
Courtesy: Douglas Lanier

13: **in strangeness:** with reserve, in aloofness

17: **nice:** petty, trifling

17: **waterish:** insubstantial, thin

18: **breed...circumstance:** root by accident or due to chance

19: **supplied:** filled by another

Act 3, Scene 3]

[The garden of the castle.]
[Enter DESDEMONA, CASSIO, and EMILIA]

DESDEMONA
  Be thou assured, good Cassio, I will do
  All my abilities in thy behalf.

EMILIA
  Good madam, do. I warrant it grieves my husband
  As if the cause were his.

DESDEMONA
  O, that's an honest fellow. Do not doubt, Cassio,   5
  But I will have my lord and you again
  As friendly as you were.

CASSIO
                Bounteous madam,
  Whatever shall become of Michael Cassio,
  He's never any thing but your true servant.   10

DESDEMONA
  I know't; I thank you. You do love my lord.
  You have known him long, and be you well assured
  He shall in strangeness stand no further off
  Than in a politic distance.

CASSIO
                Ay, but lady,   15
  That policy may either last so long,
  Or feed upon such nice and waterish diet,
  Or breed itself so out of circumstance,
  That I, being absent and my place supplied,
  My general will forget my love and service.   20

22: **give thee warrant of:** promise you

23: **perform it:** fulfill my obligation

24: **article:** detail

25: **watch him tame:** (from falconry) the practice of forcing a bird to stay awake in order to domesticate it

26: **board:** dining table

26: **shrift:** confessional

29: **thy solicitor:** petitioner, i.e., Desdemona

30: **give thy cause away:** i.e., give up

35: **purposes:** i.e., pleading his case

36: **your discretion:** as you see fit

DESDEMONA
>Do not doubt that. Before Emilia here
>I give thee warrant of thy place. Assure thee,
>If I do vow a friendship, I'll perform it
>To the last article. My lord shall never rest;
>I'll watch him tame and talk him out of patience; 25
>His bed shall seem a school, his board a shrift;
>I'll intermingle every thing he does
>With Cassio's suit. Therefore be merry, Cassio,
>For thy solicitor shall rather die
>Than give thy cause away. 30

EMILIA
>Madam, here comes my lord.

CASSIO
>Madam, I'll take my leave.

DESDEMONA
>Why, stay, and hear me speak.

CASSIO
>Madam, not now. I am very ill at ease,
>Unfit for mine own purposes. 35

DESDEMONA
>Well, do your discretion.

[Exit CASSIO]
[Enter OTHELLO and IAGO]

IAGO
>Ha! I like not that.

OTHELLO
>What dost thou say?

IAGO
>Nothing, my lord, or if — I know not what.

OTHELLO
>Was not that Cassio parted from my wife? 40

46: **suitor:** petitioner

51: **his present reconciliation take:** i.e., immediately restore Cassio to your (Othello's) favor

53: **that errs...cunning:** i.e., his fault was an accident, not deliberate

IAGO
    Cassio, my lord! No, sure, I cannot think it
    That he would steal away so guilty-like,
    Seeing your coming.

OTHELLO
                I do believe 'twas he.

DESDEMONA
    How now, my lord!   45
    I have been talking with a suitor here,
    A man that languishes in your displeasure.

OTHELLO
    Who is 't you mean?

DESDEMONA
    Why, your lieutenant, Cassio. Good my lord,
    If I have any grace or power to move you,   50
    His present reconciliation take,
    For if he be not one that truly loves you,
    That errs in ignorance and not in cunning,
    I have no judgment in an honest face.
    I prithee, call him back.   55

OTHELLO
                Went he hence now?

DESDEMONA
    Ay, faith, so humbled
    That he hath left part of his grief with me
    To suffer with him. Good love, call him back.

OTHELLO
    Not now, sweet Desdemon. Some other time.   60

DESDEMONA
    But shall 't be shortly?

OTHELLO
                The sooner, sweet, for you.

65: **dinner:** lunch, midday meal (supper = evening meal)

72: **trespass:** offense

75: **private cheque:** personal rebuke

78: **mammering on:** hesitantly

80: **dispraisingly:** disparagingly

82: **bring him in:** i.e., back into Othello's favor

Franchelle Stewart Dorn as Emilia, Ron Canada as Iago, Patrice Johnson as Desdemona, and Patrick Stewart as Othello in The Shakespeare Theatre's 1997–1998 production directed by Jude Kelly
Photo: Carol Rosegg

85: **boon:** granted favor, fulfilled wish

88: **sue to:** beg, entreat

88: **peculiar profit:** special benefit

DESDEMONA
Shall 't be tonight at supper?

OTHELLO
                    No, not tonight.

DESDEMONA
Tomorrow dinner, then?   65

OTHELLO
                    I shall not dine at home;
I meet the captains at the citadel.

DESDEMONA
Why, then, tomorrow night or Tuesday morn,
On Tuesday noon or night, on Wednesday morn.
I prithee, name the time, but let it not   70
Exceed three days. In faith, he's penitent,
And yet his trespass, in our common reason —
Save that, they say, the wars must make examples
Out of their best — is not almost a fault
To incur a private cheque. When shall he come?   75
Tell me, Othello, I wonder in my soul,
What you would ask me that I should deny
Or stand so mammering on. What? Michael Cassio,
That came a-wooing with you, and so many a time,
When I have spoke of you dispraisingly,   80
Hath ta'en your part, to have so much to do
To bring him in! Trust me, I could do much, —

OTHELLO
Prithee, no more. Let him come when he will;
I will deny thee nothing.

DESDEMONA
                    Why, this is not a boon.   85
'Tis as I should entreat you wear your gloves,
Or feed on nourishing dishes, or keep you warm,
Or sue to you to do a peculiar profit
To your own person. Nay, when I have a suit

90: **touch:** test by the touchstone, probe

91: **poise:** weight, importance

91: **weight:** consequence, importance

92: **fearful:** uncertain

98: **Be as...teach you:** do whatever you want

100: **wretch:** creature (used as a word of tenderness, perhaps mixed with pity)

Set rendering of "First Jealousy" from the 1951 staging by Orson Welles at
St. James Theatre
Rare Book and Special Collections Library, University of Illinois at Urbana-Champaign

Wherein I mean to touch your love indeed,   90
It shall be full of poise and difficult weight
And fearful to be granted.

OTHELLO
                    I will deny thee nothing.
Whereon, I do beseech thee, grant me this,
To leave me but a little to myself.   95

DESDEMONA
Shall I deny you? No. Farewell, my lord.

OTHELLO
Farewell, my Desdemona. I'll come to thee straight.

DESDEMONA
Emilia, come. Be as your fancies teach you.
Whate'er you be, I am obedient.
                    [Exeunt DESDEMONA and EMILIA]

OTHELLO
Excellent wretch! Perdition catch my soul   100
But I do love thee! And when I love thee not,
Chaos is come again.

IAGO
My noble lord —

OTHELLO
                    What dost thou say, Iago?

IAGO
Did Michael Cassio, when you wooed my lady,   105
Know of your love?

OTHELLO
He did, from first to last. Why dost thou ask?

IAGO
But for a satisfaction of my thought;
No further harm.

110: **why:** of what consequence, what

114: **Discern'st thou...that:** i.e., Did you perceive something in that
(discern'st = discern, perceive, aught = anything)

118: **for aught I know:** i.e., to my knowledge (Cassio is honest)

127: **of my counsel:** in Othello's confidence

OTHELLO
Why of thy thought, Iago?   110

IAGO
I did not think he had been acquainted with her.

OTHELLO
O, yes, and went between us very oft.

IAGO
Indeed?

OTHELLO
Indeed? Ay, indeed! Discern'st thou aught in that?
Is he not honest?   115

IAGO
Honest, my lord?

OTHELLO
Honest! Ay, honest.

IAGO
My lord, for aught I know.

OTHELLO
What dost thou think?

IAGO
Think, my lord?   120

OTHELLO
Think, my lord!
By heaven, thou echoes me
As if there were some monster in thy thought
Too hideous to be shown. Thou dost mean something;
I heard thee say even now. Thou lik'st not that,   125
When Cassio left my wife. What didst not like?
And when I told thee he was of my counsel
In my whole course of wooing, thou cried'st, "Indeed!"

129: **purse:** crease, press together

131: **conceit:** idea

135: **for:** because

137: **stops:** pauses, hesitations

139: **tricks of custom:** customary tricks

139: **just:** honest

140: **close:** hidden, secret

140: **dilations:** accusations

146: **Or those...seem none:** i.e., Men who are not honest should not appear to be honest

And didst contract and purse thy brow together,
As if thou then hadst shut up in thy brain   130
Some horrible conceit. If thou dost love me,
Show me thy thought.

IAGO
  My lord, you know I love you.

OTHELLO
               I think thou dost;
And, for I know thou 'rt full of love and honesty   135
And weigh'st thy words before thou giv'st them breath,
Therefore these stops of thine fright me the more.
For such things in a false disloyal knave
Are tricks of custom, but in a man that's just,
They are close dilations, working from the heart   140
That passion cannot rule.

IAGO
            For Michael Cassio,
I dare be sworn I think that he is honest.

OTHELLO
  I think so too.

IAGO
             Men should be what they seem,   145
Or those that be not, would they might seem none!

OTHELLO
  Certain, men should be what they seem.

IAGO
  Why, then, I think Cassio's an honest man.

OTHELLO
  Nay, yet there's more in this.
I prithee, speak to me as to thy thinkings   150
As thou dost ruminate, and give thy worst of thoughts
The worst of words.

155: **all slaves are free to:** i.e., slaves can keep their thoughts private

157–158: **As where's...intrude not:** i.e., whose soul or mind hasn't occasionally entertained bad thoughts?

159: **uncleanly apprehensions:** filthy, impure thoughts

160: **leets:** manor court, courts which oversee a private jurisdiction

160: **law-days:** court days

162: **thy friend:** i.e., himself, Othello

163–164: **If thou...thoughts:** i.e., If you think he has been wronged and do not tell him

166: **vicious:** wrong

167: **plague:** torment

168: **to spy into:** seek out

168: **jealousy:** suspicion

169: **shapes:** creates, imagines

170: **conceits:** judges

172: **his:** i.e., Iago's

172: **scattering:** scattered, distracted

tracks 12-13

176-216:
Hugh Quarshie as Othello, Anton Lesser as Iago
Paul Robeson as Othello, Jose Ferrer as Iago

181: **filches:** steals, pilfers

IAGO

Good my lord, pardon me.
Though I am bound to every act of duty,
I am not bound to that all slaves are free to.   155
Utter my thoughts? Why, say they are vile and false,
As where's that palace whereinto foul things
Sometimes intrude not? Who has a breast so pure,
But some uncleanly apprehensions
Keep leets and law-days and in session sit   160
With meditations lawful?

OTHELLO

Thou dost conspire against thy friend, Iago,
If thou but think'st him wronged and mak'st his ear
A stranger to thy thoughts.

IAGO

I do beseech you, —   165
Though I perchance am vicious in my guess,
As, I confess, it is my nature's plague
To spy into abuses and oft my jealousy
Shapes faults that are not — that your wisdom yet,
From one that so imperfectly conceits,   170
Would take no notice, nor build yourself a trouble
Out of his scattering and unsure observance.
It were not for your quiet nor your good,
Nor for my manhood, honesty, or wisdom,
To let you know my thoughts.   175

OTHELLO

What dost thou mean?

IAGO

Good name in man and woman, dear my lord,
Is the immediate jewel of their souls.
Who steals my purse steals trash; 'tis something, nothing;
'Twas mine, 'tis his, and has been slave to thousands.   180
But he that filches from me my good name
Robs me of that which not enriches him
And makes me poor indeed.

tracks 12-13

176-216:
Hugh Quarshie as Othello, Anton Lesser as Iago
Paul Robeson as Othello, Jose Ferrer as Iago

Line 188: "O, beware, my lord, of jealousy": Raul Julia as Othello and Christopher
Walken as Iago in the Public Theater's 1991 production directed by Joe Dowling
Photo: George E. Joseph

190: **the meat it feeds on:** i.e., the jealous person
190–191: **that cuckold...wronger:** Iago suggests that the man who knows his wife
has been unfaithful is much happier if he does not love her or her lover
(unlike Othello, who loves Desdemona and Cassio)
195: **Poor...enough:** proverb
196: **fineless:** infinite
201: **I'ld:** a contraction meaning "I would"
206: **exsufflicate and blown surmises:** i.e., overblown, inflated guesses or
conjectures
207: **inference:** suggestion, allegation

OTHELLO
By heaven, I'll know thy thoughts.

IAGO
You cannot, if my heart were in your hand,   185
Nor shall not, whilst 'tis in my custody.

OTHELLO
Ha!

IAGO
                         O, beware, my lord, of jealousy.
It is the green-eyed monster which doth mock
The meat it feeds on. That cuckold lives in bliss   190
Who, certain of his fate, loves not his wronger,
But, O, what damnèd minutes tells he o'er
Who dotes, yet doubts, suspects, yet strongly loves!

OTHELLO
O, misery!

IAGO
Poor and content is rich and rich enough,   195
But riches fineless is as poor as winter
To him that ever fears he shall be poor.
Good heaven, the souls of all my tribe defend
From jealousy!

OTHELLO
                         Why, why is this?   200
Think'st thou I'ld make a life of jealousy
To follow still the changes of the moon
With fresh suspicions? No, to be once in doubt
Is to be resolved. Exchange me for a goat
When I shall turn the business of my soul   205
To such exsufflicate and blown surmises
Matching thy inference. 'Tis not to make me jealous
To say my wife is fair, feeds well, loves company,
Is free of speech, sings, plays, and dances well.
Where virtue is, these are more virtuous.   210

tracks 12-13

176-216:
Hugh Quarshie as Othello, Anton Lesser as Iago
Paul Robeson as Othello, Jose Ferrer as Iago

212: **revolt:** indiscretion

Lines 213–214: "For she had eyes and chose me. No, Iago, / I'll see before I doubt; when I doubt, prove": André Braugher as Iago and Avery Brooks as Othello in The Shakespeare Theatre's 1990–1991 production directed by Harold Scott
Photo: Joan Marcus

219: **franker:** more honest or open
222: **wear your eye thus:** keep wary and alert (probably spoken with a specific gesture)
224: **self-bounty:** inherent kindness
225: **country disposition:** the character of our countrymen (i.e., the Venetians)
226: **pranks:** licentious tricks
227: **best conscience:** i.e., the best they can hope for (for their conscience)
231: **looks:** facial expressions, moods
235: **seeming:** facade, false front
236: **close as oak:** i.e., entirely blind (possibly referring to the close grain of oak)

Nor from mine own weak merits will I draw
The smallest fear or doubt of her revolt,
For she had eyes and chose me. No, Iago,
I'll see before I doubt; when I doubt, prove;
And on the proof, there is no more but this: 215
Away at once with love or jealousy!

IAGO

I am glad of it, for now I shall have reason
To show the love and duty that I bear you
With franker spirit. Therefore, as I am bound,
Receive it from me. I speak not yet of proof.   220
Look to your wife; observe her well with Cassio;
Wear your eye thus, not jealous nor secure.
I would not have your free and noble nature,
Out of self-bounty, be abused. Look to 't.
I know our country disposition well.   225
In Venice they do let heaven see the pranks
They dare not show their husbands. Their best conscience
Is not to leave 't undone but keep 't unknown.

OTHELLO

Dost thou say so?

IAGO

She did deceive her father, marrying you,   230
And when she seemed to shake and fear your looks,
She loved them most.

OTHELLO

            And so she did.

IAGO

               Why, go to then.
She that, so young, could give out such a seeming   235
To seal her father's eyes up close as oak —
He thought 'twas witchcraft — but I am much to blame.
I humbly do beseech you of your pardon
For too much loving you.

245: **moved:** distressed

246–247: **strain my speech to grosser issues:** exaggerate the meaning or consequences of my words

251: **success:** outcome

Line 253: "My lord, I see you're moved": James Earl Jones as Othello and Mitchell Ryan as Iago in the Public Theater's 1964 production directed by Gladys Vaughan
Photo: George E. Joseph

259: **affect:** like, be pleased with

259: **proposèd matches:** suitors

260: **clime:** country, region

260: **degree:** social rank

OTHELLO
                    I am bound to thee forever.   240

IAGO
    I see this hath a little dashed your spirits.

OTHELLO
    Not a jot, not a jot.

IAGO
                    I' faith, I fear it has.
    I hope you will consider what is spoke
    Comes from my love. But I do see you're moved.   245
    I am to pray you not to strain my speech
    To grosser issues nor to larger reach
    Than to suspicion.

OTHELLO
    I will not.

IAGO
                    Should you do so, my lord,   250
    My speech should fall into such vile success
    As my thoughts aim not at. Cassio's my worthy friend —
    My lord, I see you're moved.

OTHELLO
                    No, not much moved.
    I do not think but Desdemona's honest.   255

IAGO
    Long live she so! And long live you to think so!

OTHELLO
    And yet, how nature erring from itself, —

IAGO
    Ay, there's the point. As, to be bold with you,
    Not to affect many proposèd matches
    Of her own clime, complexion, and degree,   260
    Whereto we see in all things nature tends —

262: **rank:** foul smelling, corrupted (with a pun referring to degree)
263: **foul...unnatural:** disproportionate number of unnatural thoughts
264: **in position:** in making this assertion
266: **will:** desire (a pun meaning both her willfulness and sexual desire)
267: **her country forms:** look and appearance of her countrymen
274: **unfolds:** tells

Lines 273–274: "Why did I marry? This honest creature doubtless / Sees and knows more, much more, than he unfolds": Avery Brooks as Othello in The Shakespeare Theatre's 1990–1991 production directed by Harold Scott
Photo: Joan Marcus

276: **scan:** analyze
277: **have his place:** i.e., have his rank and position returned to him
281: **strain his entertainment:** press hard for his case
282: **importunity:** urgency
284: **too busy:** intrusive, meddlesome
286: **free:** (of suspicion)
287: **government:** self-control

Foh! One may smell in such a will most rank,
Foul disproportion, thoughts unnatural.
But pardon me, I do not in position
Distinctly speak of her, though I may fear   265
Her will, recoiling to her better judgment,
May fall to match you with her country forms
And happily repent.

OTHELLO
Farewell, farewell.
If more thou dost perceive, let me know more;   270
Set on thy wife to observe. Leave me, Iago.

IAGO
                                                    [Going]

My lord, I take my leave.

OTHELLO
Why did I marry? This honest creature doubtless
Sees and knows more, much more, than he unfolds.

IAGO
                                                [Returning]
My lord, I would I might entreat your honour   275
To scan this thing no further; leave it to time.
Though it be fit that Cassio have his place —
For sure he fills it up with great ability —
Yet, if you please to hold him off awhile,
You shall by that perceive him and his means.   280
Note, if your lady strain his entertainment
With any strong or vehement importunity,
Much will be seen in that. In the meantime,
Let me be thought too busy in my fears —
As worthy cause I have to fear I am —   285
And hold her free, I do beseech your honour.

OTHELLO
Fear not my government.

290: **qualities:** character, aspects of human nature
291: **haggard:** 1) intractable, wild, 2) a wild untrained hawk
292: **jesses:** straps of leather and silk with which hawks were tied by the legs
293: **let her down the wind:** set her free, release her
294: **Haply:** perhaps
295: **soft parts of conversation:** gracious or pleasant sociability
296: **chamberers:** courtly gentlemen with drawing room graces and elegant turns of phrase

Lines 294–295: "Haply, for I am black / And have not the soft parts of conversation / That chamberers have": John Kani as Othello in The Market Theater's 1987 production directed by Janet Suzman
Photo: Ruphin Coudyzer

297: **vale:** valley
302: **vapour:** dank fumes
305: **prerogatived:** privileged
305: **base :** lowly ranked people
306: **destiny unshunnable:** i.e., inevitable
307: **forked plague:** i.e., horned cuckold (in popular iconography, a cuckold was depicted as having horns)
308: **quicken:** come to life

IAGO
  I once more take my leave.

                                                       [Exit]

OTHELLO
  This fellow's of exceeding honesty
  And knows all qualities, with a learned spirit,   290
  Of human dealings. If I do prove her haggard,
  Though that her jesses were my dear heartstrings,
  I'ld whistle her off and let her down the wind
  To prey at fortune. Haply, for I am black
  And have not those soft parts of conversation   295
  That chamberers have, or for I am declined
  Into the vale of years, — yet that's not much —
  She's gone. I am abused, and my relief
  Must be to loathe her. O, curse of marriage,
  That we can call these delicate creatures ours   300
  And not their appetites! I had rather be a toad
  And live upon the vapour of a dungeon
  Than keep a corner in the thing I love
  For others' uses. Yet, 'tis the plague of great ones;
  Prerogatived are they less than the base;   305
  'Tis destiny unshunnable, like death.
  Even then this forked plague is fated to us
  When we do quicken. Look where she comes.
                [Enter DESDEMONA and EMILIA]
  If she be false, O, then heaven mocks itself!
  I'll not believe 't.   310

DESDEMONA
             How now, my dear Othello!
  Your dinner, and the generous islanders
  By you invited, do attend your presence.

OTHELLO
  I am to blame.

DESDEMONA
             Why do you speak so faintly?   315
  Are you not well?

317: **upon my forehead here:** his temples (also suggesting the horns of a cuckold)

318: **with watching:** from lack of sleep

324–367:
Patience Tomlinson as Emilia, Anton Lesser as Iago
Dorothy Gould as Emilia, Richard Haddon Haines as Iago

321: **napkin:** handkerchief

326: **wayward:** contrary, capricious

328: **he:** i.e., Othello

328: **conjured:** solemnly entreated

329: **reserves:** keep (the handkerchief) close to her

330: **ta'en out:** copied

333: **I nothing:** possibly "I am nothing" or "I know nothing"

335: **chide:** scold

336: **a thing:** an object (in general) with a vulgar pun

336: **common:** a taunt, left dangling to suggesting Emilia is loose

OTHELLO
    I have a pain upon my forehead here.

DESDEMONA
    'Faith, that's with watching. 'Twill away again.
    Let me but bind it hard; within this hour
    It will be well.   320

OTHELLO
                    Your napkin is too little.
                [He puts the handkerchief from him, and it drops]
    Let it alone. Come, I'll go in with you.

DESDEMONA
    I am very sorry that you are not well.
                    [Exeunt OTHELLO and DESDEMONA]

EMILIA
    I am glad I have found this napkin.
    This was her first remembrance from the Moor.   325
    My wayward husband hath a hundred times
    Wooed me to steal it, but she so loves the token,
    For he conjured her she should ever keep it,
    That she reserves it evermore about her
    To kiss and talk to. I'll have the work ta'en out,   330
    And give 't Iago. What he will do with it
    Heaven knows, not I.
    I nothing but to please his fantasy.

                                            [Enter Iago]

IAGO
    How now! What do you here alone?

EMILIA
    Do not you chide; I have a thing for you.   335

IAGO
    A thing for me? It is a common thing —

EMILIA
    Ha!

tracks 14–15

324–367:
Patience Tomlinson as Emilia, Anton Lesser as Iago
Dorothy Gould as Emilia, Richard Haddon Haines as Iago

Line 339–340: "What will you give me now / For that same handkerchief?":
Franchelle Stewart Dorn as Emilia and Ron Canada as Iago in The Shakespeare
Theatre's 1997–1998 production directed by Jude Kelly
Photo: Carol Rosegg

346: **faith:** interjection "in faith"

349: **wench:** woman (not necessarily used in contempt)

353: **import:** importance

354: **run mad:** become mad

355: **lack it:** find it missing

IAGO
  To have a foolish wife.

EMILIA
  O, is that all? What will you give me now
  For that same handkerchief?   340

IAGO
                    What handkerchief?

EMILIA
  What handkerchief?
  Why, that the Moor first gave to Desdemona
  That which so often you did bid me steal.

IAGO
  Hast stol'n it from her?   345

EMILIA
  No, faith. She let it drop by negligence,
  And to th' advantage I, being here, took 't up.
  Look, here it is.

IAGO
                    A good wench; give it me.

EMILIA
  What will you do with 't, that you have been so earnest   350
  To have me filch it?

IAGO
                                             [Snatching it]

  Why, what's that to you?

EMILIA
  If it be not for some purpose of import,
  Give 't me again. Poor lady, she'll run mad
  When she shall lack it.   355

tracks 14-15

324–367:
Patience Tomlinson as Emilia, Anton Lesser as Iago
Dorothy Gould as Emilia, Richard Haddon Haines as Iago

356: **Be not...on 't:** i.e., do not confess to knowing where it is

363: **conceits:** ideas

364–365: **Which....blood:** at first they do not seem distasteful (i.e., dangerous) but with a little persistence begin to work

368: **poppy:** the source for opium, which dulls the senses

368: **mandragora:** mandrake, a soporific

371: **owedst:** had

374: **avaunt:** exclamation of contempt uttered to drive one away

374: **the rack:** a torture device on which victims hands and feet were attached and stretched in opposite directions

378: **sense:** understanding, knowledge

382: **wanting:** having need for (i.e., not knowing it was stolen)

IAGO

Be not acknown on 't. I have use for it.
Go, leave me.

[Exit EMILIA]

I will in Cassio's lodging lose this napkin,
And let him find it. Trifles light as air
Are to the jealous confirmations strong   360
As proofs of holy writ. This may do something;
The Moor already changes with my poison.
Dangerous conceits are in their natures poisons,
Which at the first are scarce found to distaste,
But with a little act upon the blood   365
Burn like the mines of Sulphur.

[Enter OTHELLO]

            I did say so.
Look, where he comes! Not poppy, nor mandragora,
Nor all the drowsy syrups of the world,
Shall ever medicine thee to that sweet sleep   370
Which thou owedst yesterday.

OTHELLO

            Ha, ha, false to me?

IAGO

Why, how now, general! No more of that.

OTHELLO

Avaunt! Be gone! Thou hast set me on the rack.
I swear 'tis better to be much abused   375
Than but to know 't a little.

IAGO

            How now, my lord?

OTHELLO

What sense had I of her stol'n hours of lust?
I saw 't not, thought it not, it harmed not me.
I slept the next night well, was free and merry,   380
I found not Cassio's kisses on her lips.
He that is robbed, not wanting what is stol'n,
Let him not know 't, and he's not robbed at all.

386: **pioneers:** pioneers, i.e., construction workers and physical laborers

389: **plumed:** feathered, as on parade

391: **trump:** trumpet

392: **fife:** a type of flute

394: **circumstance:** ceremony

395: **mortal engines:** machines that cause death (i.e., cannons)

396: **Jove:** from mythology, the supreme god, a.k.a. Jupiter, also the god of thunder and weather

396: **dread clamours:** i.e., thunderclaps

396: **counterfeit:** copy, imitate

397: **occupation:** work (he has lost all pleasure in it) and his ability to concentrate

400: **ocular:** of the eye (i.e., let him see it with his own eyes)

406: **probation:** proof

IAGO
I am sorry to hear this.

OTHELLO
I had been happy if the general camp, 385
Pioneers and all, had tasted her sweet body,
So I had nothing known. O, now, forever
Farewell the tranquil mind! Farewell content!
Farewell the plumed troop and the big wars,
That make ambition virtue! O, farewell! 390
Farewell the neighing steed and the shrill trump,
The spirit-stirring drum, th' ear-piercing fife,
The royal banner, and all quality,
Pride, pomp and circumstance of glorious war!
And, O you mortal engines, whose rude throats 395
The immortal Jove's dread clamours counterfeit,
Farewell! Othello's occupation's gone!

IAGO
Is 't possible, my lord?

OTHELLO
Villain, be sure thou prove my love a whore!
Be sure of it. Give me the ocular proof, 400
Or by the worth of man's eternal soul,
Thou hadst been better have been born a dog
Than answer my waked wrath!

IAGO
                    Is 't come to this?

OTHELLO
Make me to see 't, or, at the least, so prove it 405
That the probation bear no hinge nor loop
To hang a doubt on, or woe upon thy life!

IAGO
My noble lord —

413: **damnation:** either Othello's damnation for taking his revenge or Iago's damnation for inflicting suffering on Othello

417: **mine office:** my resignation

418: **vice:** sin

421: **profit:** good lesson

422: **sith:** since

428: **just:** honest, truthful

429–430: **Fresh as Dian's visage:** clear and pure as the (full) moon

430: **Dian:** Diana, Roman goddess of the moon and of chastity

433: **were satisfied:** i.e., knew one way or the other

OTHELLO
  If thou dost slander her and torture me,
  Never pray more. Abandon all remorse.   410
  On horror's head horrors accumulate;
  Do deeds to make heaven weep, all earth amazed;
  For nothing canst thou to damnation add
  Greater than that.

IAGO
             O grace! O heaven, forgive me!   415
  Are you a man? Have you a soul or sense?
  God be wi' you; take mine office. O wretched fool
  That lov'st to make thine honesty a vice!
  O monstrous world! Take note, take note, O world,
  To be direct and honest is not safe.   420
  I thank you for this profit, and from hence
  I'll love no friend, sith love breeds such offence.

OTHELLO
  Nay, stay. Thou shouldst be honest.

IAGO
  I should be wise, for honesty's a fool
  And loses that it works for.   425

OTHELLO
          By the world,
  I think my wife be honest and think she is not;
  I think that thou art just and think thou art not.
  I'll have some proof. Her name that was as fresh
  As Dian's visage is now begrimed and black   430
  As mine own face. If there be cords, or knives,
  Poison, or fire, or suffocating streams,
  I'll not endure it. Would I were satisfied!

IAGO
  I see, sir, you are eaten up with passion.
  I do repent me that I put it to you.   435
  You would be satisfied?

439: **supervisor:** observer

439: **grossly gape:** stare with mouth open

440: **topped:** literally under a man (engaging in sexual intercourse)

443: **prospect:** sight

444: **bolster:** cushion each other (with their bodies)

448: **prime:** in heat

449: **salt:** lecherous

449: **in pride:** in heat

449: **gross:** dull, stupid

451: **imputation:** insinuation, strong implication

454: **living:** valid

455: **office:** task

457: **pricked:** spurred on, incited

458: **lay:** slept (next to each other on the same bunk)

459: **raging tooth:** toothache

461: **loose of soul:** unrestrained, uninhibited

OTHELLO
                    Would? Nay, and I will.

IAGO
    And may, but, how? How satisfied, my lord?
    Would you, the supervisor, grossly gape on,
    Behold her, topped?   440

OTHELLO
                    Death and damnation! O!

IAGO
    It were a tedious difficulty, I think,
    To bring them to that prospect. Damn them then,
    If ever mortal eyes do see them bolster
    More than their own. What then? How then?   445
    What shall I say? Where's satisfaction?
    It is impossible you should see this,
    Were they as prime as goats, as hot as monkeys,
    As salt as wolves in pride, and fools as gross
    As ignorance made drunk. But yet, I say,   450
    If imputation and strong circumstances,
    Which lead directly to the door of truth,
    Will give you satisfaction, you may have't.

OTHELLO
    Give me a living reason she's disloyal.

IAGO
    I do not like the office,   455
    But, sith I am entered in this cause so far,
    Pricked to 't by foolish honesty and love,
    I will go on. I lay with Cassio lately,
    And, being troubled with a raging tooth,
    I could not sleep.   460
    There are a kind of men so loose of soul
    That in their sleeps will mutter their affairs;
    One of this kind is Cassio.
    In sleep I heard him say, "Sweet Desdemona,

466: **gripe:** grip, grasp

Line 472: "O monstrous, monstrous!": Bill McCallum as Iago and Lester Purry as Othello in the Guthrie Theater's 2003 production directed by Joe Dowling
Photo: T. Charles Erickson

474: **denoted:** indicated

474: **foregone:** previous

474: **conclusion:** experience

475: **a shrewd doubt:** highly suspicious

Let us be wary, let us hide our loves." 465
And then, sir, would he gripe and wring my hand,
Cry, "O sweet creature!" and then kiss me hard,
As if he plucked up kisses by the roots
That grew upon my lips: then laid his leg
Over my thigh, and sighed, and kissed; and then 470
Cried, "Cursed fate that gave thee to the Moor!"

OTHELLO
O monstrous, monstrous!

IAGO
     Nay, this was but his dream.

OTHELLO
But this denoted a foregone conclusion.
'Tis a shrewd doubt, though it be but a dream. 475

IAGO
And this may help to thicken other proofs
That do demonstrate thinly.

OTHELLO
     I'll tear her all to pieces.

IAGO
Nay, but be wise. Yet we see nothing done;
She may be honest yet. Tell me but this: 480
Have you not sometimes seen a handkerchief
Spotted with strawberries in your wife's hand?

OTHELLO
I gave her such a one. 'Twas my first gift.

IAGO
I know not that, but such a handkerchief —
I am sure it was your wife's — did I today 485
See Cassio wipe his beard with.

490: **the slave:** i.e., Cassio

Lines 493–495: "All my fond love thus do I blow to heaven. / 'Tis gone. / Arise, black vengenance, from thy hollow hell!": André Braugher as Iago and Avery Brooks as Othello in The Shakespeare Theatre's 1990–1991 production directed by Harold Scott
Photo: Joan Marcus

496: **crown and hearted:** crown= logic, heart=feeling

497: **fraught:** load, contents

498: **aspics:** a venomous snake

502: **Pontic sea:** the Black sea

503: **compulsive:** forced, constrained

504: **retiring:** reverse flow or tide

505: **Propontic:** the sea of Marmora, which connects the Black Sea to the Mediterranean

505: **Hellespont:** the Dardanelles, a straight that links the Sea of Marmora to the Mediterranean

507: **humble:** kind, benevolent

OTHELLO
                    If it be that —

IAGO
  If it be that, or any that was hers,
  It speaks against her with the other proofs.

OTHELLO
  O, that the slave had forty thousand lives!   490
  One is too poor, too weak for my revenge.
  Now do I see 'tis true. Look here, Iago,
  All my fond love thus do I blow to heaven.
  'Tis gone.
  Arise, black vengeance, from thy hollow hell!   495
  Yield up, O love, thy crown and hearted throne
  To tyrannous hate! Swell, bosom, with thy fraught,
  For 'tis of aspics' tongues!

IAGO
                    Yet be content.

OTHELLO
  O, blood, blood, blood!   500

IAGO
  Patience, I say. Your mind perhaps may change.

OTHELLO
  Never, Iago. Like to the Pontic sea,
  Whose icy current and compulsive course
  Ne'er feels retiring ebb but keeps due on
  To the Propontic and the Hellespont,   505
  Even so my bloody thoughts with violent pace
  Shall ne'er look back, ne'er ebb to humble love,
  Till that a capable and wide revenge
  Swallow them up. Now, by yond marble heaven,
                                        [Kneels]
  In the due reverence of a sacred vow   510
  I here engage my words.

514: **clip us round about:** surround us

516: **execution:** action

519: **what bloody business ever:** no matter how bloody the business is

522: **put thee to 't:** assign a task to him

527: **lewd minx:** lascivious, wanton woman

528: **withdraw:** go inside

529: **furnish me:** equip me

530: **fair devil:** i.e., Desdemona

IAGO
>   Do not rise yet.

>   *[Kneels]*

Witness, you ever-burning lights above,
You elements that clip us round about,
Witness that here, Iago doth give up   515
The execution of his wit, hands, heart,
To wronged Othello's service! Let him command,
And to obey shall be in me remorse,
What bloody business ever.

>   *[They rise]*

OTHELLO
>   I greet thy love   520
Not with vain thanks, but with acceptance bounteous,
And will upon the instant put thee to 't.
Within these three days let me hear thee say
That Cassio's not alive.

IAGO
My friend is dead. 'Tis done at your request.   525
But let her live.

OTHELLO
Damn her, lewd minx! O, damn her!
Come, go with me apart. I will withdraw,
To furnish me with some swift means of death
For the fair devil. Now art thou my lieutenant.   530

IAGO
I am your own forever.

>   *[Exeunt]*

1: **lies:** sleeps, lodges

2: **lies:** a pun meaning "sleeps" as well as "be dishonest"

4: **stabbing:** 1) kill with a weapon, 2) betray (stab in the back)

5: **go to:** an interjection

6: **where I lie:** 1) where I lodge, and 2) where I tell lies

8: **devise:** make up

11: **inquire him out:** ask about

12: **catechize:** instruct by questions and appropriate answers

Act 3, Scene 4]

[Enter DESDEMONA, EMILIA, and Clown]

DESDEMONA
Do you know, sirrah, where Lieutenant Cassio lies?

Clown
I dare not say he lies anywhere.

DESDEMONA
Why, man?

Clown
He's a soldier, and for one to say a soldier lies, 'tis stabbing.

DESDEMONA
Go to. Where lodges he?   5

Clown
To tell you where he lodges is to tell you where I lie.

DESDEMONA
Can anything be made of this?

Clown
I know not where he lodges, and for me to devise a
lodging and say he lies here or he lies there were
to lie in mine own throat.   10

DESDEMONA
Can you inquire him out, and be edified by report?

Clown
I will catechize the world for him; that is, make
questions, and by them, answer.

15: **moved:** applied to

16: **compass:** scope, range

16: **wit:** intellect

18: **should:** did

21: **crusadoes:** Portuguese coins

21: **but:** though

22: **baseness:** meanness, ill thought

26: **the sun where he was born:** his astrological sign

27: **humours:** moods

DESDEMONA

Seek him; bid him come hither. Tell him I have
moved my lord on his behalf and hope all will be well.   15

Clown

To do this is within the compass of man's wit, and
therefore I will attempt the doing it.

[Exit]

DESDEMONA

Where should I lose that handkerchief, Emilia?

EMILIA

I know not, madam.

DESDEMONA

Believe me, I had rather have lost my purse   20
Full of crusadoes. And, but my noble Moor
Is true of mind and made of no such baseness
As jealous creatures are, it were enough
To put him to ill thinking.

EMILIA

Is he not jealous?   25

DESDEMONA

Who, he? I think the sun where he was born
Drew all such humours from him.

EMILIA

Look where he comes.

DESDEMONA

I will not leave him now till Cassio
Be called to him.   30

[Enter OTHELLO]

How is 't with you, my lord?

33: **hardness:** difficulty

33: **dissemble:** give false appearance (i.e., not show his real mood)

40: **sequester:** separation, a retreat

44: **frank:** liberal

50: **chuck:** a term of endearment (an indication that in spite of his doubts, Othello still feels affection for her)

OTHELLO
  Well, my good lady.
  [*Aside*] O, hardness to dissemble! —
  How do you, Desdemona?

DESDEMONA
                    Well, my good lord.   35

OTHELLO
  Give me your hand. This hand is moist, my lady.

DESDEMONA
  It yet hath felt no age nor known no sorrow.

OTHELLO
  This argues fruitfulness and liberal heart.
  Hot, hot, and moist, this hand of yours requires
  A sequester from liberty, fasting and prayer,   40
  Much castigation, exercise devout;
  For here's a young and sweating devil here,
  That commonly rebels. 'Tis a good hand,
  A frank one.

DESDEMONA
  You may, indeed, say so,   45
  For 'twas that hand that gave away my heart.

OTHELLO
  A liberal hand. The hearts of old gave hands.
  But our new heraldry is hands, not hearts.

DESDEMONA
  I cannot speak of this. Come now, your promise.

OTHELLO
  What promise, chuck?   50

DESDEMONA
  I have sent to bid Cassio come speak with you.

52: **salt:** bitter

52: **sorry:** painful

52: **rheum:** runny, stuffy nose

52: **offends:** bothers

68: **fancies:** sexual interests

70: **take heed on 't:** take care of it

71: **darling:** favorite

72: **perdition:** devastation

OTHELLO
I have a salt and sorry rheum offends me;
Lend me thy handkerchief.

DESDEMONA
                        Here, my lord.

OTHELLO
That which I gave you.   55

DESDEMONA
                        I have it not about me.

OTHELLO
Not?

DESDEMONA
                        No, faith, my lord.

OTHELLO
                        That's a fault.
That handkerchief   60
Did an Egyptian to my mother give.
She was a charmer, and could almost read
The thoughts of people. She told her while she kept it,
'Twould make her amiable and subdue my father
Entirely to her love, but if she lost it   65
Or made gift of it, my father's eye
Should hold her loathed, and his spirits should hunt
After new fancies. She, dying, gave it me,
And bid me, when my fate would have me wived,
To give it her. I did so, and, take heed on 't,   70
Make it a darling like your precious eye.
To lose 't or give 't away were such perdition
As nothing else could match.

DESDEMONA
                        Is 't possible?

76: **sibyl:** chief prophetess at any of the oracles, temples dedicated to the gods in ancient Greece

76–77: **sibyl...compasses:** a 200-year old prophetess

79: **hallowed:** holy

80: **mummy:** a preparation for magical purposes, made from dead bodies

85: **wherefore:** why

OTHELLO
'Tis true. There's magic in the web of it.   75
A sibyl that had numbered in the world
The sun to course two hundred compasses,
In her prophetic fury sewed the work.
The worms were hallowed that did breed the silk,
And it was dyed in mummy which the skillful   80
Conserved of maidens' hearts.

DESDEMONA
                    I' faith, is 't true?

OTHELLO
Most veritable; therefore look to 't well.

DESDEMONA
Then would to God that I had never seen 't!

OTHELLO
Ha? Wherefore?   85

DESDEMONA
Why do you speak so startingly and rash?

OTHELLO
Is 't lost? Is 't gone? Speak, is 't out o' th' way?

DESDEMONA
Heaven bless us!

OTHELLO
Say you?

DESDEMONA
It is not lost, but what an if it were?   90

OTHELLO
How?

95: **put me from my suit:** distract her from her petition (on Cassio's behalf)

97: **misgives:** has a presentiment of evil

99: **sufficient:** adequate, capable

104: **founded:** built, based

107: **in sooth:** in truth

DESDEMONA
    I say it is not lost.

OTHELLO
                Fetch 't, let me see 't.

DESDEMONA
    Why, so I can, sir, but I will not now.
    This is a trick to put me from my suit.   95
    Pray you, let Cassio be received again.

OTHELLO
    Fetch me the handkerchief. My mind misgives.

DESDEMONA
    Come, come.
    You'll never meet a more sufficient man.

OTHELLO
    The handkerchief!   100

DESDEMONA
                I pray, talk me of Cassio.

OTHELLO
    The handkerchief!

DESDEMONA
              A man that all his time
    Hath founded his good fortunes on your love,
    Shared dangers with you, —   105

OTHELLO
    The handkerchief!

DESDEMONA
    In sooth, you are to blame.

OTHELLO
    Zounds!

                                  [Exit]

111: **wonder:** miracle

113: **shows us a man:** shows us a man's true nature

114: **all but:** nothing but

118: **importune:** urge

122: **exist:** be, live (in Othello's good graces)

123: **office:** duty

125: **mortal:** fatal

127: **purposed:** intended

127: **futurity:** the future

128: **ransom:** return, deliver

130: **clothe me...content:** appear contended

131: **shut myself up:** i.e., follow

134: **advocation:** pleading

134: **in tune:** appropriate to the time and mood

EMILIA
Is not this man jealous?

DESDEMONA
I ne'er saw this before. 110
Sure, there's some wonder in this handkerchief;
I am most unhappy in the loss of it.

EMILIA
'Tis not a year or two shows us a man.
They are all but stomachs, and we all but food.
They eat us hungerly, and when they are full, 115
They belch us. — Look you, Cassio and my husband!
[Enter CASSIO and IAGO]

IAGO
There is no other way. 'Tis she must do 't.
And, lo, the happiness! Go and importune her.

DESDEMONA
How now, good Cassio! What's the news with you?

CASSIO
Madam, my former suit. I do beseech you 120
That by your virtuous means, I may again
Exist and be a member of his love,
Whom I with all the office of my heart
Entirely honour. I would not be delayed.
If my offence be of such mortal kind 125
That nor my service past nor present sorrows
Nor purposed merit in futurity
Can ransom me into his love again,
But to know so must be my benefit;
So shall I clothe me in a forced content 130
And shut myself up in some other course
To fortune's alms.

DESDEMONA
Alas, thrice-gentle Cassio!
My advocation is not now in tune.
My lord is not my lord, nor should I know him, 135

136: **favour:** outward appearance

139: **blank:** the aim, the center (as in the center of a target or a rifle scope)

145: **unquietness:** agitation

147: **ranks:** soldiers under his command

149: **puffed:** blew up

150: **of moment:** momentary, fleeting

151: **matter in 't:** substance, serious meaning

153: **state:** relating to government

154: **unhatched:** unknown

154: **practice:** custom

156: **puddled:** made cloudy, darkened

157–158: **Men...object:** men become preoccupied with trivial matters, though the true causes of their discontent are major

159: **indues:** endows

162: **observances:** reverential attention

163: **bridal:** nuptial festival

163: **beshrew me:** woe to me (mild oath)

164: **unhandsome:** incompetent

164: **warrior:** (because she is fighting for Cassio's cause)

165: **arraigning:** summoning before a court

166: **suborned:** testified falsely

Were he in favour as in humour altered.
So help me every spirit sanctified,
As I have spoken for you all my best
And stood within the blank of his displeasure
For my free speech. You must awhile be patient.   140
What I can do I will, and more I will
Than for myself I dare. Let that suffice you.

IAGO
  Is my lord angry?

EMILIA
                            He went hence but now,
  And certainly in strange unquietness.   145

IAGO
  Can he be angry? I have seen the cannon
  When it hath blown his ranks into the air,
  And, like the devil, from his very arm
  Puffed his own brother — and is he angry?
  Something of moment then. I will go meet him.   150
  There's matter in 't indeed if he be angry.

DESDEMONA
  I prithee, do so.

                                               [Exit IAGO]

                            Something sure of state,
  Either from Venice, or some unhatched practice
  Made demonstrable here in Cyprus to him,   155
  Hath puddled his clear spirit. And in such cases
  Men's natures wrangle with inferior things,
  Though great ones are their object. 'Tis even so,
  For let our finger ache, and it indues
  Our other healthful members even to that sense   160
  Of pain. Nay, we must think men are not gods,
  Nor of them look for such observances
  As fit the bridal. Beshrew me much, Emilia,
  I was, unhandsome warrior as I am,
  Arraigning his unkindness with my soul.   165
  But now I find I had suborned the witness,
  And he's indicted falsely.

169: **conception :** evil thought

169: **toy:** folly

175: **begot...on itself:** i.e., jealousy feeds on itself

179: **fit:** in a suitable mood

179: **move your suit:** plead your case

Lines 184–185: "How is it with you, my most fair Bianca? / I' faith, sweet love, I was coming to your house": Neil McCarthy as Cassio and Gaynor Young as Bianca in The Market Theater's 1987 production directed by Janet Suzman
Photo: Ruphin Coudyzer

EMILIA
Pray heaven it be state matters, as you think,
And no conception nor no jealous toy
Concerning you.   170

DESDEMONA
Alas the day! I never gave him cause.

EMILIA
But jealous souls will not be answered so.
They are not ever jealous for the cause,
But jealous for they're jealous. It is a monster
Begot upon itself, born on itself.   175

DESDEMONA
Heaven keep that monster from Othello's mind!

EMILIA
Lady, amen.

DESDEMONA
I will go seek him. — Cassio, walk hereabout.
If I do find him fit, I'll move your suit
And seek to effect it to my uttermost.   180

CASSIO
I humbly thank your ladyship.
                              [Exeunt DESDEMONA and EMILIA]
                                          [Enter BIANCA]

BIANCA
Save you, friend Cassio!

CASSIO
                    What make you from home?
How is it with you, my most fair Bianca?
I' faith, sweet love, I was coming to your house.   185

188: **eight score eight hours:** score = 20, thus 8(20) + 8 = 168 hours

192: **leaden:** heavy

193: **in a more continuate time:** in a time unbroken by other business

198: **feel a cause:** see a reason

201: **throw...teeth:** and exclamatory expression

210: **wherefore:** why

BIANCA
And I was going to your lodging, Cassio.
What, keep a week away? Seven days and nights?
Eight score eight hours? And lovers' absent hours,
More tedious than the dial eight score times?
O weary reck'ning!   190

CASSIO
                    Pardon me, Bianca.
I have this while with leaden thoughts been pressed,
But I shall in a more continuate time
Strike off this score of absence. Sweet Bianca,
                    [Giving her DESDEMONA's handkerchief]
Take me this work out.   195

BIANCA
                    O Cassio, whence came this?
This is some token from a newer friend.
To the felt absence now I feel a cause.
Is 't come to this? Well, well.

CASSIO
                    Go to, woman!   200
Throw your vile guesses in the devil's teeth
From whence you have them. You are jealous now
That this is from some mistress some remembrance.
No, by my faith, Bianca.

BIANCA
                    Why, whose is it?   205

CASSIO
I know not, sweet. I found it in my chamber.
I like the work well, ere it be demanded,
As like enough it will, I would have it copied.
Take it, and do 't, and leave me for this time.

BIANCA
Leave you! Wherefore?   210

211: **attend here on:** wait here for

212: **no addition:** not honorable

213: **womaned:** in the company of a woman

217: **bring:** come with

221: **circumstanced:** submit to circumstances

CASSIO
  I do attend here on the general
  And think it no addition, nor my wish,
  To have him see me womaned.

BIANCA
             Why, I pray you?

CASSIO
  Not that I love you not.   215

BIANCA
  But that you do not love me.
  I pray you, bring me on the way a little,
  And say if I shall see you soon at night.

CASSIO
  'Tis but a little way that I can bring you,
  For I attend here, but I'll see you soon.   220

BIANCA
  'Tis very good. I must be circumstanced.

[Exeunt]

[Othello

Act 4

5: **unauthorized:** unjustifiable

9: **hypocrisy...devil:** i.e., hypocritical in the face of evil to appear bad while actually meaning no harm

11: **tempt:** test

12: **venial slip:** In the Roman Catholic Church, a "venial sin" is a minor infraction, committed without knowledge or deliberate intent; a "slip" is even less serious

16: **bestow 't:** contraction for "bestow it"

Act 4, Scene 1]

[Enter OTHELLO and IAGO]

IAGO
  Will you think so?

OTHELLO
                Think so, Iago?

IAGO
                        What,
  To kiss in private?

OTHELLO
                An unauthorized kiss!   5

IAGO
  Or to be naked with her friend in bed
  An hour or more, not meaning any harm?

OTHELLO
  Naked in bed, Iago, and not mean harm?
  It is hypocrisy against the devil!
  They that mean virtuously, and yet do so,   10
  The devil their virtue tempts, and they tempt heaven.

IAGO
  So they do nothing, 'tis a venial slip,
  But if I give my wife a handkerchief, —

OTHELLO
  What then?

IAGO
  Why, then, 'tis hers, my lord, and, being hers,   15
  She may, I think, bestow 't on any man.

19: **essence...not seen:** i.e., it is an abstract aspect of the spirit

20: **They have it...not:** i.e., people who seem honorable often are not

24: **raven:** a traditional omen of bad luck

24: **infected:** cursed

25: **boding:** foreboding or foreshadowing bad luck

Lines 23–25: "it comes o'er my memory, / As doth the raven o'er the infected house, / Boding to all — he had my handkerchief": Ron Canada as Iago and Patrick Stewart as Othello in The Shakespeare Theatre's 1997–1998 production directed by Jude Kelly
Photo: Carol Rosegg

30–34: **Or heard him...must blab:** i.e., knaves who have dallied with women, either by seducing them or giving in to their seductions, can't help but brag about it

31: **importunate :** urgent, pressing

32: **dotage:** excessive fondness

33: **cannot choose:** have no choice

37: **unswear:** swear it is not true

OTHELLO
> She is protectress of her honour too.
> May she give that?

IAGO
> Her honour is an essence that's not seen.
> They have it very oft that have it not.   20
> But, for the handkerchief, —

OTHELLO
> By heaven, I would most gladly have forgot it.
> Thou said'st — it comes o'er my memory,
> As doth the raven o'er the infected house,
> Boding to all — he had my handkerchief.   25

IAGO
> Ay, what of that?

OTHELLO
> > That's not so good now.

IAGO
> > What
> If I had said I had seen him do you wrong?
> Or heard him say — as knaves be such abroad,   30
> Who having, by their own importunate suit
> Or voluntary dotage of some mistress,
> Convincèd or supplied them, cannot choose
> But they must blab —

OTHELLO
> > Hath he said any thing?   35

IAGO
> He hath, my lord, but be you well assured,
> No more than he'll unswear.

OTHELLO
> > What hath he said?

41: **lie:** (Iago leaves this word hanging with deliberate ambiguity)
43: **on her:** (tell lies) about her, but can also be taken in a more literal sense to mean lie on top of her

tracks 16-17

38–54:
Hugh Quarshie as Othello, Anton Lesser as Iago
Paul Robeson as Othello, Jose Ferrer as Iago

44: **We say...belie her:** i.e., we say "lie on her" when they (people) tell lies about her
45: **fulsome:** disgusting
46: **be hanged:** popular expression meaning "be damned" in a general sense
47: **First, to be...confess:** Othello reverses the proverb, "Confess and be hanged."
48: **shadowing:** full of shapes and images
49: **Pish:** interjection of contempt or disgust

Lines 51–52: "Work on, / My medicine, work!": Patrick Stewart as Othello and Ron Canada as Iago in The Shakespeare Theatre's 1997–1998 production directed by Jude Kelly
Photo: Carol Rosegg

54: **reproach:** disgrace, infamy
58: **epilepsy:** a brain disorder causing strange sensations, convulsions, muscle spasms, and loss of consciousness

IAGO
'Faith, that he did — I know not what he did.

OTHELLO
What? What?   40

IAGO
Lie —

OTHELLO
                    With her?

IAGO
                    With her, on her, what you will.

OTHELLO
Lie with her? Lie on her? We say "lie on her" when they belie her.
Lie with her? Zounds, that's fulsome. — Handkerchief — confes-   45
sions — handkerchief! — To confess and be hanged for his labour.
First, to be hanged, and then to confess. — I tremble at it. Nature
would not invest herself in such shadowing passion without some
instruction. It is not words that shake me thus. Pish! Noses, ears,
and lips — Is 't possible? — Confess — handkerchief! — O devil! —   50
                                        [Falls in a trance]

IAGO
Work on,
My medicine, work! Thus credulous fools are caught,
And many worthy and chaste dames even thus,
All guiltless, meet reproach. — What, ho! My lord!
My lord, I say! Othello!   55
                                        [Enter CASSIO]
                    How now, Cassio?

CASSIO
What's the matter?

IAGO
My lord is fall'n into an epilepsy.
This is his second fit; he had one yesterday.

60: **rub...temples:** Cassio inadvertently reinforces Iago's plot by pointing out Othello's temples, the place where a cuckold's horns are said to grow.

61: **forbear:** hold off

62: **his :** its

72: **hornèd:** i.e., a cuckold

72: **monster:** an unnatural creature

72: **beast:** a wild or domesticated animal

74: **civil:** decent, well-mannered (with a linguistic quibble or pun on "of the city," or "civilized")

77: **yoked:** married

78: **may draw:** is in the same situation

79: **unproper:** 1) not one's own, and 2) indecent

80: **peculiar:** exclusively one's own

81: **arch-mock:** main jest

82: **lip:** kiss

82: **secure:** (apparently) carefree and unsuspecting

82: **couch:** bed

CASSIO
  Rub him about the temples.   60

IAGO
                    No, forbear.
  The lethargy must have his quiet course.
  If not, he foams at mouth and by and by
  Breaks out to savage madness. Look, he stirs.
  Do you withdraw yourself a little while,   65
  He will recover straight. When he is gone,
  I would on great occasion speak with you.

                                              [Exit CASSIO]

  How is it, general? Have you not hurt your head?

OTHELLO
  Dost thou mock me?

IAGO
                    I, mock you not, by heaven.   70
  Would you would bear your fortune like a man!

OTHELLO
  A hornèd man's a monster and a beast.

IAGO
  There's many a beast then in a populous city,
  And many a civil monster.

OTHELLO
  Did he confess it?   75

IAGO
                    Good sir, be a man.
  Think every bearded fellow that's but yoked
  May draw with you? There's millions now alive
  That nightly lie in those unproper beds
  Which they dare swear peculiar. Your case is better.   80
  O, 'tis the spite of hell, the fiend's arch-mock,
  To lip a wanton in a secure couch
  And to suppose her chaste! No, let me know,
  And knowing what I am, I know what she shall be.

87: **patient list:** within the bounds of patience (list = boundary, limit)

91: **'scuse:** excuse

91: **ecstasy:** fainting fit, a swoon

92: **anon:** soon

93: **encave:** hide

94: **fleers:** sneers

98: **cope:** meet (in this instance, for the purposes of having sex)

99: **mark:** observe

99: **marry:** exclamation

100: **in spleen:** in a fit of passion

108: **selling her desires:** i.e., selling her body

109: **it:** she

110: **strumpet:** wanton woman

110: **plague:** curse

OTHELLO
 O, thou art wise. 'Tis certain.   85

IAGO
     Stand you awhile apart.
 Confine yourself but in a patient list.
 Whilst you were here o'erwhelmed with your grief —
 A passion most unsuiting such a man —
 Cassio came hither. I shifted him away   90
 And laid good 'scuses upon your ecstasy,
 Bade him anon return and here speak with me,
 The which he promised. Do but encave yourself
 And mark the fleers, the gibes, and notable scorns
 That dwell in every region of his face,   95
 For I will make him tell the tale anew —
 Where, how, how oft, how long ago, and when
 He hath, and is again to cope your wife.
 I say but mark his gesture. Marry, patience!
 Or I shall say you are all in all in spleen 100
 And nothing of a man.

OTHELLO
    Dost thou hear, Iago?
 I will be found most cunning in my patience;
 But — dost thou hear? — most bloody.

IAGO
     That's not amiss,   105
 But yet keep time in all. Will you withdraw?
         [OTHELLO retires]

 Now will I question Cassio of Bianca,
 A housewife that by selling her desires
 Buys herself bread and clothes. It is a creature
 That dotes on Cassio — as 'tis the strumpet's plague 110
 To beguile many and be beguiled by one.
 He, when he hears of her, cannot refrain
 From the excess of laughter. Here he comes.
         [Enter CASSIO]

Line 114: "As he shall smile, Othello shall go mad": Orson Welles's sketch of "Second Jealousy" from the 1951 staging at St. James Theatre

Rare Book and Special Collections Library, University of Illinois at Urbana-Champaign

115: **unbookish:** unsophisticated, ignorant
118: **addition:** title (i.e., lieutenant)
119: **want:** lack, absence

121–168:
Anton Lesser as Iago, Roger May as Cassio, Hugh Quarshie as Othello,
Allison Pettit as Bianca

122: **speed:** be successful
123: **caitiff:** wretch
126: **rogue:** rascal (unusual usage, usually refers to a man)
127: **faintly:** without zeal or conviction
129: **importunes:** urges, solicits
130: **o'er:** over
130: **go to:** a general expression meaning "get on with it"
131: **gives it out:** announces, publicly declares

As he shall smile, Othello shall go mad,
And his unbookish jealousy must construe   115
Poor Cassio's smiles, gestures, and light behaviors
Quite in the wrong. – How do you, lieutenant?

CASSIO
The worser that you give me the addition
Whose want even kills me.

IAGO
Ply Desdemona well, and you are sure on 't.   120
                                                    [Speaking lower]

Now, if this suit lay in Bianca's power,
How quickly should you speed!

CASSIO
                    Alas, poor caitiff!

OTHELLO
Look, how he laughs already!

IAGO
I never knew woman love man so.   125

CASSIO
Alas, poor rogue! I think, i' faith, she loves me.

OTHELLO
Now he denies it faintly and laughs it out.

IAGO
Do you hear, Cassio?

OTHELLO
                    Now he importunes him
To tell it o'er. Go to. Well said, well said.   130

IAGO
She gives it out that you shall marry her.
Do you intend it?

121–168:
*Anton Lesser as Iago, Roger May as Cassio, Hugh Quarshie as Othello,
Allison Pettit as Bianca*

track 18

134: **triumph:** exult

135: **customer:** Cassio is referring to himself as being a customer of Bianca's sexual services (see line 107-109)

136: **unwholesome:** morally tainted

138: **cry:** gossip

141: **scored me:** 1) considered my reputation, and 2) branded me

142: **monkey:** i.e., Bianca

143: **flattery:** delusion

146: **sea-bank:** seashore

147: **thither:** there

147: **bauble:** trinket, plaything (i.e., Bianca)

147: **by this hand:** exclamation "I swear"

149: **imports:** conveys, shows

CASSIO
  Ha, ha, ha!

OTHELLO
  Do you triumph, Roman? Do you triumph?

CASSIO
  I marry her? What, a customer? Prithee, bear some charity to my   135
  wit. Do not think it so unwholesome. Ha, ha, ha!

OTHELLO
  So, so, so, so. They laugh that win.

IAGO
  'Faith, the cry goes that you shall marry her.

CASSIO
  Prithee, say true!

IAGO
  I am a very villain else.   140

OTHELLO
  Have you scored me? Well.

CASSIO
  This is the monkey's own giving out. She is persuaded I will marry
  her out of her own love and flattery, not out of my promise.

OTHELLO
  Iago beckons me; now he begins the story.

CASSIO
  She was here even now; she haunts me in every place. I was the   145
  other day talking on the sea-bank with certain Venetians, and
  thither comes the bauble, and, by this hand, she falls me thus
  about my neck —

OTHELLO
  Crying, "O dear Cassio!" as it were; his gesture imports it.

track 18

121–168:
*Anton Lesser as Iago, Roger May as Cassio, Hugh Quarshie as Othello,
Allison Pettit as Bianca*

150: **lolls:** leans to one side

152: **plucked:** took

153: **nose:** possibly also a euphemism for penis

156: **fitchew:** polecat (reputed to be very amorous and lecherous), thus meaning
lascivious woman

156: **marry:** indeed

158: **dam:** mother

160: **take out:** copy

160: **work:** design

160: **piece of work:** story

162: **minx:** a pert and wanton woman

162: **token:** gift

163: **hobbyhorse:** term of contempt for a loose person

166: **should be:** appears to be

167: **an:** if

168: **when you are next prepared for:** i.e., when next I am ready for you
(which may be never)

CASSIO

So hangs, and lolls, and weeps upon me, so shakes, and pulls me.   150
Ha, ha, ha!

OTHELLO

Now he tells how she plucked him to my chamber. O, I see that
nose of yours but not that dog I shall throw it to.

CASSIO

Well, I must leave her company.

IAGO

Before me, look where she comes.   155

[Enter BIANCA]

CASSIO

'Tis such another fitchew! Marry, a perfumed one. —
What do you mean by this haunting of me?

BIANCA

Let the devil and his dam haunt you! What did you mean by that
same handkerchief you gave me even now? I was a fine fool to
take it. I must take out the work? A likely piece of work that you   160
should find it in your chamber and not know who left it there!
This is some minx's token, and I must take out the work? There,
give it your hobbyhorse. Wheresoever you had it, I'll take out no
work on 't.

CASSIO

How now, my sweet Bianca? How now? How now?   165

OTHELLO

By heaven, that should be my handkerchief!

BIANCA

An you'll come to supper tonight, you may. An you will not, come
when you are next prepared for.

[Exit]

170: **rail:** revile, scold

173: **fain:** willingly, gladly

177: **vice:** transgression, sin

181: **prizes:** values

IAGO
After her, after her.

CASSIO
'Faith, I must; she'll rail in the street else.   170

IAGO
Will you sup there?

CASSIO
'Faith, I intend so.

IAGO
Well, I may chance to see you, for I would very fain speak with you.

CASSIO
Prithee, come, will you?

IAGO
Go to; say no more.   175
                                              [Exit CASSIO]

OTHELLO
                                                [Advancing]
How shall I murder him, Iago?

IAGO
Did you perceive how he laughed at his vice?

OTHELLO
O, Iago!

IAGO
And did you see the handkerchief?

OTHELLO
Was that mine?   180

IAGO
Yours by this hand! And to see how he prizes the foolish woman,
your wife! She gave it him, and he hath giv'n it his whore.

183: nine years a-killing: take nine years to kill him i.e., have him die a slow death

183: fair: beautiful or honorable

187: it: i.e., his chest

188–189: she might...tasks: i.e., she would have power even over an emperor (an interesting inversion of the precepts of courtly love, where a woman's power over a man was strongest before he was granted unlimited access to her)

193: plenteous: copious

195: condition: disposition

199: over: of

199: iniquity: sin

Lines 197–198: "O, Iago, the pity of it, Iago!": Raul Julia as Othello and Richard Dreyfuss as Iago in the Public Theater's 1978–1979 production directed by Wilford Leach
Photo: George E. Joseph

199: patent: permission

201: messes: small pieces

OTHELLO
I would have him nine years a-killing. A fine woman, a fair
woman, a sweet woman!

IAGO
Nay, you must forget that.   185

OTHELLO
Ay, let her rot and perish and be damned tonight, for she shall not
live. No, my heart is turned to stone; I strike it, and it hurts my
hand. O, the world hath not a sweeter creature! She might lie by
an emperor's side and command him tasks.

IAGO
Nay, that's not your way.   190

OTHELLO
Hang her! I do but say what she is: so delicate with her needle, an
admirable musician! O, she will sing the savageness out of a bear!
Of so high and plenteous wit and invention!

IAGO
She's the worse for all this.

OTHELLO
O, a thousand, thousand times! And then, of so gentle a condition!   195

IAGO
Ay, too gentle.

OTHELLO
Nay, that's certain, but yet the pity of it, Iago! O Iago, the pity of
it, Iago!

IAGO
If you are so fond over her iniquity, give her patent to offend, for
if it touch not you, it comes near nobody.   200

OTHELLO
I will chop her into messes! Cuckold me?

205: **expostulate:** converse

206: **unprovide my mind:** weaken my resolve

Lines 205–207: "I'll not expostulate her, lest her body and beauty unprovide my mind again. This night, Iago.": Raul Julia as Othello and Christopher Walken as Iago in the Public Theater's 1991 production directed by Joe Dowling
Photo: George E. Joseph

211: **undertaker:** a pun meaning a) undertake the task of killing him and b) become the undertaker, i.e., the one who buries him

218: **save you:** exclamation, derived from "God save you"

IAGO
O, 'tis foul in her.

OTHELLO
With mine officer.

IAGO
That's fouler.

OTHELLO
Get me some poison, Iago. This night. I'll not expostulate with   205
her, lest her body and beauty unprovide my mind again. This
night, Iago.

IAGO
Do it not with poison. Strangle her in her bed, even the bed she
hath contaminated.

OTHELLO
Good, good. The justice of it pleases; very good.   210

IAGO
And for Cassio, let me be his undertaker. You shall hear more by
midnight.

OTHELLO
Excellent good.
                                                                [A trumpet within]

What trumpet is that same?

IAGO
I warrant something from Venice.   215
'Tis Lodovico. This comes from the duke.
See, your wife's with him.
                        [Enter LODOVICO, DESDEMONA, and Attendants]

LODOVICO
Save you, worthy general!

221: instrument of their pleasures: i.e., the letter that conveys the orders (pleasures) of the duke and senators

228: unkind: ungentle, hard-hearted

232: call: speak

232: paper: i.e., the letter

OTHELLO
> With all my heart, sir.

LODOVICO
> The duke and senators of Venice greet you.   220
>> *[Gives him a letter]*

OTHELLO
> I kiss the instrument of their pleasures.
>> *[Opens the letter, and reads]*

DESDEMONA
> And what's the news, good cousin Lodovico?

IAGO
> I am very glad to see you, signior.
> Welcome to Cyprus.

LODOVICO
> I thank you. How does Lieutenant Cassio?   225

IAGO
> Lives, sir.

DESDEMONA
> Cousin, there's fall'n between him and my lord
> An unkind breach, but you shall make all well.

OTHELLO
> Are you sure of that?

DESDEMONA
> My lord?   230

OTHELLO
>> *[Reads]*

> "This fail you not to do, as you will —"

LODOVICO
> He did not call; he's busy in the paper.
> Is there division 'twixt my lord and Cassio?

235: **atone:** reconcile

235: **love:** affection

243: **glad on 't:** i.e., glad they are going home and glad for Cassio

Stage direction: Striking her: Laurence Olivier as Othello and Maggie Smith
as Desdemona in Stuart Burge's 1965 movie production
Courtesy: Douglas Lanier

DESDEMONA
A most unhappy one. I would do much
To atone them for the love I bear to Cassio.   235

OTHELLO
Fire and brimstone!

DESDEMONA
                                My lord?

OTHELLO
                                                Are you wise?

DESDEMONA
What, is he angry?

LODOVICO
                                May be th' letter moved him;   240
For, as I think, they do command him home,
Deputing Cassio in his government.

DESDEMONA
Trust me, I am glad on 't.

OTHELLO
                                Indeed?

DESDEMONA
                                                My lord?   245

OTHELLO
I am glad to see you mad.

DESDEMONA
                                Why, sweet Othello, —

OTHELLO
                                                                        [Striking her]

    Devil!

251: **very much:** it is a major occurrence, a terrible thing

252: **Make her amends:** apologize to her

255: **crocodile:** the crocodile was thought to be a deceptive creature; "crocodile tears"

265: **turn and turn:** i.e., she is changeable, deceptive

DESDEMONA
I have not deserved this.

LODOVICO
My lord, this would not be believed in Venice,   250
Though I should swear I saw 't. 'Tis very much.
Make her amends. She weeps.

OTHELLO
                    O devil, devil!
If that the earth could teem with woman's tears,
Each drop she falls would prove a crocodile.   255
Out of my sight!

DESDEMONA
I will not stay to offend you.

                                                        [Going]

LODOVICO
Truly an obedient lady.
I do beseech your lordship call her back.

OTHELLO
Mistress!   260

DESDEMONA
                    My lord?

OTHELLO
                              What would you with her, sir?

LODOVICO
Who, I, my lord?

OTHELLO
Ay; you did wish that I would make her turn.
Sir, she can turn and turn, and yet go on   265
And turn again; and she can weep, sir, weep;
And she's obedient, as you say, obedient,

268: **Proceed you...tears:** (spoken to Desdemona)

269: **well-painted:** well-painted like a prostitute or well-painted in deception

269: **O well-painted passion:** (spoken to Desdemona)

271: **mandate:** government order

275: **goats and monkeys:** Othello is still obsessing over Iago's words. See 3.3.448.

277: **sufficient:** capable

277–278: **the nature whom:** i.e., the one whose nature

279: **shot of...chance:** war images reflecting Othello's former reputation as a great general

282: **safe:** sound, intact

282: **light of brain:** insane

283: **He's that he is:** Iago leaves this ambiguous to allow Lodovico's imagination to assume the worst

283: **censure:** judgment, opinion

284–285: **If what he might...he were:** i.e., if he is not, in fact, insane, I wish he were (for that would at least explain his actions)

287: **not so well:** not good, not appropriate

287–288: **yet I...the worst:** i.e., I wish I knew this was the worst of his abuses

289: **use:** habit, custom

290: **work upon his blood:** enrage him

Very obedient. — Proceed you in your tears. —
Concerning this, sir, — O well-painted passion! —
I am commanded home. — Get you away;   270
I'll send for you anon. — Sir, I obey the mandate
And will return to Venice. — Hence, avaunt!
                                        [Exit DESDEMONA]
Cassio shall have my place. And, sir, tonight,
I do entreat that we may sup together.
You are welcome, sir, to Cyprus. — Goats and monkeys!   275
                                                [Exit]

LODOVICO
Is this the noble Moor whom our full senate
Call all in all sufficient? Is this the nature
Whom passion could not shake? Whose solid virtue,
The shot of accident, nor dart of chance,
Could neither graze nor pierce?   280

IAGO
He is much changed.

LODOVICO
Are his wits safe? Is he not light of brain?

IAGO
He's that he is. I may not breathe my censure
What he might be. If what he might, he is not,
I would to heaven he were!   285

LODOVICO
What, strike his wife?

IAGO
'Faith, that was not so well, yet would I knew
That stroke would prove the worst!

LODOVICO
                    Is it his use?
Or did the letters work upon his blood   290
And new-create this fault?

293: **honesty in me:** decent or honorable for me

295: **courses:** actions, conduct

295: **denote:** indicate (his character)

IAGO
  Alas, alas!
  It is not honesty in me to speak
  What I have seen and known. You shall observe him,
  And his own courses will denote him so   295
  That I may save my speech. Do but go after,
  And mark how he continues.

LODOVICO
  I am sorry that I am deceived in him.

                                                              [Exeunt]

5: Each syllable...them: i.e., every word they exchanged

10: mask: part of a woman's attire at that time

Act 4, Scene 2]

OTHELLO
You have seen nothing then?

EMILIA
Nor ever heard, nor ever did suspect.

OTHELLO
Yes, you have seen Cassio and she together.

EMILIA
But then I saw no harm, and then I heard
Each syllable that breath made up between them.   5

OTHELLO
What, did they never whisper?

EMILIA
Never, my lord.

OTHELLO
Nor send you out o' th' way?

EMILIA
Never.

OTHELLO
To fetch her fan, her gloves, her mask, nor nothing?   10

EMILIA
Never, my lord.

OTHELLO
That's strange.

13: **durst:** dare not

15: **remove your thought:** forget the idea

15: **bosom:** heart

17: **serpent's curse:** a biblical reference to the story of Adam and Eve, in which they are banished from paradise

22: **bawd:** procuress, a pimp

23: **a subtle whore:** i.e., Desdemona

24: **a closet lock and key:** i.e., a locked closet or chamber (filled with villainous secrets)

25: **do 't:** do it (i.e., pray)

27: **chuck:** Othello still refers to her with an affectionate pet name

32: **function:** job, duties

33: **procreants:** ones who procreate (i.e., husbands and wives)

35: **mystery:** calling, occupation (i.e., as a procuress)

35: **dispatch:** make haste

EMILIA
  I durst, my lord, to wager she is honest.
  Lay down my soul at stake. If you think other,
  Remove your thought; it doth abuse your bosom.   15
  If any wretch have put this in your head,
  Let heaven requite it with the serpent's curse!
  For, if she be not honest, chaste, and true,
  There's no man happy; the purest of their wives
  Is foul as slander.   20

OTHELLO
                    Bid her come hither. Go.
                                              [Exit EMILIA]

  She says enough, yet she's a simple bawd
  That cannot say as much. This is a subtle whore,
  A closet lock and key of villainous secrets
  And yet she'll kneel and pray. I have seen her do 't.   25
                    [Enter DESDEMONA with EMILIA]

DESDEMONA
  My lord, what is your will?

OTHELLO
                    Pray you, chuck, come hither.

DESDEMONA
  What is your pleasure?

OTHELLO
                    Let me see your eyes.
  Look in my face.   30

DESDEMONA
                    What horrible fancy's this?

OTHELLO
  [To EMILIA] Some of your function, mistress.
  Leave procreants alone and shut the door.
  Cough or cry "hem" if anybody come.
  Your mystery, your mystery! Nay, dispatch.   35
                                              [Exit EMILIA]

36: **import:** mean

43: **like one of heaven:** i.e., like an angel

44: **be double damned:** i.e., damned not only for lying, but also for appearing to be so innocent and pure

45: **honest:** faithful

50: **heavy:** sad, full of sorrow

52: **haply:** by chance

52–53: **if haply...calling back:** if you suspect my father was instrumental in commanding you back home

DESDEMONA
    Upon my knees, what doth your speech import?
    I understand a fury in your words,
    But not the words.

OTHELLO
    Why? What art thou?

DESDEMONA
                        Your wife, my lord, your true   40
        and loyal wife.

OTHELLO
                    Come, swear it, damn thyself,
    Lest, being like one of heaven, the devils themselves
    Should fear to seize thee. Therefore, be double damned.
    Swear thou art honest.   45

DESDEMONA
                    Heaven doth truly know it.

OTHELLO
    Heaven truly knows that thou art false as hell.

DESDEMONA
    To whom, my lord? With whom? How am I false?

OTHELLO
    Ah Desdemon, away, away, away!

DESDEMONA
    Alas the heavy day! Why do you weep?   50
    Am I the motive of these tears, my lord?
    If haply you my father do suspect
    An instrument of this your calling back,
    Lay not your blame on me. If you have lost him,
    I have lost him too.   55

60: **Given...hopes:** i.e., enslaved him and his deepest desires

63: **fixed:** permanent, like a statue or shrine

63: **for the time of scorn:** i.e., to be ridiculed and scorned for all time

66: **garnered:** collected and stowed away like a treasure

67: **bear no life:** an echo of line 65: ("bear that too"); die, and possibly also by extension, have no children

68: **current:** life force, energy

70: **cistern:** receptacle of water

71: **knot:** copulate (used for toads)

71: **gender:** engender, breed

71: **complexion:** face

73: **grim:** terrifying

74: **esteems:** holds, considers

75: **shambles:** slaughterhouses, butchers' shops

76: **quicken:** enliven, come to life, become pregnant

76: **blowing:** i.e., of the wind

80: **ignorant:** i.e., committed in ignorance, unintentional

81: **paper:** (metaphorically) skin

81: **book:** (metaphorically) Desdemona's skin or face

82: **What committed:** what sin have you committed

83: **Committed:** perpetrated, also sometimes used to mean surrender (as in her fidelity)

83: **public commoner:** whore

84: **forges:** blacksmith's fires, therefore red hot with anger

OTHELLO
     Had it pleased heaven
To try me with affliction, had they rained
All kinds of sores and shames on my bare head,
Steeped me in poverty to the very lips,
Given to captivity me and my utmost hopes,   60
I should have found in some place of my soul
A drop of patience. But, alas, to make me
A fixed figure for the time of scorn
To point his slow unmoving finger at!
Yet could I bear that too, well, very well.   65
But there, where I have garnered up my heart,
Where either I must live or bear no life,
The fountain from the which my current runs
Or else dries up — to be discarded thence!
Or keep it as a cistern for foul toads   70
To knot and gender in! — Turn thy complexion there.
Patience, thou young and rose-lipped cherubin.
Ay, there look grim as hell!

DESDEMONA
I hope my noble lord esteems me honest.

OTHELLO
O, ay, as summer flies are in the shambles   75
That quicken even with blowing. O thou weed
Who art so lovely fair and smell'st so sweet
That the sense aches at thee. Would thou hadst
ne'er been born!

DESDEMONA
Alas, what ignorant sin have I committed?   80

OTHELLO
Was this fair paper, this most goodly book,
Made to write "whore" upon? What committed?
Committed? O thou public commoner!
I should make very forges of my cheeks
That would to cinders burn up modesty   85

87: **stops the nose at it:** plugs its nose

87: **moon winks:** the moon goes dark, turns away. (Diana, the goddess of the moon, is also the goddess of chastity)

88: **bawdy:** unchaste

91: **strumpet:** prostitute

95: **vessel:** i.e., her body

96: **unlawful:** i.e., touch by anyone other than her lawful husband

99: **saved:** go to heaven

102: **I cry you mercy:** I pray for God's mercy on you

103: **took:** mistook, thought you to be

106: **office:** duty

106: **Saint Peter:** biblical saint who guards heaven's gates

107: **keep:** guard

Did I but speak thy deeds. What committed?
Heaven stops the nose at it, and the moon winks.
The bawdy wind that kisses all it meets
Is hushed within the hollow mine of earth
And will not hear it. What committed?   90
Impudent strumpet!

DESDEMONA
                By heaven, you do me wrong.

OTHELLO
Are you not a strumpet?

DESDEMONA
                No, as I am a Christian.
If to preserve this vessel for my lord   95
From any other foul unlawful touch
Be not to be a strumpet, I am none.

OTHELLO
What, not a whore?

DESDEMONA
                No, as I shall be saved.

OTHELLO
Is 't possible?   100

DESDEMONA
O, heaven forgive us!

OTHELLO
                I cry you mercy, then.
I took you for that cunning whore of Venice
That married with Othello.

                                  [Raising his voice]
                You, mistress,   105
That have the office opposite to Saint Peter
And keep the gate of hell!

109: **course:** business

110: **counsel:** secret

111: **conceive:** think

113: **half asleep:** senseless, numb

Lines 119–120: "I have none. Do not talk to me, Emilia. / I cannot weep, nor answer have I none": Franchelle Stewart Dorn as Emilia and Patrice Johnson as Desdemona in The Shakespeare Theatre's 1997–1998 production directed by Jude Kelly
Photo: Carol Rosegg

121: **water:** tears

121: **prithee:** please

[Enter EMILIA]

You, you, ay, you!
We have done our course. There's money for your pains.
I pray you, turn the key and keep our counsel.   110

[Exit]

EMILIA
  Alas, what does this gentleman conceive?
  How do you, madam? How do you, my good lady?

DESDEMONA
  'Faith, half asleep.

EMILIA
  Good madam, what's the matter with my lord?

DESDEMONA
  With who?   115

EMILIA
  Why, with my lord, madam.

DESDEMONA
  Who is thy lord?

EMILIA
                      He that is yours, sweet lady.

DESDEMONA
  I have none. Do not talk to me, Emilia.
  I cannot weep, nor answer have I none   120
  But what should go by water. Prithee, tonight
  Lay on my bed my wedding sheets. Remember,
  And call thy husband hither.

EMILIA
                      Here's a change indeed!

[Exit]

125: **meet:** fitting, appropriate

125: **used:** treated

126: **I been behaved:** I behaved

126–127: **How have...misuse:** i.e., How have I behaved that he might criticize me so harshly for the smallest transgression?

131: **chid:** scolded

132: **a child to chiding:** unused to being scolded

134: **bewhored:** called her a whore

135: **despite:** malice, contemptuous hate

135: **heavy terms:** severe expressions of hate

140: **in his drink:** drunk

141: **laid such terms:** applied such words

141: **callat:** woman of ill repute

DESDEMONA

    'Tis meet I should be used so, very meet.   125
    How have I been behaved, that he might stick
    The small'st opinion on my least misuse?

                    [Enter EMILIA with IAGO]

IAGO

    What is your pleasure, madam? How is 't with you?

DESDEMONA

    I cannot tell. Those that do teach young babes
    Do it with gentle means and easy tasks.   130
    He might have chid me so; for in good faith,
    I am a child to chiding.

IAGO

               What's the matter, lady?

EMILIA

    Alas, Iago, my lord hath so bewhored her,
    Thrown such despite and heavy terms upon her   135
    As true hearts cannot bear.

DESDEMONA

    Am I that name, Iago?

IAGO

               What name, fair lady?

DESDEMONA

    Such as she says my lord did say I was.

EMILIA

    He called her whore. A beggar in his drink   140
    Could not have laid such terms upon his callat.

IAGO

    Why did he so?

149: **beshrew:** mild oath

150: **trick:** vicious or foolish action

152: **eternal:** damned, abhorrent

153: **busy and insinuating:** meddling and ingratiating

154: **cogging:** deceiving

154: **cozening:** cheating

154: **office:** position, rank

158: **halter:** hangman's noose

161: **abused:** deceived

162: **base:** not noble, common, cheap

162: **scurvy:** vile, contemptible

DESDEMONA
    I do not know; I am sure I am none such.

IAGO
    Do not weep, do not weep. Alas the day!

EMILIA
    Hath she forsook so many noble matches,   145
    Her father and her country and her friends,
    To be called whore? Would it not make one weep?

DESDEMONA
    It is my wretched fortune.

IAGO
                        Beshrew him for 't!
    How comes this trick upon him?   150

DESDEMONA
                        Nay, heaven doth know.

EMILIA
    I will be hanged if some eternal villain,
    Some busy and insinuating rogue,
    Some cogging, cozening slave, to get some office,
    Have not devised this slander. I'll be hanged else.   155

IAGO
    Fie, there is no such man. It is impossible.

DESDEMONA
    If any such there be, heaven pardon him!

EMILIA
    A halter pardon him! And hell gnaw his bones!
    Why should he call her whore? Who keeps her company?
    What place? What time? What form? What likelihood?   160
    The Moor's abused by some most villainous knave,
    Some base notorious knave, some scurvy fellow.

163: **companions:** i.e., dishonorable men
163: **thou'dst:** you should
163: **unfold:** be revealed or discovered
167: **within door:** softly, so no one outside can hear
169: **turned...without:** turned your way of thinking inside out
170: **made you to suspect me:** i.e., Iago once suspected Emilia had an affair with Othello

Lines 172–173: "Alas Iago, / What shall I do to win my lord again?": Joyce Redman as Emilia, Maggie Smith as Desdemona, and Frank Finlay as Iago in Stuart Burge's 1965 movie production
Courtesy: Douglas Lanier

176: **will:** intentions
177: **discourse of thought:** in her thoughts
179: **them:** themselves (i.e., her eyes, ears and senses)
182: **beggarly divorcement:** penniless divorce
183: **Comfort forswear me:** I renounce all comforts
187: **addition:** title, rank
188: **world's mass of vanity:** all the vanity in the world
190: **does him offence:** upsets him
191: **chide with you:** take it out on you

O heaven, that such companions thou'dst unfold,
And put in every honest hand a whip
To lash the rascals naked through the world   165
Even from the east to the west!

IAGO
                              Speak within door.

EMILIA
O, fie upon them! Some such squire he was
That turned your wit the seamy side without
And made you to suspect me with the Moor.   170

IAGO
You are a fool! Go to.

DESDEMONA
                    Alas, Iago,
What shall I do to win my lord again?
Good friend, go to him, for by this light of heaven,
I know not how I lost him. Here I kneel.   175
If e'er my will did trespass 'gainst his love,
Either in discourse of thought or actual deed,
Or that mine eyes, mine ears, or any sense,
Delighted them in any other form,
Or that I do not yet, and ever did,   180
And ever will — though he do shake me off
To beggarly divorcement — love him dearly,
Comfort forswear me! Unkindness may do much,
And his unkindness may defeat my life
But never taint my love. I cannot say, "whore."   185
It does abhor me now I speak the word,
To do the act that might the addition earn
Not the world's mass of vanity could make me.

IAGO
I pray you, be content. 'Tis but his humour.
The business of the state does him offence,   190
And he does chide with you.

193: **warrant:** swear

195: **stays the meat:** wait for food

199: **What in the contrary:** i.e., how is that not true

200: **daff'st me:** puts me aside, evades me

200: **device:** trick

201: **conveniency:** advantage, opportunity

201: **than:** that

202: **the least advantage of hope:** at least more hope

201–202: **keep'st from me...of hope:** i.e., Keep opportunities away from him and drawing him along with small amount hope

207: **no kin together:** unrelated

DESDEMONA
    If 'twere no other —

IAGO
                    'Tis but so, I warrant.
                                        [Trumpets within]
    Hark, how these instruments summon to supper!
    The messengers of Venice stays the meat.   195
    Go in, and weep not. All things shall be well.
                    [Exeunt DESDEMONA and EMILIA]
                            [Enter RODERIGO]
    How now, Roderigo!

RODERIGO
    I do not find that thou deal'st justly with me.

IAGO
    What in the contrary?

RODERIGO
    Every day thou daff'st me with some device, Iago, and rather, as   200
    it seems to me now, keep'st from me all conveniency than suppli-
    est me with the least advantage of hope. I will indeed no longer
    endure it, nor am I yet persuaded to put up in peace what already
    I have foolishly suffered.

IAGO
    Will you hear me, Roderigo?   205

RODERIGO
    'Faith, I have heard too much, for your words and performances
    are no kin together.

IAGO
    You charge me most unjustly.

209: **naught:** nothing

209: **wasted myself...means:** wasted all of my money and resources

211: **votarist:** an acolyte or devotee of the church

214: **go to:** expression of dismissal

215: **go to:** a quibble on the meaning of "go to"; Iago means it as a casual dismissal, while Roderigo takes it to mean "go to" Desdemona (for an extramarital affair)

216: **scurvy:** contemptible

216: **fobbed:** tricked, deluded

218: **make myself known:** speak to her directly and explain my situation

219: **give over:** give up

221: **satisfaction of:** amends from

222: **You have said now:** i.e., you have said your piece

223: **intendment:** intention

224: **mettle:** fighting spirit

226–227: **exception:** objection

227: **directly:** openly, honestly

RODERIGO

With naught but truth. I have wasted myself out of my means.
The jewels you have had from me to deliver to Desdemona would   210
half have corrupted a votarist. You have told me she hath
received them and returned me expectations and comforts of sudden respect and acquaintance, but I find none.

IAGO

Well, go to. Very well.

RODERIGO

"Very well?" " Go to?" I cannot go to, man, nor 'tis not very well!   215
Nay, I think it is scurvy and begin to find myself fobbed in it.

IAGO

Very well.

RODERIGO

I tell you 'tis not very well. I will make myself known to
Desdemona. If she will return me my jewels, I will give over my
suit and repent my unlawful solicitation. If not, assure yourself, I   220
will seek satisfaction of you.

IAGO

You have said now.

RODERIGO

Ay, and said nothing but what I protest intendment of doing.

IAGO

Why, now I see there's mettle in thee and even from this instant
to build on thee a better opinion than ever before. Give me thy   225
hand, Roderigo. Thou hast taken against me a most just exception, but yet, I protest, I have dealt most directly in thy affair.

RODERIGO

It hath not appeared.

134: **engines:** instruments of torture, deadly plots

235: **compass:** reach

236: **depute:** substitute

236–237: **depute Cassio in Othello's place:** i.e., promote Cassio to Othello's current position

240: **Mauritania:** a country in Northern Africa

241: **abode:** stay

241: **lingered:** protracted, extended

242: **determinate:** decisive, certain

IAGO

I grant indeed it hath not appeared, and your suspicion is not
without wit and judgment. But, Roderigo, if thou hast that in   230
thee indeed, which I have greater reason to believe now than ever
— I mean purpose, courage and valour — this night show it. If
thou the next night following enjoy not Desdemona, take me
from this world with treachery and devise engines for my life.

RODERIGO

Well, what is it? Is it within reason and compass?   235

IAGO

Sir, there is especial commission come from Venice to depute
Cassio in Othello's place.

RODERIGO

Is that true? Why, then Othello and Desdemona return again to
Venice.

IAGO

O, no. He goes into Mauritania and takes away with him the fair   240
Desdemona, unless his abode be lingered here by some accident,
wherein none can be so determinate as the removing of Cassio.

RODERIGO

How do you mean, removing of him?

IAGO

Why, by making him uncapable of Othello's place — knocking
out his brains.   245

RODERIGO

And that you would have me to do?

247: **profit:** benefit

248: **harlotry:** harlot, prostitute

249: **honourable fortune:** i.e., his promotion

249: **thence:** from that place

250: **fashion:** contrive

250: **fall out:** occur

251: **second:** back up

252: **between us:** with both our efforts

254: **bound:** obligated

254: **put it on:** inflict it on

254: **high:** well into

IAGO

  Ay, if you dare do yourself a profit and a right. He sups tonight
  with a harlotry, and thither will I go to him. He knows not yet of
  his honourable fortune. If you will watch his going thence, which
  I will fashion to fall out between twelve and one, you may take   250
  him at your pleasure. I will be near to second your attempt, and
  he shall fall between us. Come, stand not amazed at it, but go
  along with me. I will show you such a necessity in his death
  that you shall think yourself bound to put it on him. It is now high
  supper time, and the night grows to waste. About it!   255

RODERIGO

  I will hear further reason for this.

IAGO

  And you shall be satisfied.

                                               [Exeunt]

Set rendering of "Willow Scene" from the 1951 staging by Orson Welles at St. James Theatre

Rare Book and Special Collections Library, University of Illinois at Urbana-Champaign

8: **be returned:** return to you

9: **forthwith:** shortly

Act 4, Scene 3]

[Enter OTHELLO, LODOVICO, DESDEMONA,
EMILIA and Attendants]

LODOVICO
I do beseech you, sir, trouble yourself no further.

OTHELLO
O, pardon me. 'Twill do me good to walk.

LODOVICO
Madam, good night. I humbly thank your ladyship.

DESDEMONA
Your honour is most welcome.

OTHELLO
                    Will you walk, sir? —   5
O, Desdemona, —

DESDEMONA
My lord?

OTHELLO
Get you to bed on the instant; I will be returned
forthwith. Dismiss your attendant there. Look't be done.

DESDEMONA
I will, my lord.   10
[Exeunt OTHELLO, LODOVICO, and Attendants]

EMILIA
How goes it now? He looks gentler than he did.

12: **incontinent:** immediately

14: **dismiss:** send (Emilia) away for the night

17: **nightly wearing:** nightclothes

20: **approve:** adore

21: **cheques:** rebukes

24: **All's one:** all's the same

25: **shroud:** wrap in cloth in preparation for burial

track 19

28–60:
Emma Fielding as Desdemona, Patience Tomlinson as Emilia

31: **an old thing:** i.e., the song

31: **fortune:** (bad) luck

34: **hang...one side:** over to one side (like a sad or insane person)

DESDEMONA
He says he will return incontinent,
and hath commanded me to go to bed,
And bid me to dismiss you.

EMILIA
                    Dismiss me?   15

DESDEMONA
It was his bidding. Therefore, good Emilia,
Give me my nightly wearing and adieu.
We must not now displease him.

EMILIA
Ay. Would you had never seen him!

DESDEMONA
So would not I. My love doth so approve him   20
That even his stubbornness, his cheques, his frowns —
Prithee, unpin me, — have grace and favour in them.

EMILIA
I have laid those sheets you bade me on the bed.

DESDEMONA
All's one. Good faith, how foolish are our minds!
If I do die before, prithee, shroud me   25
In one of those same sheets.

EMILIA
                    Come, come, you talk.

DESDEMONA
My mother had a maid called Barbary.
She was in love, and he she loved proved mad
And did forsake her. She had a song of "willow,"   30
An old thing 'twas, but it expressed her fortune,
And she died singing it. That song tonight
Will not go from my mind. I have much to do,
But to go hang my head all at one side
And sing it like poor Barbary. Prithee, dispatch.   35

track 19

28–60:
Emma Fielding as Desdemona, Patience Tomlinson as Emilia

42: **nether:** lower, bottom

Line 46: "*Sing willow, willow, willow*": Dorothy Gould as Emilia and Joanna Weinberg as Desdemona in The Market Theater's 1987 production directed by Janet Suzman

Photo: Ruphin Coudyzer

50: **Lay by these:** lay these (items) here

54: **let nobody...approve:** In her distraction, Desdemona confuses her own feeling and those of the song

EMILIA
Shall I go fetch your nightgown?

DESDEMONA
                    No, unpin me here.
This Lodovico is a proper man.

EMILIA
A very handsome man.

DESDEMONA
He speaks well.   40

EMILIA
I know a lady in Venice would have walked barefoot
to Palestine for a touch of his nether lip.

DESDEMONA
                                              [Singing]
          The poor soul sat sighing by a sycamore tree,
          Sing all a green willow.
          Her hand on her bosom, her head on her knee,   45
          Sing willow, willow, willow.
          The fresh streams ran by her, and murmured her
          moans;
          Sing willow, willow, willow;
          Her salt tears fell from her, and softened the stones; —
Lay by these. —   50
                                              [Singing]
          Sing willow, willow, willow;
Prithee, hie thee. He'll come anon. —
                                              [Singing]
          Sing all a green willow must be my garland.
          Let nobody blame him; his scorn I approve, —
Nay, that's not next. — Hark! Who is 't that knocks?   55

EMILIA
It's the wind.

track 19

28–60:
Emma Fielding as Desdemona, Patience Tomlinson as Emilia

59: **court:** seek favor from

59: **moe:** more

59: **couch:** lie in bed with

tracks 20-21

64–110:
Uta Hagen as Desdemona, Edith King as Emilia
Joanna Weinberg as Desdemona, Dorothy Gould as Emilia

66: **gross:** shocking, unseemly

68: **such a deed:** i.e., abuse your husband by being unfaithful

70: **by this heavenly light:** an oath meaning "no, by heaven"

71: **by this heavenly light:** by this actual source of light (i.e., Emilia would not be faithful where she can be seen)

72: **do 't:** do it (i.e., be unfaithful)

DESDEMONA

[Singing]
    I called my love false love; but what said he then?
    Sing willow, willow, willow.
    If I court moe women, you'll couch with moe men. —
So, get thee gone. Good night. Mine eyes do itch;   60
Doth that bode weeping?

EMILIA
'Tis neither here nor there.

DESDEMONA
I have heard it said so. O, these men, these men!
Dost thou in conscience think — tell me, Emilia, —
That there be women do abuse their husbands   65
In such gross kind?

EMILIA
There be some such, no question.

DESDEMONA
Wouldst thou do such a deed for all the world?

EMILIA
Why, would not you?

DESDEMONA
No, by this heavenly light!   70

EMILIA
Nor I neither by this heavenly light.
I might do 't as well i' the dark.

DESDEMONA
Wouldst thou do such a deed for all the world?

EMILIA
The world's a huge thing. It is a great price
For a small vice.   75

tracks 20-21

64–110:
Uta Hagen as Desdemona, Edith King as Emilia
Joanna Weinberg as Desdemona, Dorothy Gould as Emilia

76: **in troth:** In truth

78: **joint-ring:** a ring with joints in it, thus consisting of two halves making a whole like a husband and wife

78–79: **measures of a lawn:** property, land

79: **petty:** small

79-80: **exhibition:** allowance

82: **purgatory:** a biblical place of atonement between heaven and hell

83: **beshrew:** curse

84: **for the whole world:** Desdemona continues to mean "not for anything, not ever" while Emilia takes a more literal meaning

85: **i' th' world:** i.e., in this world (the real one)

86: **labour:** i.e., your infidelity

89: **to the vantage:** in addition

90: **store:** populate

90: **played for:** i.e., traded their bodies for

92: **do fall:** (morally)

93: **our treasures:** jewels and/or sexual favors

95: **restraint:** restrictions

96: **scant:** limit, reduce

96: **former having:** previous allowance, pin-money

96: **in despite:** for spite

97: **galls:** resentment

97: **grace:** virtue

102: **change us for others:** i.e., have sex with other women

DESDEMONA
In troth, I think thou wouldst not.

EMILIA
In troth, I think I should and undo't when I had done. Marry, I
would not do such a thing for a joint-ring, nor for measures of
lawn, nor for gowns, petticoats, nor caps, nor any petty exhibition. But for all the whole world! Why, who would not make her   80
husband a cuckold to make him a monarch? I should venture
purgatory for 't.

DESDEMONA
Beshrew me, if I would do such a wrong
For the whole world.

EMILIA
Why the wrong is but a wrong i' th' world. And having the world   85
for your labour, 'tis a wrong in your own world, and you might
quickly make it right.

DESDEMONA
I do not think there is any such woman.

EMILIA
Yes, a dozen, and as many to the vantage as would
store the world they played for.   90
But I do think it is their husbands' faults
If wives do fall. Say that they slack their duties,
And pour our treasures into foreign laps.
Or else break out in peevish jealousies,
Throwing restraint upon us. Or say they strike us,   95
Or scant our former having in despite.
Why, we have galls, and though we have some grace,
Yet have we some revenge. Let husbands know
Their wives have sense like them. They see and smell
And have their palates both for sweet and sour   100
As husbands have. What is it that they do
When they change us for others? Is it sport?

tracks 20-21

64–110:
Uta Hagen as Desdemona, Edith King as Emilia
Joanna Weinberg as Desdemona, Dorothy Gould as Emilia

103: **affection:** disposition

107: **use us:** behave well toward us

108: **ills:** evils

109: **such uses:** i.e., bad behaviors

110: **pick bad from bad:** copy or follow bad behavior

110: **by bad mend:** i.e., by recognizing it, be able to learn from it

I think it is. And doth affection breed it?
I think it doth. Is 't frailty that thus errs?
It is so too. And have not we affections,   105
Desires for sport, and frailty, as men have?
Then let them use us well. Else let them know,
The ills we do, their ills instruct us so.

DESDEMONA
Good night, good night. Heaven me such uses send,
Not to pick bad from bad, but by bad mend!   110
[Exeunt]

[Othello

Act 5

1: **bulk:** shelter, a jutting portion of a building

1: **straight:** immediately

2: **rapier:** a type of two-edged sword

2: **bare:** unsheathed

2: **home:** to the target (i.e., his heart)

4: **makes:** makes our fortunes

6: **miscarry:** fail, be unsuccessful

7: **take thy stand:** position oneself in preparation of a fight

11: **quat:** pimple, postule

11: **to the sense:** to the quick

14: **makes my gain:** is to my advantage

14: **live Roderigo:** if Roderigo lives

15: **calls me:** will demand of me

16: **bobbed:** filched

19–20: **a daily...ugly:** Iago indicates his jealousy of Cassio, but whether "a daily beauty" means that Cassio is physically better looking than Iago or that Cassio's life is more upstanding and pure is a matter of debate

21: **unfold:** reveal

Act 5, Scene 1]

[Enter IAGO and RODERIGO]

IAGO
Here, stand behind this bulk. Straight will he come.
Wear thy good rapier bare, and put it home.
Quick, quick; fear nothing; I'll be at thy elbow.
It makes us, or it mars us. Think on that,
And fix most firm thy resolution.   5

RODERIGO
Be near at hand; I may miscarry in 't.

IAGO
Here, at thy hand: be bold, and take thy stand.

[Retires]

RODERIGO
I have no great devotion to the deed,
And yet he hath given me satisfying reasons.
'Tis but a man gone. Forth my sword! He dies.   10

IAGO
I have rubbed this young quat almost to the sense,
And he grows angry. Now, whether he kill Cassio,
Or Cassio him, or each do kill the other,
Every way makes my gain. Live Roderigo,
He calls me to a restitution large   15
Of gold and jewels that I bobbed from him
As gifts to Desdemona.
It must not be. If Cassio do remain,
He hath a daily beauty in his life
That makes me ugly. And besides, the Moor   20
May unfold me to him. There stand I in much peril.
No, he must die. But so, I hear him coming.

[Enter CASSIO]

25: **coat:** might also refer to protective clothing (armor) or even undergarments

26: **make proof:** test (the integrity)

35: **minion:** darling (used pejoratively here), i.e., Desdemona

35: **your dear:** i.e., Cassio

36: **unblest:** unblessed, cursed

36: **hies:** makes haste, hurries closer

36: **strumpet:** i.e., Desdemona

37: **forth of:** from

Set rendering of "Street" from the 1951 staging by Orson Welles at St. James Theatre

Rare Book and Special Collections Library, University of Illinois at Urbana-Champaign

RODERIGO
    I know his gait, 'tis he. — Villain, thou diest!

                    [Makes a pass at CASSIO]

CASSIO
    That thrust had been mine enemy indeed
    But that my coat is better than thou know'st.   25
    I will make proof of thine.

                    [Draws, and wounds RODERIGO]

RODERIGO
                    O, I am slain!

                    *[IAGO from behind wounds CASSIO
                            in the leg, and exit]*

CASSIO
    I am maimed for ever. Help, ho! Murder! Murder!

                                    [Falls]
                            [Enter OTHELLO]

OTHELLO
    The voice of Cassio. Iago keeps his word.

RODERIGO
    O, villain that I am!   30

OTHELLO
                    It is even so.

CASSIO
    O, help, ho! Light! A surgeon!

OTHELLO
    'Tis he. — O brave Iago, honest and just,
    That hast such noble sense of thy friend's wrong.
    Thou teachest me. Minion, your dear lies dead,   35
    And your unblest fate hies. Strumpet, I come.
    Forth of my heart, those charms, thine eyes, are blotted.
    Thy bed, lust-stained, shall with lust's blood be spotted.

                                    [Exit]
                    [Enter LODOVICO and GRATIANO]

39: **watch:** night guard

39: **passage:** pedestrians

40: **mischance:** misfortune

40: **direful:** dreadful, dismal

43: **villain:** (Roderigo is referring to himself)

44: **heavy:** dark and dismal

45: **counterfeits:** false cries (designed to trick or lure passersby)

49: **shirt:** without coat, vest or armour

CASSIO
What, ho! No watch? No passage? Murder! Murder!

GRATIANO
'Tis some mischance; the voice is very direful.   40

CASSIO
O, help!

LODOVICO
Hark!

RODERIGO
O wretched villain!

LODOVICO
Two or three groan. It is a heavy night.
These may be counterfeits. Let's think 't unsafe   45
To come in to the cry without more help.

RODERIGO
Nobody come? Then shall I bleed to death.

LODOVICO
Hark!

[Enter IAGO]

GRATIANO
Here's one comes in his shirt, with light and weapons.

IAGO
Who's there? Whose noise is this that cries on murder?   50

LODOVICO
We do not know.

IAGO
                    Did not you hear a cry?

55: **ancient:** next in command under lieutenant

58: **spoiled:** destroyed

60: **lieutenant:** (note that Iago flatters by "promoting" Cassio from ancient to lieutenant)

62: **make away:** escape

64: **what:** who (what person)

CASSIO
Here, here! For heaven's sake, help me!

IAGO
What's the matter?

GRATIANO
This is Othello's ancient, as I take it.   55

LODOVICO
The same indeed, a very valiant fellow.

IAGO
What are you here that cry so grievously?

CASSIO
Iago? O, I am spoiled, undone by villains!
Give me some help.

IAGO
O me, lieutenant! What villains have done this?   60

CASSIO
I think that one of them is hereabout,
And cannot make away.

IAGO
O treacherous villains!
[*To LODOVICO and GRATIANO*] What are you there? Come in, and
give some help.   65

RODERIGO
O, help me there!

CASSIO
That's one of them.

IAGO
O murd'rous slave! O villain!
[Stabs RODERIGO]

73: **prove us:** ascertain our value to be

73: **praise us:** give us our due praise

79: **cut in two:** deeply cut

RODERIGO
O damned Iago! O inhuman dog!

IAGO
Kill men i' th' dark! — Where be these bloody thieves? —   70
How silent is this town! — Ho! murder! murder! —
What may you be? Are you of good or evil?

LODOVICO
As you shall prove us, praise us.

IAGO
Signior Lodovico?

LODOVICO
He, sir.   75

IAGO
I cry you mercy. Here's Cassio, hurt by villains.

GRATIANO
Cassio!

IAGO
How is 't, brother?

CASSIO
My leg is cut in two.

IAGO
                    Marry, heaven forbid!   80
Light, gentlemen; I'll bind it with my shirt.

                                        [Enter BIANCA]

BIANCA
What is the matter, ho? Who is 't that cried?

IAGO
Who is 't that cried?

86: **notable:** infamous

90: **garter:** a string or fabric band used to keep stockings from falling down (Iago wants it to bind Cassio's leg)

90: **chair:** stretcher

93: **trash:** i.e., Bianca

100: **even he:** i.e., that same man

BIANCA
>O my dear Cassio!
>My sweet Cassio! O Cassio, Cassio, Cassio!   85

IAGO
>O notable strumpet! Cassio, may you suspect
>Who they should be that have thus mangled you?

CASSIO
>No.

GRATIANO
>I am sorry to find you thus. I have been to seek you.

IAGO
>Lend me a garter. So. — O, for a chair,   90
>To bear him easily hence!

BIANCA
>Alas, he faints! O Cassio, Cassio, Cassio!

IAGO
>Gentlemen all, I do suspect this trash
>To be a party in this injury.
>Patience awhile, good Cassio. Come, come;   95
>Lend me a light. Know we this face or no?
>Alas my friend and my dear countryman,
>Roderigo? No! Yes, sure. O heaven, Roderigo!

GRATIANO
>What, of Venice?

IAGO
>Even he, sir. Did you know him?   100

GRATIANO
>   Know him? Ay!

103: **accidents:** events

104: **neglected you:** i.e., failed you (by not issuing proper greetings)

110: **for you:** as for you

111: **labour:** efforts

111: **he that lies slain:** (spoken to Cassio)

112: **dear friend:** i.e., Roderigo

114: **out o' the air:** i.e., indoors

116: **gastness:** ghastliness, haggard look

117: **anon:** shortly, soon

119: **guiltiness will speak:** i.e., her guilt will show in her face

121: **'Las:** alas

IAGO
> Signior Gratiano? I cry you gentle pardon.
> These bloody accidents must excuse my manners
> That so neglected you.

GRATIANO
>   I am glad to see you.   105

IAGO
> How do you, Cassio? — O, a chair, a chair!

GRATIANO
> Roderigo!

IAGO
> He, he, 'tis he. [*A chair is brought in*] O, that's well said. The chair!
> Some good man bear him carefully from hence.
> I'll fetch the general's surgeon. [*To BIANCA*] For you, mistress,   110
> Save you your labour. — He that lies slain here, Cassio,
> Was my dear friend. What malice was between you?

CASSIO
> None in the world, nor do I know the man.

IAGO
> [*To BIANCA*] What, look you pale? — O, bear him out o' the air.
>   *[CASSIO and RODERIGO are borne off]*
> Stay you, good gentlemen. — Look you pale, mistress? —   115
> Do you perceive the gastness of her eye? —
> Nay, if you stare, we shall hear more anon. —
> Behold her well. I pray you, look upon her.
> Do you see, gentlemen? Nay, guiltiness will speak,
> Though tongues were out of use.   120
>   *[Enter EMILIA]*

EMILIA
> 'Las, what's the matter? What's the matter, husband?

123: **scaped:** escaped

127: **supped:** had supper

128: **shake :** tremble

129: **therefore shake not:** i.e., do not tremble for that reason

131: **fie:** expression of distain

132: **of life:** in life

135: **dressed:** his wounds cleaned and bandaged

136: **tell 's:** tell us

138: **happ'd:** happened

140: **makes me:** makes his fortunes

140: **fordoes:** destroys

IAGO
> Cassio hath here been set on in the dark
> By Roderigo and fellows that are scaped.
> He's almost slain, and Roderigo dead.

EMILIA
> Alas, good gentleman! Alas, good Cassio!   125

IAGO
> This is the fruit of whoring. Prithee, Emilia,
> Go know of Cassio where he supped tonight.
> [*To BIANCA*] What, do you shake at that?

BIANCA
> He supped at my house, but I therefore shake not.

IAGO
> O, did he so? I charge you, go with me.   130

EMILIA
> O, fie upon thee, strumpet!

BIANCA
> I am no strumpet; but of life as honest
> As you that thus abuse me.

EMILIA
>   As I? Foh! Fie upon thee!

IAGO
> Kind gentlemen, let's go see poor Cassio dressed. —   135
> Come, mistress, you must tell 's another tale. —
> Emilia run you to the citadel,
> And tell my lord and lady what hath happ'd.
> Will you go on afore? [*Aside*] This is the night
> That either makes me or fordoes me quite.   140
>   *[Exeunt]*

1-22:
Paul Scofield as Othello
Hugh Quarshie as Othello

5: **monumental:** used to make statues and monuments
5: **alabaster:** a type of marble
7: **put out the light:** i.e., extinguish the light of the candle
7: **then put out the light:** i.e., extinguish her life
8: **flaming minister:** i.e., burning torch
9: **restore:** relight (if he puts out a candle, he can relight its flame)
10: **should I repent me:** if I regret my actions
10: **put out thy light:** i.e., end Desdemona's life
11: **cunning'st:** skillful
11: **pattern:** example
11: **excelling:** sublime
12: **Promethean:** related to Prometheus, the titan in Greek mythology responsible for defying the Gods in order to bring fire to humankind
13: **relume:** relight
14: **give it vital growth:** i.e., bring it back to life
15: **must needs:** will, by necessity,
17: **Justice:** Justice is often depicted in early imagery as a blindfolded woman holding scales and a sword
17: **break her sword:** give up retribution or punishment
21: **this sorrow's heavenly:** (proverbial) like God's love

Act 5, Scene 2]

[Enter OTHELLO and DESDEMONA in her bed]

OTHELLO
It is the cause, it is the cause, my soul.
Let me not name it to you, you chaste stars.
It is the cause. Yet I'll not shed her blood,
Nor scar that whiter skin of hers than snow
And smooth as monumental alabaster.   5
Yet she must die, else she'll betray more men.
Put out the light, and then put out the light.
If I quench thee, thou flaming minister,
I can again thy former light restore
Should I repent me. But once put out thy light,   10
Thou cunning'st pattern of excelling nature,
I know not where is that Promethean heat
That can thy light relume. When I have plucked the rose,
I cannot give it vital growth again.
It must needs wither. I'll smell it on the tree.   15
                                                    [Kissing her]

Oh balmy breath, that dost almost persuade
Justice to break her sword! One more, one more.
Be thus when thou art dead, and I will kill thee
And love thee after. One more, and that's the last.
So sweet was ne'er so fatal. I must weep,   20
But they are cruel tears. This sorrow's heavenly;
It strikes where it doth love. She wakes.

DESDEMONA
Who's there? Othello?

OTHELLO
                    Ay, Desdemona.

DESDEMONA
Will you come to bed, my lord?   25

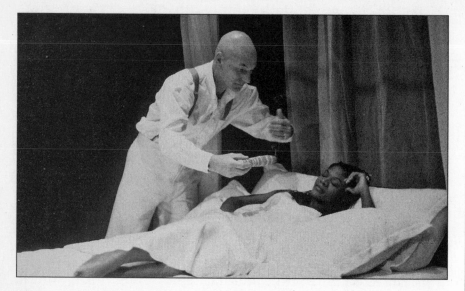

Patrick Stewart as Othello and Patrice Johnson as Desdemona in The Shakespeare Theatre's 1997–1998 production directed by Jude Kelly

Photo: Carol Rosegg

28: **bethink:** can think

29: **unreconciled:** not yet confessed

30: **solicit:** pray

30: **straight:** immediately

32: **walk by:** be nearby

34: **forefend:** forbid

34: **kill thy soul:** Within a Christian worldview, one must confess all one's sins before death in order to be accepted into heaven

OTHELLO
Have you prayed tonight, Desdemon?

DESDEMONA
                    Ay, my lord.

OTHELLO
If you bethink yourself of any crime
Unreconciled as yet to heaven and grace,
Solicit for it straight.   30

DESDEMONA
Alas, my lord, what do you mean by that?

OTHELLO
Well, do it, and be brief. I will walk by.
I would not kill thy unprepared spirit.
No, heaven forfend! I would not kill thy soul.

DESDEMONA
Talk you of killing?   35

OTHELLO
                    Ay, I do.

DESDEMONA
                            Then heaven have mercy on me!

OTHELLO
                            Amen, with all my heart!

DESDEMONA
If you say so, I hope you will not kill me.

OTHELLO
Hum!   40

DESDEMONA
And yet I fear you, for you are fatal then
When your eyes roll so. Why I should fear I know not,
Since guiltiness I know not, but yet I feel I fear.

Line 44: "Think on thy sins": Jordan Baker as Desdemona and Avery Brooks as Othello in The Shakespeare Theatre's 1990–1991 production, directed by Harold Scott
Photo: Joan Marcus

45: **loves I bear to you:** i.e., her sin is that she loves him too much

47: **unnatural:** inhuman in the highest degree

48: **nether:** lower

49: **passion:** strong emotion

49: **frame:** i.e., body, skeleton

50: **portents:** bad omens

51: **point on me:** point toward me

OTHELLO
Think on thy sins.

DESDEMONA
They are loves I bear to you.   45

OTHELLO
Ay, and for that thou diest.

DESDEMONA
That death's unnatural that kills for loving.
Alas, why gnaw you so your nether lip?
Some bloody passion shakes your very frame.
These are portents, but yet I hope, I hope,   50
They do not point on me.

OTHELLO
Peace, and be still!

DESDEMONA
I will so. What's the matter?

OTHELLO
That handkerchief which I so loved and gave thee,
Thou gav'st to Cassio.   55

DESDEMONA
No, by my life and soul!
Send for the man, and ask him.

OTHELLO
Sweet soul, take heed,
Take heed of perjury. Thou art on thy deathbed.

DESDEMONA
Ay, but not yet to die.   60

62: **freely:** without inhibitions or concerns

63: **article:** item of sin

64: **conception:** idea

70: **warranty:** permission, allowance

72: **in's:** in his

73: **stone:** harden

80: **confessed:** sworn it (the accusation) is true

OTHELLO
                    Yes, presently.
Therefore confess thee freely of thy sin,
For to deny each article with oath
Cannot remove nor choke the strong conception
That I do groan withal. Thou art to die.   65

DESDEMONA
Then Lord have mercy on me!

OTHELLO
                    I say, amen.

DESDEMONA
And have you mercy too! I never did
Offend you in my life; never loved Cassio
But with such general warranty of heaven   70
As I might love. I never gave him token.

OTHELLO
By heaven, I saw my handkerchief in's hand.
O perjured woman! Thou dost stone my heart,
And makes me call what I intend to do
A murder, which I thought a sacrifice.   75
I saw the handkerchief.

DESDEMONA
                    He found it then.
I never gave it him. Send for him hither.
Let him confess a truth.

OTHELLO
                    He hath confessed.   80

DESDEMONA
What, my lord?

OTHELLO
That he hath used thee.

Orson Welles's sketch of "Bedroom" from the 1951 staging at St. James Theatre
Rare Book and Special Collections Library, University of Illinois at Urbana-Champaign

87: **ta'en order for 't:** i.e., ensured it

88: **interprets:** deciphers, conjectures

96: **strive:** resist

97: **but:** only

DESDEMONA
          How? Unlawfully?

OTHELLO
               Ay.

DESDEMONA
   He will not say so.   85

OTHELLO
          No, his mouth is stopped.
   Honest Iago hath ta'en order for 't.

DESDEMONA
   O, my fear interprets! What, is he dead?

OTHELLO
   Had all his hairs been lives, my great revenge
   Had stomach for them all.   90

DESDEMONA
   Alas! He is betrayed and I undone.

OTHELLO
   Out, strumpet! Weep'st thou for him to my face?

DESDEMONA
   O, banish me, my lord, but kill me not!

OTHELLO
   Down, strumpet!

DESDEMONA
   Kill me tomorrow. Let me live tonight!   95

OTHELLO
   Nay, if you strive —

DESDEMONA
   But half an hour!

98: being done: i.e., having been decided, being inevitable

109: by and by: in a moment, soon

109: she's dead: referring to Desdemona

110: she: referring to Emilia

Line 112: "Still as the grave": John Kani as Othello and Joanna Weinberg as Desdemona in The Market Theater's 1987 production directed by Janet Suzman
Photo: Ruphin Coudyzer

112: shall she: referring to Emilia

113: she stirs: referring to Desdemona

114: if she come: referring to Emilia

OTHELLO
                    Being done, there is no pause.

DESDEMONA
But while I say one prayer!

OTHELLO
                    It is too late.   100
                                              [He stifles her]

EMILIA
                                                   [Within]

My lord, my lord! What, ho! My lord, my lord!

OTHELLO
What noise is this? Not dead? Not yet quite dead?
I that am cruel am yet merciful.
I would not have thee linger in thy pain.
So, so.   105

EMILIA
                                                   [Within]

                    What, ho! My lord, my lord!

OTHELLO
                    Who's there?

EMILIA
                                                   [Within]

O, good my lord, I would speak a word with you!

OTHELLO
Yes. 'Tis Emilia. By and by. She's dead.
'Tis like she comes to speak of Cassio's death.   110
The noise was here. Ha! No more moving?
Still as the grave. Shall she come in? Were't good?
I think she stirs again. No. What's best to do?
If she come in, she'll sure speak to my wife.
My wife! My wife! What wife? I have no wife.   115

116: **insupportable:** intolerable

116: **heavy:** dismal, grim

Line 116: "O insupportable! O heavy hour!": Raul Julia as Othello and
Kathryn Meisle as Desdemona in the Public Theater's 1991 production directed
by Joe Dowling.
Photo: George E. Joseph

118: **affrighted globe:** frightened earth

119: **yawn:** gape in fear

119: **alteration:** momentous change (because Desdemona is now dead)

123: **soft:** hush

130: **she comes:** referring to the moon

130: **wont:** accustomed

131: **makes men mad:** (madness was thought to be caused by increased proximity
of the moon)

O insupportable! O heavy hour!
Methinks it should be now a huge eclipse
Of sun and moon, and that the affrighted globe
Should yawn at alteration.

EMILIA
                                                                         [Within]
                    I do beseech you   120
That I may speak with you, O, good my lord!

OTHELLO
I had forgot thee. O, come in, Emilia.
Soft, by and by. Let me the curtains draw.
Where art thou?
                                       [Unlocks the door]
                                         [Enter EMILIA]
                    What's the matter with thee now?   125

EMILIA
O, my good lord, yonder's foul murders done!

OTHELLO
What, now?

EMILIA
But now, my lord.

OTHELLO
It is the very error of the moon.
She comes more nearer earth than she was wont   130
And makes men mad.

EMILIA
Cassio, my lord, hath killed a young Venetian
Called Roderigo.

OTHELLO
                    Roderigo killed!
And Cassio killed!   135

138: **sweet revenge:** (the music of) sweet revenge

139: **falsely:** wrongly

Lines 143–144: "O lady, speak again! / Sweet Desdemona! O sweet mistress, speak!": Sada Thompson as Emilia, Julienne Marie as Desdemona, and James Earl Jones as Othello in the Public Theater's 1964 production directed by Gladys Vaughan
Photo: George E. Joseph

EMILIA

No, Cassio is not killed.

OTHELLO

Not Cassio killed! Then murder's out of tune,
And sweet revenge grows harsh.

DESDEMONA

O, falsely, falsely murdered!

EMILIA

Alas, what cry is that?   140

OTHELLO

That? What?

EMILIA

Out, and alas! That was my lady's voice.
Help! Help, ho! Help! O lady, speak again!
Sweet Desdemona! O sweet mistress, speak!

DESDEMONA

A guiltless death I die.   145

EMILIA

O, who hath done this deed?

DESDEMONA

Nobody. I myself. Farewell
Commend me to my kind lord. O, farewell!

[Dies]

OTHELLO

Why, how should she be murdered?

EMILIA

Alas, who knows?   150

OTHELLO

You heard her say herself it was not I.

156: **blacker:** darker, more evil (with a racist slur on his color)

157: **folly:** wantonness

158: **belie:** tell lies about her

159: **false as water:** i.e., water goes wherever it can flow

160–197:
Patience Tomlinson as Emilia, Hugh Quarshie as Othello
Dorothy Gould as Emilia, John Kani as Othello

161: **true:** faithful

162: **top:** have sexual intercourse with

162: **else:** otherwise

163: **all depth in hell:** the lowest regions of hell

164: **but:** except

164: **just:** justifiable

165: **extremity:** extreme action

168: **false to wedlock:** unfaithful

EMILIA
She said so. I must needs report the truth.

OTHELLO
She's like a liar, gone to burning hell.
'Twas I that killed her.

EMILIA
                              O, the more angel she,   155
And you the blacker devil!

OTHELLO
She turned to folly, and she was a whore.

EMILIA
Thou dost belie her, and thou art a devil.

OTHELLO
She was false as water.

EMILIA
                              Thou art rash as fire, to say   160
That she was false. O, she was heavenly true!

OTHELLO
Cassio did top her. Ask thy husband else.
O, I were damned beneath all depth in hell
But that I did proceed upon just grounds
To this extremity. Thy husband knew it all.   165

EMILIA
My husband?

OTHELLO
Thy husband.

EMILIA
That she was false to wedlock?

tracks 24-25

160–197:
Patience Tomlinson as Emilia, Hugh Quarshie as Othello
Dorothy Gould as Emilia, John Kani as Othello

171: **chrysolite:** a green precious stone

178: **iterance:** repetition

179: **mocks:** mockery, fools

184: **pernicious:** wicked

185: **Rot half a grain a day:** i.e., die a slow, torturous death

186: **filthy bargain:** i.e., marrying Othello (filthy = a continued slur, as in line 156)

OTHELLO
　Ay, with Cassio. Nay, had she been true,
　If heaven would make me such another world　　　　170
　Of one entire and perfect chrysolite,
　I'ld not have sold her for it.

EMILIA
　My husband?

OTHELLO
　　　　　　　Ay, 'twas he that told me first.
　An honest man he is and hates the slime　　　　　175
　That sticks on filthy deeds.

EMILIA
　　　　　　My husband?

OTHELLO
　What needs this iterance, woman? I say, thy husband.

EMILIA
　O, mistress, villainy hath made mocks with love.
　My husband say that she was false?　　　　　　180

OTHELLO
　　　　　　He, woman;
　I say, thy husband. Dost understand the word?
　My friend, thy husband, honest, honest Iago.

EMILIA
　If he say so, may his pernicious soul
　Rot half a grain a day! He lies to the heart.　　　185
　She was too fond of her most filthy bargain.

OTHELLO
　Ha?

tracks 24-25

160–197:
Patience Tomlinson as Emilia, Hugh Quarshie as Othello
Dorothy Gould as Emilia, John Kani as Othello

189: **worthy heaven** : worthy of heaven

190: **worthy her:** worthy of her

191: **you were best:** i.e., be quiet

192–193: **Thou hast...to be hurt:** you can't harm me half as much as I can tolerate

193: **gull:** fool, dupe

194: **ignorant as dirt:** continued slur (see lines 156 and 186)

195: **make thee known:** i.e., tell the authorities about you

200: **lay:** justify

202: **disprove:** prove him false

205: **full:** heavy (with sorrow)

207: **apt:** plausible

EMILIA

Do thy worst.
This deed of thine is no more worthy heaven
Than thou wast worthy her.   190

OTHELLO

Peace, you were best.

EMILIA

Thou hast not half that power to do me harm
As I have to be hurt. O gull, o dolt,
As ignorant as dirt! Thou hast done a deed. —
I care not for thy sword; I'll make thee known,   195
Though I lost twenty lives. — Help! Help, ho! Help!
The Moor hath killed my mistress! Murder! Murder!
                    [Enter MONTANO, GRATIANO, and IAGO]

MONTANO

What is the matter? How now, general!

EMILIA

O, are you come, Iago? You have done well,
That men must lay their murders on your neck.   200

GRATIANO

What is the matter?

EMILIA

Disprove this villain, if thou be'st a man.
He says thou told'st him that his wife was false.
I know thou didst not; thou'rt not such a villain.
Speak, for my heart is full.   205

IAGO

I told him what I thought, and told no more
Than what he found himself was apt and true.

EMILIA

But did you ever tell him she was false?

213: **charm your tongue:** be silent

214: **bound:** obliged

217: **set the murder on:** instigated the murder

219: **strange:** extraordinary

225: **charge:** order

IAGO
I did.

EMILIA
You told a lie, an odious, damnèd lie!   210
Upon my soul, a lie, a wicked lie!
She false with Cassio? — Did you say with Cassio?

IAGO
With Cassio, mistress. Go to, charm your tongue.

EMILIA
I will not charm my tongue. I am bound to speak:
My mistress here lies murdered in her bed, —   215

All
O heavens forfend!

EMILIA
And your reports have set the murder on.

OTHELLO
Nay, stare not, masters. It is true, indeed.

GRATIANO
'Tis a strange truth.

MONTANO
O monstrous act!   220

EMILIA
                    Villainy, villainy, villainy!
I think upon 't, I think. I smell 't. O villainy! —
I thought so then. — I'll kill myself for grief. —
O villainy, villainy!

IAGO
What, are you mad? I charge you, get you home.   225

227: **'Tis proper I obey him:** compare line 3.3.333: "I nothing but to please his fantasy"

232: **e'er:** ever

232: **lift up eye:** looked up (from a position of humility)

234: **uncle:** referring to Gratiano

236: **shows:** appears

238: **match:** marriage

238: **mortal:** fatal

239: **shore:** cut

239: **his old thread:** his life. According to Greek Mythology, each life is a thread spun by the Fates, and death occurs whenever a thread is cut

239: **in twain:** in two

240: **turn:** act

241: **his better angel:** his conscience

242: **reprobation:** eternal damnation

246: **gratify:** reward

246: **works:** efforts

247: **recognizance:** token, gift

EMILIA
    Good gentlemen, let me have leave to speak.
    'Tis proper I obey him, but not now.
    Perchance, Iago, I will ne'er go home.

OTHELLO
    O, O, O!

                                                   [He falls on the bed]

EMILIA
                 Nay, lay thee down and roar.   230
    For thou hast killed the sweetest innocent
    That e'er did lift up eye.

OTHELLO
                                                  [Rising]
                 O, she was foul!
    I scarce did know you, uncle. There lies your niece,
    Whose breath, indeed, these hands have newly stopped.   235
    I know this act shows horrible and grim.

GRATIANO
    Poor Desdemona! I am glad thy father's dead.
    Thy match was mortal to him, and pure grief
    Shore his old thread in twain. Did he live now,
    This sight would make him do a desperate turn.   240
    Yea, curse his better angel from his side
    And fall to reprobation.

OTHELLO
    'Tis pitiful, but yet Iago knows
    That she with Cassio hath the act of shame
    A thousand times committed. Cassio confessed it,   245
    And she did gratify his amorous works
    With that recognizance and pledge of love
    Which I first gave her. I saw it in his hand.
    It was a handkerchief, an antique token
    My father gave my mother.   250

253: **'Twill out:** It will be out, it will be said

254: **liberal as the north:** freely as the north (wind)

Stage direction: **offers:** attempts

262: **by fortune:** by chance, luck

EMILIA

O heaven! O heavenly powers!

IAGO

Come, hold your peace.

EMILIA

'Twill out, 'twill out! I peace?
No, I will speak as liberal as the north.
Let heaven and men and devils, let them all,   255
All, all, cry shame against me, yet I'll speak.

IAGO

Be wise, and get you home.

EMILIA

I will not.

[IAGO offers to stab EMILIA]

GRATIANO

Fie!
Your sword upon a woman?   260

EMILIA

O thou dull Moor, that handkerchief thou speak'st of
I found by fortune and did give my husband;
For often, with a solemn earnestness,
More than indeed belonged to such a trifle,
He begged of me to steal 't.   265

IAGO

Villainous whore!

EMILIA

She give it Cassio? No, alas! I found it,
And I did give 't my husband.

IAGO

Filth, thou liest!

271: **coxcomb:** fool

272: **do with:** want to do (such horrible things)

273: **stones:** thunderbolts

280: **without:** from outside

281: **rather:** instead (if he tries to pass)

281: **villain:** Iago

282: **'tis:** he is

283: **not valiant neither:** a double negative used for emphasis

284: **whipster:** insignificant or contemptible fellow

288: **play the swan:** the swan is said to sing a mournful song before it dies, hence the expression "swan song"

EMILIA

By heaven, I do not! I do not, gentlemen.   270
O murderous coxcomb, what should such a fool
Do with so good a wife?

OTHELLO

               Are there no stones in heaven
But what serve for the thunder? — Precious villain!

[He runs at IAGO; IAGO, from behind,
stabs EMILIA, and exits]

GRATIANO

The woman falls. Sure, he hath killed his wife.   275

EMILIA

Ay, ay. O, lay me by my mistress' side.

GRATIANO

He's gone, but his wife's killed.

MONTANO

'Tis a notorious villain. — Take you this weapon
Which I have here recovered from the Moor.
Come, guard the door without. Let him not pass,   280
But kill him rather. I'll after that same villain,
For 'tis a damnèd slave.

[Exeunt MONTANO and GRATIANO]

OTHELLO

            I am not valiant neither,
But every puny whipster gets my sword.
But why should honour outlive honesty?   285
Let it go all.

EMILIA

What did thy song bode, lady?
Hark, canst thou hear me? I will play the swan,
And die in music.

[Singing]

Willow, willow, willow, —   290

295: **ice-brook's temper:** a Spanish sword-making technique made by plunging hot steel into a cold river

298: **perforce:** necessarily

300: **naked:** without a sword or weapon

303: **a better:** i.e., weapon

303: **sustain:** maintain a place

305: **little:** insignificant, not powerful

307: **twenty times:** twenty times greater than

307: **stop:** obstacle, block

310: **butt:** goal

311: **sea-mark:** navigational reference point at sea

312: **go back:** step back

113: **man:** organize, attempt

314: **retires:** retreats/dies

315: **ill-starred:** ill-fated, cursed

316: **compt:** judgment day

Moor, she was chaste. She loved thee, cruel Moor,
So come my soul to bliss, as I speak true.
So speaking as I think, I die, I die.

[Dies]

OTHELLO
I have another weapon in this chamber.
It is a sword of Spain, the ice-brook's temper.   295
O, here it is. Uncle, I must come forth.

GRATIANO

[Within]

If thou attempt it, it will cost thee dear.
Thou hast no weapon, and perforce must suffer.

OTHELLO
Look in upon me then and speak with me,
Or, naked as I am, I will assault thee.   300
[Enter GRATIANO]

GRATIANO
What is the matter?

OTHELLO
                    Behold, I have a weapon.
A better never did itself sustain
Upon a soldier's thigh. I have seen the day
That, with this little arm and this good sword,   305
I have made my way through more impediments
Than twenty times your stop. But, O vain boast,
Who can control his fate? 'Tis not so now.
Be not afraid, though you do see me weaponed.
Here is my journey's end, here is my butt   310
And very sea-mark of my utmost sail.
Do you go back dismayed? 'Tis a lost fear.
Man but a rush against Othello's breast,
And he retires. Where should Othello go?
Now, how dost thou look now? O ill-starred wench!   315
Pale as thy smock! When we shall meet at compt,

322: **sulphur:** brimstone, the material which feeds the fires of hell

323: **steep-down:** precipitous

327: **viper:** poisonous snake, i.e., Iago

328: **I look…feet:** to see if they are cloven, like the Devil

329: **If that thou be'st:** If you are

Stage direction: Wounds IAGO: Ensemble in Stuart Burge's 1965 movie production
Courtesy: Douglas Lanier

333: **in my sense:** in my state

This look of thine will hurl my soul from heaven,
And fiends will snatch at it. Cold, cold, my girl!
Even like thy chastity. O cursèd, cursèd slave!
Whip me, ye devils,   320
From the possession of this heavenly sight!
Blow me about in winds, roast me in sulphur,
Wash me in steep-down gulfs of liquid fire!
O Desdemon! Dead Desdemon. Dead! Oh, oh!

> *[Enter LODOVICO, CASSIO, MONTANO,*
> *and IAGO, with Officers]*

LODOVICO
Where is this rash and most unfortunate man?   325

OTHELLO
That's he that was Othello. Here I am.

LODOVICO
Where is that viper? Bring the villain forth.

> *[IAGO is brought forth]*

OTHELLO
I look down towards his feet, but that's a fable.
If that thou be'st a devil, I cannot kill thee.

> *[Wounds IAGO]*

LODOVICO
Wrench his sword from him.   330

IAGO
          I bleed, sir, but not killed.

OTHELLO
I am not sorry neither. I'ld have thee live,
For in my sense, 'tis happiness to die.

LODOVICO
O thou Othello, that was once so good,
Fall'n in the practice of a cursèd slave,   335
What shall be said to thee?

338: **honourable murderer:** Othello is making a distinction between one who kills with malice and one who kills for honor

340: **part:** partly

341: **consent:** agree (to murder), collude

350: **torments:** torture

350: **ope:** open

352: **understand:** learn

355: **imports:** signifies, explains

OTHELLO
Why, anything.
An honourable murderer, if you will,
For nought I did in hate but all in honour.

LODOVICO
This wretch hath part confessed his villainy.   340
Did you and he consent in Cassio's death?

OTHELLO
Ay.

CASSIO
Dear general, I never gave you cause.

OTHELLO
I do believe it, and I ask your pardon.
Will you, I pray, demand that demi-devil   345
Why he hath thus ensnared my soul and body?

IAGO
Demand me nothing. What you know, you know.
From this time forth, I never will speak word.

LODOVICO
What, not to pray?

GRATIANO
Torments will ope your lips.   350

OTHELLO
Well, thou dost best.

LODOVICO
Sir, you shall understand what hath befallen,
Which, as I think, you know not. Here is a letter
Found in the pocket of the slain Roderigo,
And here another. The one of them imports   355
The death of Cassio to be undertook
By Roderigo.

359: **heathenish:** savage

359: **gross:** shocking

360: **discontented paper:** letter filled with dissatisfaction

362: **this damned villain:** Othello

363: **belike:** apparently

364: **satisfied:** gratified

365: **pernicious caitiff:** malicious wretch

371: **wrought:** came to fulfill

374: **upbraids:** reproaches, accuses

375: **brave me:** attack

376: **cast:** thrown (i.e., drawn into)

376: **spake:** spoke

379: **forsake:** abandon, leave

380: **taken off:** relieved of duty

381: **this slave:** Iago

382: **cunning cruelty:** ingenious torture

OTHELLO
  O villain!

CASSIO
           Most heathenish and most gross!

LODOVICO
  Now here's another discontented paper,   360
  Found in his pocket too, and this, it seems,
  Roderigo meant to have sent this damned villain,
  But that belike Iago in the interim
  Came in and satisfied him.

OTHELLO
           O thou pernicious caitiff!   365
  How came you, Cassio, by that handkerchief
  That was my wife's?

CASSIO
           I found it in my chamber,
  And he himself confessed but even now
  That there he dropped it for a special purpose   370
  Which wrought to his desire.

OTHELLO
           O fool, fool, fool!

CASSIO
  There is besides in Roderigo's letter
  How he upbraids Iago that he made him
  Brave me upon the watch. Whereon it came   375
  That I was cast, and even but now he spake,
  After long seeming dead, Iago hurt him,
  Iago set him on.

LODOVICO
  You must forsake this room, and go with us.
  Your power and your command is taken off,   380
  And Cassio rules in Cyprus. For this slave,
  If there be any cunning cruelty

384: **close prisoner rest:** remain a closely watched prisoner

387–409:
Paul Robeson as Othello
John Kani as Othello

391: **extenuate:** soften, lessen in severity

392: **aught:** anything

395: **perplexed:** confounded, confused, bewildered

396: **base :** unsophisticated, primitive

398: **melting:** softening, i.e., peace time

401: **Aleppo:** a city in Syria once famous as a commercial center

403: **traduced:** defamed

405: **smote:** killed

406: **period:** ending, conclusion

407: **is marred:** i.e., has been spoken in vain

408: **ere:** before

That can torment him much and hold him long,
It shall be his. You shall close prisoner rest,
Till that the nature of your fault be known   385
To the Venetian state. — Come, bring him away.

OTHELLO
Soft you, a word or two before you go.
I have done the state some service, and they know 't.
No more of that. I pray you, in your letters
When you shall these unlucky deeds relate,   390
Speak of me as I am. Nothing extenuate,
Nor set down aught in malice. Then must you speak
Of one that loved not wisely but too well;
Of one not easily jealous, but being wrought
Perplexed in the extreme; of one whose hand,   395
Like the base Judean, threw a pearl away
Richer than all his tribe; of one whose subdued eyes,
Albeit unused to the melting mood,
Drops tears as fast as the Arabian trees
Their medicinal gum. Set you down this,   400
And say besides, that in Aleppo once,
Where a malignant and a turbaned Turk
Beat a Venetian and traduced the state,
I took by th' throat the circumcisèd dog
And smote him, thus.   405

                                     [Stabs himself]

LODOVICO
O bloody period!

GRATIANO
                    All that's spoke is marred.

OTHELLO
I kissed thee, ere I killed thee. No way but this,
Killing myself, to die upon a kiss.

                          [Falls on the bed, and dies]

411: **great of heart:** passionate, proud

413: **fell:** cruel

414: **loading:** burden (of corpses)

417: **seize upon:** claim

418: **succeed:** i.e., Gratiano inherits Othello's fortunes

John Kani as Othello and Joanna Weinberg as Desdemona in The Market Theater's 1987 production directed by Janet Suzman

Photo: Ruphin Coudyzer

CASSIO

    This did I fear, but thought he had no weapon,   410
    For he was great of heart.

LODOVICO

               [*To IAGO*] O Spartan dog,
    More fell than anguish, hunger, or the sea!
    Look on the tragic loading of this bed.
    This is thy work. — The object poisons sight.   415
    Let it be hid. — Gratiano, keep the house,
    And seize upon the fortunes of the Moor,
    For they succeed on you. — To you, lord governor,
    Remains the censure of this hellish villain:
    The time, the place, the torture. O, enforce it!   420
    Myself will straight aboard, and to the state
    This heavy act with heavy heart relate.

                                                      [Exeunt]

The Cast Speaks

Marie Macaisa

In the text of the play, directors, actors, and other interpreters of Shakespeare's work find a wealth of information. A hallmark of Shakespeare's writing is to tell us more than we need to know about a particular character, more than is needed to understand the plot. For example, in Iago, we are presented with a myriad of motivations for him to destroy Othello and Desdemona's marriage. Janet Suzman, director of the acclaimed 1987 Johannesburg *Othello*, offers the following: "he's jealous of Cassio's advancement; he's suspicious that the Moor has had a fling with his wife Emilia; he despises Othello because he's black or because he's credulous; he's disgusted with Desdemona for breaking the rules of white Venice." Yet, despite the spate of reasons, we remain very much uncertain of his primary motivation, an uncertainty that Shakespeare reinforces with Iago's response to Othello's direct question: "Demand me nothing: what you know, you know: / From this time forth I never will speak word."

While providing extra information, Shakespeare (like all playwrights and unlike novelists) also leaves gaps. We are thus coaxed to fill in the missing information ourselves, either through reasonable surmises (we can guess that Gertrude and Claudius were attracted to each other before Old Hamlet died) or through back stories we supply on our own (the idea that Mercutio was disappointed in love, not present in the text, to explain his attitude). This mix, simultaneously knowing too much and not enough about the characters, enables us to paint vivid, varied interpretations of the same play.

In staging a play, directors create a vision for their production starting from the text but also moving beyond that, by making decisions on what *isn't* in the text. In collaboration with actors, they flesh out the characters: they discuss what they might be like, they create stories that explain their actions, they determine motivations, and they speculate on the nature of their relationships. In Shakespeare they have a rich text to draw on and hundreds of years of performances for inspiration. Thus we, the audience, can experience a play anew each time we see a different production: perhaps it is in an unfamiliar setting, perhaps it is in a scene or characterization we hadn't noticed in the past, perhaps it is in the realization that we somehow sympathize with different characters now (for example, the parents Lord and Lady Capulet instead of the teenage lovers Romeo and Juliet). Whatever the case, a closer look into one cast's interpretation creates an opportunity for us to make up our own minds about their stories and in the process, gain new insights not just into a play hundreds of years old but, quite possibly, ourselves.

ACTORS FROM THE LONDON STAGE, 2005

Now in its thirtieth year, Actors From The London Stage (AFTLS) is one of the oldest established touring Shakespeare theater companies in the world. Their approach to performance is a unique one: in each tour, five classically trained actors, working without a director and guided only by the text, work through the staging of the play by themselves. Each actor plays multiple roles, using only simple props and costumes along with their voice and bearing, to delineate the characters from each other. The sets are minimal. Through it all, their emphasis is on Shakespeare's words. According to Professor Peter Holland, their current academic director, "The aim is to make Shakespeare's words exert their magic and their power in performance. The actors ask the audience to perform that same kind of imaginative engagement that Shakespeare was thinking about when, in the Prologue to *Henry V*, he instructed his spectators:

> Think, when we talk of horses, that you see them,
> Printing their proud hoofs i' th' receiving earth
> For 'tis your thoughts that now must deck our kings."

The following actors were interviewed in February, 2005, in the middle of their tour of *Othello*:

Andrew Dennis (Othello, Clown, Gentleman)
Gemma Larke (Desdemona, Bianca, Montano, Second Senator, Officer)
George May (Cassio, Brabantio, Lodovico, Officer)
Paul McCleary (Iago, Duke)
Julia Watson (Emilia, Roderigo, Gratiano, First Senator)

A group discussion was held, and they were asked about their characters, their main relationships, and scenes in the play. In many cases, because the group had worked on the scenes together, the actors had a lot to contribute about characters not their own. Keep in mind that their thoughts and ideas represent but one interpretation of the play. You may be surprised, you may agree or disagree strongly with some of their choices. That is exactly the point.

APPROACHING THE PLAY

Working without a director provides challenges but also opportunities for the actors. The actors elaborate on their approach to the play and what the absence of a director means for the production.

Paul McCleary: Part of the way this happens is that we end up working from within the play. We're not trying to put a gloss on it or an interpretation that is for now, or tomorrow, or the future sometime. We have to come to the characters and find their interrelationships all within the play.

Julia Watson: The director feels an obligation to have some kind of view on the play, but from where we're coming, all we have are the words. We have no set, very few costumes, hardly any props; so really, we can only let the play speak for itself. And if any of us have views on the play, they have to be filtered through four other people.

George May: When you work with a director, you're often trying to fit into his plan.

Paul McCleary: And he's hired you with a plan in mind.

George May: With this approach, you can't just sit there and wait for someone to tell you what to do. You've got to volunteer and say, "I think this is what happens." You've much more at stake in a personal way, because you really have to make the decisions yourself.

In fact, the actors are responsible for everything you see on stage: the sets, costumes, and props, in addition to the performance. Serendipity played a role in their costume design.

Paul McCleary: Sometimes things just happened accidentally. Gemma, Julia, and I were walking along Oxford Street in London, and I noticed a shop and said, "Let's go have a look in here." We found some things we thought we could use as uniforms that suggested a military tone. These things can be dressed very blankly, these tours—almost like rehearsal clothes. We decided we wanted to give the play a military feel. The fact that it happens to a soldier and it involves a group of people on a military campaign is important to the play, we felt.

Julia Watson: We found jackets, desert combats but with a sort of a World War II style, and paratrooper berets. It's a great mixture. We didn't want it to look American, and we didn't want it to look British. We wanted to give a suggestion. As women we ran into problems because we're both playing men, we're both playing soldiers. Yet we're also playing women, so we had to have costumes that would fit in all of those as much as we could. Because there are no combats for girls, we tried on the men's combats and looked ridiculous in them because they're cut so differently. It's quite difficult.

For the set and the props, the actors settled on nine chairs and a briefcase of goodies including cups, wine bottles, and torches. They have had to be creative with the staging of key scenes. For one of the final scenes, they cut out the character of Cassio entirely. They used army blankets stuffed with pillows to suggest extra bodies. And, lacking a bed, the murder of Desdemona happens in full view of the audience.

Andrew Dennis: We don't have a bed or curtains, so Othello and Desdemona fight standing up. I strangle Desdemona standing up and she fights for her life. It's horrible, and the audience witnesses it all.

THE CHARACTERS AND THEIR RELATIONSHIPS
While each actor is responsible for his or her own character, the group collaborates on the interpretation. In a sense, they are all directors for one another.

DESDEMONA
Gemma Larke: Desdemona is the daughter of Brabantio. She's had a sheltered upbringing with no mother figure, so I see her as having lived a very sheltered life. As she got older, she kind of looked after her father too. In the play they talked about dinners that Othello would attend. She'd be eavesdropping on the conversations but also being a part of it, and then she would get called on to serve as well. Brabantio never saw any relationship between them. She fell in love with his words and that is the witchcraft and the magic of Othello, I think. It's his language.

She saw beneath color; it wasn't an obstacle. She saw the foppishness of Roderigo and all these other suitors and that wasn't good enough for her. That's the strength of this character; she didn't accept what she didn't feel was right and I think she has a lot of grace and dignity because of that. And strength.

Andrew Dennis as Othello and Gemma Larke as Desdemona

Julia Watson: Something interesting you might want to talk about is the scene where they first arrive in Cyprus. Iago talks quite raunchily, talks about sex, in fact, in front of Desdemona, who is still a virgin at this point. You might want to talk about the fact that she's not cowed by that at all, although she's been incredibly protected by her father, partly because she's a commodity to him. Who he marries his daughter to was very important for his status.

George May: The dowry as well.

Gemma Larke: Othello is off at sea and the stakes are high. He hasn't landed yet, and there's a terrible storm. We don't know where Othello is; Cyprus is completely alien to her and she's with people she doesn't know, and Iago is being quite rude in front of her. She's trying to fit in, but she does say that her outside shows that she's laughing and joking but really it's a façade.

> I am not merry; but I do beguile
> The thing I am, by seeming otherwise.

Julia Watson: It does show her feistiness and her ability to be in control because she takes Iago on.

Gemma Larke: Yes, she really does. She really trusts Iago, I think. Well, she takes the trust that Othello has for him. She goes to him and asks for his help and she wants him to talk to Othello. She doesn't see the bad in Iago.

Desdemona's great trust and faith in Othello leave her vulnerable to the consequences of Iago's manipulation. She's puzzled by the change in Othello's behavior but attributes it to matters of state because she knows she's given him no reason to be jealous or upset with her. She tries very hard to understand, asking Emilia and even approaching Iago, who malevolently affirms her mistaken guess. She pleads her case to the very end.

Gemma Larke: In rehearsals I was playing it as if she was shocked by the change in him and kind of went against it, getting a bit angry. That turned out to be the wrong choice. She is a very active person and she would have

Gemma Larke as Desdemona

tried to understand what was wrong with Othello and talk to him, because I think they really communicate well with each other. But it's also early in their relationship; I don't feel that they know each other particularly well, but that's exciting because they've got a whole life together, and it turns so, so terribly. That's the shock. She never gave up, and to her death, she pleads her innocence. And she lays no blame on Othello whatsoever, to the very end. Which is an amazing, amazing thing to do.

DESDEMONA AND EMILIA

Gemma Larke: We played that Emilia doesn't think much of Desdemona in the beginning.

Julia Watson: There's not much detail in this part of the play, when Othello asks Iago for his wife, look after Desdemona. Emilia is a soldier's wife and there's no suggestion that she's ever been a servant. So we understand from looking at the text, although it's not written explicitly, that Emilia doesn't normally wait on other women. She's used to being a soldier's wife and trekking around behind Iago, or staying at home while he goes off to campaigns. Presumably, they can live on his soldier's pay; he's doing quite well as a soldier. So I think she's fairly fed up that she's being dragged to Cyprus on this long voyage to look after this chit of a girl, really.

I think Emilia is pretty racist. And the way I'm playing it, I think there's something faintly disgusting about this relationship. In fact, when they kiss, I turn away, because I don't want to see it. For me, I think Emilia grows to respect Desdemona and by the willow scene is desperate for this very young girl, who she can see is just spiraling out of control. Yet, one has to remember that she has taken the handkerchief.

Stealing that handkerchief, that seems to me most bizarre. Why does she do this when she knows what weight it has to Desdemona? She doesn't know that the Moor thinks it's magical. Whether she believes that or not, and whether he's telling Desdemona a lie when he says there's magic in the web of it, we don't know. Maybe he's making up a story to give it more weight. Yet she takes it. She knows that Desdemona reserves it "evermore about her/ to kiss and talk to." Othello "conjured her she should ever keep it." She knows this is terribly important. But she does say, what I'm going to do is I'm going to have it copied and then I'll give it to Iago. So I'll stick it back and I'll cover myself.

Julia Watson as Emilia

George May: That line, "I'll have the work ta'en out" (meaning copied), is so often lost.

Gemma Larke: In the willow scene I think Desdemona wants comfort from Emilia. It's the first time she actually asks anything of Emilia in the script, for her to stay. She also asks her, "Wouldst thou do such a deed for all the world?" (i.e., cheat on your husband) because she's trying to understand. Before, she had always gone to Othello to discuss problems and this time—

Julia Watson: Well, she is in a bizarre situation. She's suddenly being completely uprooted from her home and she's with a man she doesn't really know very well. They've fallen in love in secret and they've eloped. So how long is this relationship going to last?

EMILIA AND IAGO

Julia Watson: By contrast, Emilia and Iago have been married a long time. I think if you look in terms of women's status in that world, she was owned by

Iago. When she married him, what tiny bit of wealth she might have had would have gone to him as her husband. She owns nothing. So if she leaves him, she has nothing and nowhere to go; he is her provider. I think we see from the text, although it's very underwritten, that it's an abusive relationship.

Who knows if they were ever in love? Presumably there was some kind of sexual relationship in the beginning. I'm assuming there isn't one now, because he goes on about housewives in your beds. Obviously, she pleads a headache quite a lot. The way he puts her down in front of the entire company, you don't feel that there's a great deal of love lost between them. I think he's a bully. He verbally abuses her in that first scene, but there's a suggestion that he may do other things too. She certainly understands the Moor's behavior. She recognizes his bullying tactics and has a lot to say about men and their attitude toward women. So one feels this comes from a wealth of experience. I think she's deeply unhappy, I think he (Iago) is a violent and abusive husband and she's scared of him. In the final scene she says:

> Good gentlemen, let me have leave to speak:
> 'Tis proper I obey him, but not now.
> Perchance, Iago, I will ne'er go home.

Iago and Emilia only have one scene together, the one in which she gives him the handkerchief. We play it that she's scared of him. She said that she's going to have the handkerchief copied, but within two lines, she's offering it to him. As an actress, I had to decide why she suddenly changed her mind. Certainly in Act 4 she gets a voice, and I think in that scene she speaks for women who've been abused. In the willow scene (Act 4, Scene 3) she and Desdemona come to have a sort of a mother-daughter relationship and the killing of the child (Desdemona) releases in her the mother tiger. We don't know if they had children. The suggestion, I suppose, is that they don't.

BIANCA

In addition to Desdemona and Emilia, there is one other female character in the play, Bianca. She's quite different from both of them. In contrast to Emilia, she's not married and seems to have a fine relationship with her partner. In contrast to Desdemona, she's definitely not a virgin. There's a question as to whether she's a Cypriot or whether she came with the women on the boat.

Gemma Larke: Well, Bianca is this, well, kind of a—

Paul McCleary: Nymphomaniac!

Gemma Larke: I come off the stage as Desdemona and come on as Bianca. And the contrast between the two characters is very great and it's really, really fun to play. She's out for what she can get. She does hassle Cassio terribly, and I think she's out for money. I don't think there's any love in her, really. She knows how to manipulate men and she's very canny. I don't know if that's right, or what. It's a sexual thing, and she knows how to get men. She's not after Cassio to marry her though, although Iago says that.

Julia Watson: "She gives it out that you shall marry her"…I think that's Iago baiting.

Gemma Larke: I think she knows there is no chance of that. But from her point of view it would be very good for her if she did get him to marry her.

Gemma Larke as Bianca and George May as Cassio

Julia Watson: Do we know if she has come from Venice with Cassio or if she's a Cypriot?

Gemma Larke: It doesn't say, but that's just the choice I've made—that he met her in Cyprus. Were we ever agreed on that?

Paul McCleary: Well, I've always thought you were on the boat with the wives coming out after him. You just follow the soldiers.

Gemma Larke: Oh my gosh, we're playing different things.

George May: You've turned up, and you're kind of the surprise. Cassio does take his job very seriously, but he's also a jolly chap. He's very fond of her, and I think he likes her when he's ready for her. Otherwise, he likes to get on with his job.

Gemma Larke: I think she breaks down his barriers in some ways because she goes straight for him.

Julia Watson: It's the perfect relationship because he doesn't have to marry her but he gets great sex. In a sense it's the only male-female relationship in the play.

Andrew Dennis: It's really unfortunate, because we've cut this quite heavily, and one that's cut is a huge chunk of Bianca in the night action scene where Cassio gets wounded (5.1). You really see her treated so inhumanly by the men in that scene. But all of that's gone, it's a shame because then it's not just a piece about racism, it's a play too about men's behavior towards women.

Despite suggestions that Bianca is a prostitute, she may have had the best relationship in the play. Of the three men who are romantically attached, her partner, Cassio, is the only one who doesn't murder his mate.

CASSIO

George May: I don't think I've totally decided on one way of playing him. Sometimes he's naive; sometimes he's the joke of the party. The text suggests he's a Florentine, so he's not part of Venetian society. Perhaps that allows him to be a mercenary solider like Othello is. He might have been able to be promoted since he's not a Venetian; they wouldn't have wanted a Venetian to be too powerful. I think he's intensely loyal and I think he also admires Othello enormously. I don't think he sees anything odd in the relationship between Desdemona and Othello; he sees it purely as true love. In my mind, there's nothing in the text to suggest that he finds the relationship disgusting or anything. I think he's very fond of Desdemona. He's obviously gone between the two of them many times and there's a suggestion that when they've fallen out or had some kind of argument or Desdemona's cross with Othello, he's often been the one that patched up the differences. He's sort of stuck his neck out a little for Othello, but at the same time he's been rewarded: Othello has promoted him.

He's also very fond of Iago. I think he sees Iago as a very efficient, very good solider. He enjoys his company. I think on occasion he finds him a bit bawdy and sometimes he kind of goes along with that.

I think he has quite a strong quality of naiveté. He thinks the best of people and sadly that does get him into trouble. He's not a strong-willed man. The whole drinking scene, he could have said no and walked away from it. But he wants to try and please everyone and ends up going along with it and drinking. Then he gets drunk very quickly and reacts very aggressively once he's drunk, which is Shakespeare's device that we just have to play along with though I'm sure it does happen. He quickly degenerates into a very aggressive character. He knows this about himself and that's why he doesn't like to drink. It's not in the text, but there is a fight and we've chosen to make that fight quite brutal. And that's his downfall.

I think the whole life of a soldier is very important to him and it's what he feels comfortable doing; it gives him the support that he needs. When that is taken away from him he feels quite lost. Then Iago comes along and says, "Look, I know how you can get it back." So he confides completely in Iago, and from then on, interestingly enough, his character says very little. It's almost like he sold his soul to the devil; he becomes a pawn in Iago's game. All he wants to do is see Othello, and he never does for the rest of the play. He sees Desdemona and then is seen by Othello, but Iago manages to manipulate things so that he doesn't see Othello, except when [Othello] is having a fit. He doesn't get a chance to talk to him or look him in the eye. They just keep missing.

Julia Watson: Except for the last scene [in the text]. But in our production, we had to cut Cassio from the last act because we just ran out of people.

Andrew Dennis: We ran out of bodies. We've included a device to bring a couple of people back on, but we just didn't have enough bodies. We didn't have enough army blankets to stuff to make into bodies.

Julia Watson: It's interesting that Cassio often is played as rather feckless because of his relationship with Bianca: another man with a bad relationship with a woman in the play. But the way you play him, he comes across as so

Julia Watson as Roderigo and Paul McCleary as Iago

charming and trying to please everybody, including Bianca. He doesn't want anyone not to like him. So all of us do end up liking him.

On the other hand, Roderigo, apparently a Venetian gentleman, is never-theless spurned by Desdemona and Brabantio (initially). Yet, as a character, Roderigo plays an important role, as the actors point out.

RODERIGO

Julia Watson: I think he's in the line of Shakespeare's characters from Sir Andrew Aguecheek. He is one of those city gentlemen. Why is Roderigo in the play apart from some light relief? He's a dupe for Iago, an easy dupe.

Paul McCleary: It shows that Iago is keeping all these different balls up in the air. He goes from Cassio to Roderigo to Othello. He manipulated all these people. It adds to the complexity of that.

Julia Watson: I think he's light [comic] relief. From the text, Iago suggests that he go and follow the army in disguise with a usurped beard. We decided a beard might be a bit much, so I just wear a mustache.

George May: He's the guy, in Brabantio's mind, whom Desdemona should have married.

Julia Watson: Except Brabantio didn't want it. Brabantio never wanted him around. In the first scene, Roderigo oddly seems more upset that Iago has gone to work for Othello and that Othello has taken Desdemona than he is concerned for Desdemona. I think Roderigo saw Desdemona as a commodity; she would have had a great dowry. He does say once that he's going to kill himself for love, but I never saw him as being desperately in love with this woman.

Gemma Larke: He hardly knows her.

Paul McCleary: He's the only Venetian male that we get to see—the most developed character of the Venetians throughout the play.

George May as Brabantio

Julia Watson: He's the prime example of a Venetian gentleman.

Paul McCleary: It helps to give a fabric to the play for when I turn around to Othello and say I know our country disposition well. If it was full of Roderigo's, god help us all. He's selfish. He thinks he can buy this woman's body and affections.

Julia Watson: I think he sees her as a commodity, as a prize. He's not in love with her for her—he hasn't gotten to know her. He may well be gay. It's just that he needs to secure his position within Venetian society.

Andrew Dennis: Speaking structurally as well, it helps us be amused by Iago. If Roderigo were a sound, solid, heartbroken chap who's been jilted by this woman, then the way Iago treats him wouldn't be so amusing; but because he's such a fool we laugh at that. It's a very clever way that Shakespeare does it because he gets us to laugh along—yeah, these people are fools aren't they?

BRABANTIO

Paul McCleary: Brabantio is clearly racist. He's happy to have the Moor there telling stories but when he runs off with his daughter—

George May: I think that is what is so shocking to Brabantio, because in a sense, he never before saw Othello as a threat to his daughter. It was inconceivable. Young men he probably wouldn't have allowed in the house but Othello, he just never thought that it would be an issue so he allowed this man in and entertained him.

Julia Watson: But also, [Othello] was the sideshow at dinner parties.

George May: He was an entertainer, an exotic outsider you brought in. Presumably Othello was a unique character in this society, so if you had him coming to your house every night, it was a certain kind of status symbol.

Julia Watson: He was highly prized, wasn't he, by the Venetian state because apparently they always had outsiders as generals, mercenaries as generals of their army. It would mean that if you had an outsider paid by the state, he couldn't turn on the state (a bit like the Vatican city having Swiss guards). Mercenaries would be less likely to usurp power and—

George May: seek it for themselves.

Andrew Dennis: The amazing thing about Brabantio is how quickly he turns around. When Roderigo identifies himself to Brabantio, Brabantio says "The worser welcome: / I have charged thee not to haunt about my doors."

Within a page or two, he says to Roderigo, "O, would you had had her!" It's amazing how quickly the transformation happened—just the speed of it.

Julia Watson: Yes. It's not that he's worried about her going off to war with Othello or marrying a soldier or being in danger. It's purely about class and race.

Paul McCleary: "To fall in love with what she fear'd to look on!" There's another line somewhere else: "Run from her guardage to the sooty bosom / Of such a thing as thou, to fear, not to delight."

OTHELLO AND IAGO

Andrew Dennis: I was probably off track a bit, and I said to Paul one day during rehearsals, "I think that Othello just knows that Iago is there and that's why he overlooks his transformation." Othello needs Iago by his side because he doesn't have the time nor does he want to forge a new relationship as close as what he has with Iago. Iago is just my right-hand man. If I want something done and I say I want it done by eight o'clock, I know it'll be done. If I drop something, metaphorically or physically speaking, I know it'll be picked up. He's not my crutch, but he's just there and I know he will always be there. So, maybe Othello's biggest downfall is he never promoted Iago, never gave Iago the position he wanted, and he kept him there because that's where he needed him to be.

Paul and I were discovering that, particularly in the two bits towards the end of that interval, in the famous "indeed scene" between Iago and Othello (3.3). It's not that Othello doesn't care, but he's in love, he's gone to Cyprus, he's had to stand up before the senate and the duke to plead his case. Iago's there—my honest and my ancient. It's always a case of how he may benefit me, not necessarily how I may benefit him. Once Paul and I sat down one morning, and we agreed there is an element of that in their relationship, it became, not necessarily easy to play, but it put me on a road. Iago's there, he's my right-hand man. Not knowing that these demons are working overtime triple time within him.

Paul McCleary: I don't know what Iago thinks of all this. That's sort of at the heart of what I've tried to do in the play. I think Iago is psychopathic. He's very arrogant in the way that a psychopath might be. In terms of Othello, he doesn't think anybody's better than himself. I felt, working through the play, that it's wrong to look for motives for Iago and that his

Andrew Dennis as Othello and Paul McCleary as Iago

apparent search in the soliloquies for motives often don't add up. He's fascinated with the human condition, which he doesn't understand. He's unsocialized, he doesn't understand emotions, and he thinks that any grand emotions, grand feelings, are hypocrisy because he doesn't get them. I think he probably got on well with Othello when Othello was just a soldier because a soldier at heart has to be a machine and doesn't have to have emotions. As soon as he gets emotions, I suppose that belittles Othello in Iago's eyes. It's vaguely offensive seeing him falling all over Desdemona when they arrive in Cyprus. And I don't think Iago likes company of women much at all.

George May: Do you think he's gay?

Paul McCleary: One feels, when I do have him under my thumb, there is a physical fascination there, but whether that's a sexual fantasy...I won't exclude it, but I don't think it's driving him. I don't think he's jealous of Desdemona in that respect. He's jealous of everybody because he thinks he can do anything that anyone else can do. I think he just despises the human race really.

George May: When he says, "From hence I will not speak another word," he conveys very little respect for anyone.

Julia Watson: He has been a victim of this world. It is a class-ridden society. He's not from the officer class, and however talented he is as a solider, however much he has put into the work, he's not going to get ahead. He's done all those campaigns, but when Othello is a general and needs a right hand man, he picks a darling of the state, Cassio, one who has never fought. Iago is in a menial role, and he had hoped to better himself. [*To Paul*] The way you play the moment when he gets told to disembark the coffers, you made a choice. You have the attitude, "Oh great. It's up to me, is it?" You don't say, "Yes, sir,"

IAGO

George May: It's interesting that the play could have been called Iago, instead of Othello. For whatever reason Shakespeare doesn't make Iago's motives clear. It all has to do with the story; it's about Othello. Iago disappears from the action once he's spun his web. Do you think Shakespeare's less interested in Iago's motivation?

Paul McCleary: Shakespeare's very clever with manipulating his audience. He knows where the story lies. I think he doesn't want the audience to get emotionally involved with Iago because then they don't have room for the tragedy, and it's a tragedy. It's about grand human beings. In a way, it's a great part to play, because any part where you get to talk to the audience a lot is great. They sort of always like you when you talk to them…The funny thing is, he's always trying to make people laugh, he's trying to amuse people, but it's almost because he doesn't understand how all of that stuff works. In the beginning of the drunk scene (2.3) I say, "There's Desdemona," and I do it in a really lewd way. But Cassio doesn't bite, so I just switch and do something else.

Julia Watson: You're much wittier with the audience in your soliloquies. It's odd that his humor doesn't always pay off with the characters in the play. I always think Iago finds a voice in the soliloquies with the audience, which he never finds with the interaction other characters on stage. Well, that's not true; he has it with Othello.

OTHELLO

Andrew Dennis: Othello falls for all this, possibly because of his honesty and trust. Plus he's had no reason in the past to doubt any of Iago's concerns. He's caught up in the whirlwind of love and romance. Within the excitement of that, Iago plants seeds of doubt. "She could have had anyone, but she chose you. Look how she spun her father around to make him think that you actually poisoned her with drugs and so forth." And Othello knows from past experience that Iago doesn't vocalize anything unless he's thought through it. Then Iago says, "I know how these people behave. You don't. I know how they behave. They'd rather hide certain things than let them be known." He now has a persistent outside voice saying, "Look, I'm watching your back, just be careful." This from someone who's always had his back in the past. His ancient. There is no reason not to believe him. These droplets of information make him start to think.

Paul McCleary: Everything I say seems to come true.

Andrew Dennis: Once the seeds are planted that's all he can then see. Desdemona may be talking about Othello, but as soon as she says the word Cassio, I'm like, "Oh God, it's true!" And again, again, and you brought him up again. Iago does a good job on him.

WHAT IF?

The lack of clear motivation for Iago fascinates the cast and they continue to explore his character and what would have happened had his plot succeeded.

Paul McCleary: If you're playing a part, you have to play him as a human being. There are signs of hypocrisy, of arrogance in all of us, isn't there? And bitterness? It's a very childlike thing. You see kids pulling legs off insects or worse. It's sort of what he does, just to see what happens.

Julia Watson: One moment in the play that always affects me, when I'm sitting off stage watching it, is when Desdemona comes to Iago after Othello has slapped her. I find it such a shocking moment that Iago, seeing the slap, seeing Desdemona, this child in such distress, still pursues that line [*4.2, assuring her it is the business of the state that has Othello so upset*]. It's a moment in our production that stands out to me as a very shocking moment. Having witnessed all that, he still pursues. To what end, I don't know, because by the second half, he in a sense has no hope of success. There is no way there will be a good outcome for him. He tells Othello to kill her, but once Othello kills her, the Venetian state is going to come down on Othello. Iago is stuck every which way.

George May: The biggest misfortune for him is that he doesn't kill Cassio. If Cassio had died and couldn't talk, he might have gotten away with it.

Julia Watson: Othello wouldn't have gotten away with. What would've happened to Iago? He wouldn't have been promoted. He wouldn't have been made general. There would be no monetary advantage.

Paul McCleary: I think it's just seeing people suffer, isn't it?

Julia Watson: That, at the end of the day, is what is so malevolent about him. If he had a goal, if he thought he could become a lieutenant and really achieve success within the army, one might find some understanding of his actions, but—

Paul McCleary: Can you honestly never admit to ever, ever being glad that...if you're not going to have something, no one should have it.

Andrew Dennis: Before 5.2 he says, "This is the night / that either makes me or fordoes me quite." So he knows he's stirred things enough. I don't know why he doesn't make sure to kill Cassio; he only wounds him. He doesn't make sure of it, even when Cassio's down.

George May: I think possibly he's going to go back to try and kill him but Lodovico and Montano are there. He's quite a coward, really, isn't he?

Andrew Dennis: Yes, he attacks Cassio from behind.

George May: He kills his wife to try and shut her up.

Julia Watson: What I find fascinating is he's never done this before. He's not a man of the first flush of youth. His wife knows he's a nasty piece of work, but she's never known he was this nasty until—

Paul McCleary: I think it has something to do with us all being in Cyprus. That's what I've always thought: that in Venice it wouldn't be like this. It's like we've all got a blank canvas, because we're all stuck there in Cyprus where we haven't got homes to go to.

Andrew Dennis: He even said in the beginning in Venice, "I am not what I am."

Despite their interesting conjectures, the cast, as with actors and scholars before them, make no definitive conclusions. The final words from one who can settle the issue is this are as follows:

IAGO
Demand me nothing. What you know, you know.
From this time forth, I never will speak word.

A Voice Coach's Perspective on Speaking Shakespeare

KEEPING SHAKESPEARE PRACTICAL

Andrew Wade

track 28

Speaking Shakespeare
Andrew Wade with Bill McCallum

Why, you might be wondering, is it so important to keep Shakespeare practical? What do I mean by practical? Why is this the way to discover how to speak the text and understand it?

Plays themselves are not simply literary events—they demand interpreters in the deepest sense of the word, and the language of Shakespeare requires, therefore, not a vocal demonstration of writing techniques but an imaginative response to that writing. The key word here is imagination. The task of the voice coach is to offer relevant choices to the actor so that the actor's imagination is titillated, excited by the language, which he or she can then share with an audience, playing on that audience's imagination. Take the word "IF"—it is only composed of two letters when written, but if you say it aloud and listen to what it implies, then your reaction, the way the word plays through you, can change the perception of meaning. "Ifffffffff"… you might hear and feel it implying "possibilities," "choices," "questioning," "trying to work something out." The saying of this word provokes active investigation of thought. What an apt word to launch a play: "If music be the food of love, play on" (Act 1, Scene 1 in *Twelfth Night, or What You Will*). How this word engages the listener and immediately sets up an involvement is about more than audibility.

How we verbalize sounds has a direct link to meaning and understanding. In the words of Touchstone in *As You Like It*, "Much virtue in if."

I was working with a company in Vancouver on *Macbeth,* and at the end of the first week's rehearsal—after having explored our voices and opening out different pieces of text to hear the possibilities of the rhythm, feeling how the meter affects the thinking and feeling, looking at structure and form— one of the actors admitted he was also a writer of soap operas and that I had completely changed his way of writing. Specifically, in saying a line like, "The multitudinous seas incarnadine / Making the green one red" he heard the complexity of meaning revealed in the use of polysyllabic words becoming monosyllabic, layered upon the words' individual dictionary definitions. The writer was reminded that merely reproducing the speech of everyday life was nowhere near as powerful and effective as language that is shaped.

Do you think soap operas would benefit from rhyming couplets? Somehow this is difficult to imagine! But, the writer's comments set me thinking. As I am constantly trying to find ways of exploring the acting process, of opening out actors' connection with language that isn't their own, I thought it would be a good idea to involve writers and actors in some practical work on language. After talking to Cicely Berry (Voice Director, the Royal Shakespeare Company) and Colin Chambers (the then RSC Production Adviser), we put together a group of writers and actors who were interested in taking part. It was a fascinating experience all round, and it broke down barriers and misconceptions.

The actors discovered, for instance, that a writer is not coming from a very different place as they are in their creative search; that an idea or an image may result from a struggle to define a gut feeling and not from some crafted, well-formed idea in the head. The physical connection of language to the body was reaffirmed. After working with a group on Yeats' poem, *Easter 1916,* Ann Devlin changed the title of the play she was writing for the Royal Shakespeare Company to *After Easter.* She had experienced the poem read aloud by a circle of participants, each voice becoming a realization of the shape of the writing. Thus it made a much fuller impact on her and caused her thinking to shift. Such practical exchanges, through language work and voice, feed and stimulate my work to go beyond making sure the actors' voices are technically sound.

It is, of course, no different when we work on a Shakespeare play. A similar connection with the language is crucial. Playing Shakespeare, in many ways, is crafted instinct. The task is thus to find the best way to tap into someone's imagination. As Peter Brook put it: "People forget that a text is dumb. To make it speak, one must create a communication machine. A living network, like a nervous system, must be made if a text which comes from far away is to touch the sensibility of the present."

This journey is never to be taken for granted. It is the process that every text must undergo every time it is staged. There is no definitive rehearsal that would solve problems or indicate ways of staging a given play. Again, this is where creative, practical work on voice can help forge new meaning by offering areas of exploration and challenge. The central idea behind my work comes back to posing the question, "How does meaning change by speaking out aloud?" It would be unwise to jump hastily to the end process for, as Peter Brook says, "Shakespeare's words are records of the words that he wanted spoken, words issuing from people's mouths, with pitch, pause and rhythm and gesture as part of their meaning. A word does not start as a word—it is the end product which begins as an impulse, stimulated by attitude and behavior which dictates the need for expression." (1)

PRACTICALLY SPEAKING

Something happens when we vocalize, when we isolate sounds, when we start to speak words aloud, when we put them to the test of our physicality, of our anatomy. We expose ourselves in a way that makes taking the language back more difficult. Our body begins a debate with itself, becomes alive with the vibrations of sound produced in the mouth or rooted deep in the muscles that aim at defining sound. In fact, the spoken words bring into play all the senses, before sense and another level of meaning are reached.

"How do I know what I think, until I see what I say," Oscar Wilde once said. A concrete illustration of this phrase was reported to me when I was leading a workshop recently. A grandmother said the work we had done that day reminded her of what her six-year-old grandson had said to his mother while they were driving through Wales: "Look, mummy, sheep! Sheep! Sheep!" "You don't have to keep telling us," the mother replied, but the boy said, "How do I know they're there, if I don't tell you?!"

Therefore, when we speak of ideas, of sense, we slightly take for granted those physical processes which affect and change their meaning. We tend to separate something that is an organic whole. In doing so, we become blind to the fact that it is precisely this physical connection to the words that enables the actors to make the language theirs.

The struggle for meaning is not just impressionistic theater mystique; it is an indispensable aspect of the rehearsal process and carries on during the life of every production. In this struggle, practical work on Shakespeare is vital and may help spark creativity and shed some light on the way meaning is born into language. After a performance of *More Words*, a show devised and directed by Cicely Berry and myself, Katie Mitchell (a former Artistic Director of The Other Place in Stratford-upon-Avon) gave me an essay by Ted Hughes that echoes with the piece. In it, Ted Hughes compares the writing of a poem—the coming into existence of words—to the capture of a wild animal. You will notice that in the following passage Hughes talks of "spirit" or "living parts" but never of "thought" or "sense." With great care and precaution, he advises, "It is better to call (the poem) an assembly of living parts moved by a single spirit. The living parts are the words, the images, the rhythms. The spirit is the life which inhabits them when they all work together. It is impossible to say which comes first, parts or spirit."

This is also true of life in words, as many are connected directly to one or several of our senses. Here Hughes talks revealingly of "the five senses," of "word," "action," and "muscle," all things which a practical approach to language is more likely to allow one to perceive and do justice to.

Words that live are those which we hear, like "click" or "chuckle," or which we see, like "freckled" or "veined," or which we taste, like "vinegar" or "sugar," or touch, like "prickle" or "oily," or smell, like "tar" or "onion," words which belong to one of the five senses. Or words that act and seem to use their muscles, like "flick" or "balance." (2)

In this way, practically working on Shakespeare to arrive at understanding lends itself rather well, I think, to what Adrian Noble (former Artistic Director of the RSC) calls "a theater of poetry." a form of art that, rooted deeply in its classical origins, would seek to awaken the imagination of its audiences through love and respect for words while satisfying our eternal craving for myths and twice-told tales.

This can only be achieved at some cost. There is indeed a difficult battle to fight and hopefully win "the battle of the word to survive." This phrase was coined by Michael Redgrave at the beginning of the 1950s, a period when theater began to be deeply influenced by more physical forms, such as mime. (3) Although the context is obviously different, the fight today is of the same nature.

LISTENING TO SHAKESPEARE

Because of the influence of television, our way of speaking as well as listening has changed. It is crucial to be aware of this. We can get fairly close to the way *Henry V* or *Hamlet* was staged in Shakespeare's time, we can try also to reconstruct the way English was spoken. But somehow, all these fall short of the real and most important goal: the Elizabethan ear. How did one "hear" a Shakespeare play? This is hardest to know. My personal view is that we will probably never know for sure. We are, even when we hear a Shakespeare play or a recording from the past, bound irrevocably to modernity. The Elizabethan ear was no doubt different from our own, as people were not spoken to or entertained in the same way. A modern voice has to engage us in a different way in order to make us truly listen in a society that seems to rely solely on the belief that image is truth, that it is more important to show rather than to tell.

Sometimes, we say that a speech in Shakespeare, or even an entire production, is not well-spoken, not up to standard. What do we mean by that? Evidently, there are a certain number of "guidelines" that any actor now has to know when working on a classical text. Yet, even when these are known, actors still have to make choices when they speak. A sound is not a sound without somebody to lend an ear to it: rhetoric is nothing without an audience.

There are a certain number of factors that affect the receiver's ear. These can be cultural factors such as the transition between different acting styles or the level of training that our contemporary ear has had. There are also personal and emotional factors. Often we feel the performance was not well-spoken because, somehow, it did not live up to our expectations of how we think it should have been performed. Is it that many of us have a self-conscious model, perhaps our own first experience of Shakespeare, that meant something to us and became our reference point for the future (some treasured performance kept under glass)? Nothing from then on can quite compare with that experience.

Most of the time, however, it is more complex than nostalgia. Take, for example, the thorny area of accent. I remind myself constantly that audibility is not embedded in Received Pronunciation or Standard American. The familiarity that those in power have with speech and the articulate confidence gained from coming from the right quarters can lead us all to hear certain types of voices as outshining others. But, to my mind, the role of theater is at least to question these assumptions so that we do not perpetuate those givens but work towards a broader tolerance.

In Canada on a production of *Twelfth Night*, I was working with an actor who was from Newfoundland. His own natural rhythms in speaking seemed completely at home with Shakespeare's. Is this because his root voice has direct links back to the voice of Shakespeare's time? It does seem that compared to British dialects, which are predominantly about pitch, many North American dialects have a wonderful respect and vibrancy in their use of vowels. Shakespeare's language seems to me very vowel-aware. How useful it is for an actor to isolate the vowels in the spoken words to hear the music they produce, the rich patterns, their direct connection to feelings. North Americans more easily respond to this and allow it to feed their speaking. I can only assume it is closer to how the Elizabethans spoke.

In *Othello* the very names of the characters have a direct connection to one vowel in particular. All the male names, except the Duke, end in the sound OH: Othello, Cassio, Iago, Brabantio, etc. Furthermore, the sound OH ripples through the play both consciously and unconsciously. "Oh" occurs repeatedly and, more interestingly, is contained within other words: "so," "soul," and "know." These words resonate throughout the play, reinforcing another level of meaning. The repeating of the same sounds affects us beyond what we can quite say.

Vowels come from deep within us, from our very core. We speak vowels before we speak consonants. They seem to reveal the feelings that require the consonants to give the shape to what we perceive as making sense.

Working with actors who are bilingual (or ones for whom English is not the native language) is fascinating because of the way it allows the actor to have an awareness of the cadence in Shakespeare. There seems to be an objective perception to the musical patterns in the text, and the use of alliteration and assonance are often more easily heard not just as literary devices, but also as means by which meaning is formed and revealed to an audience.

Every speech pattern (i.e., accent, rhythm) is capable of audibility. Each has its own music, each can become an accent when juxtaposed against another. The point at which a speech pattern becomes audible is in the dynamic of the physical making of those sounds. The speaker must have the desire to get through to a listener and must be confident that every speech pattern has a right to be heard.

SPEAKING SHAKESPEARE

So, the way to speak Shakespeare is not intrinsically tied to a particular sound; rather, it is how a speaker energetically connects to that language. Central to this is how we relate to the form of Shakespeare. Shakespeare employs verse, prose, and rhetorical devices to communicate meaning. For example, in *Romeo and Juliet*, the use of contrasts helps us to quantify Juliet's feelings: "And learn me how to lose a winning match," "Whiter than new snow upon a raven's back." These extreme opposites, "lose" and "winning," "new snow" and "raven's back," are her means to express and make sense of her feelings.

On a more personal note, I am often reminded how much, as an individual, I owe to Shakespeare's spoken word. The rather quiet and inarticulate schoolboy I once was, found in the speaking and the acting of those words a means to quench his thirst for expression.

NOTES:

(1) Peter Brook, "The Empty Space" (Harmondsworth: Penguin, 1972)
(2) Ted Hughes, "Winter Pollen" (London: Faber and Faber, 1995)
(3) Michael Redgrave, "The Actor's Ways and Means"
    (London: Heinemann, 1951)

In the Age of Shakespeare

Thomas Garvey

One of the earliest published pictures of Shakespeare's birthplace, from an original watercolor by Phoebe Dighton (1834)

The works of William Shakespeare have won the love of millions since he first set pen to paper some four hundred years ago; but at first blush, his plays can seem difficult to understand, even willfully obscure. There are so many strange words, not fancy, exactly, but often only half-familiar. And the very fabric of the language seems to spring from a world of forgotten assumptions, a vast network of beliefs and superstitions that have long been dispelled from the modern mind.

In fact, when "Gulielmus filius Johannes Shakespeare" (Latin for "William, son of John Shakespeare") was baptized in Stratford-on-Avon in 1564, English itself was only just settling into its current form; no dictionary had yet been written, and Shakespeare coined hundreds of words himself. Astronomy and medicine were entangled with astrology and the occult arts; democracy was waiting to be reborn; and even educated people believed in witches and fairies, and that the sun revolved around the Earth. Yet somehow Shakespeare still speaks to us today, in a voice as fresh and direct as the day his lines were first spoken; and to better understand both their artistic depth and enduring power, we must first understand something of his age.

REVOLUTION AND RELIGION

Shakespeare was born into a nation on the verge of global power, yet torn by religious strife. Henry VIII, the much-married father of Elizabeth I, had

From *The Book of Martyrs* (1563), this woodcut shows the Archbishop of Canterbury being burned at the stake in March 1556

Map of London ca. 1625

defied the Pope by proclaiming a new national church, with himself as its head. After Henry's death, however, his daughter Mary reinstituted Catholicism via a murderous nation-wide campaign, going so far as to burn the Archbishop of Canterbury at the stake. But after a mere five years, the childless Mary also died; and when her half-sister Elizabeth was crowned, she declared the Church of England again triumphant.

In the wake of so many religious reversals, it is impossible to know which form of faith lay closest to the English heart, and at first, Elizabeth was content with mere outward deference to the Anglican Church. Once the Pope hinted her assassination would not be a mortal sin, however, the suppression of Catholicism grew more savage, and many Catholics— including some known in Stratford—were hunted down and executed, which meant being hanged, disemboweled, and carved into quarters. Many scholars suspect that Shakespeare himself was raised a Catholic (his father's testament of faith was found hidden in his childhood home). We can speculate about the impact this religious tumult may have had on his plays. Indeed, while explicit Catholic themes, such as the description of Purgatory in *Hamlet*, are rare, the larger themes of disguise and double allegiance are prominent across the canon. Prince Hal offers false friendship to Falstaff in the histories, the heroines of the comedies are forced to disguise themselves as men, and the action of the tragedies is driven by double-dealing villains. "I am not what I am," Iago tells us (and himself) in *Othello*, summing up in a single stroke what may have been Shakespeare's formative social and spiritual experience.

If religious conflict rippled beneath the body politic like some ominous undertow, on its surface the tide of English power was clearly on the rise. The defeat of the Spanish Armada in 1588 had established Britain as a global power; by 1595 Sir Walter Raleigh had founded the colony of Virginia (named for the Virgin Queen), and discovered a new crop, tobacco, which would inspire a burgeoning international trade. After decades of strife and the threat of invasion, England enjoyed a welcome stability. As the national coffers grew, so did London; over the course of Elizabeth's reign, the city would nearly double in size to a population of some 200,000.

Hornbook from Shakespeare's lifetime

A 1639 engraving of a scene from a royal state visit of Marie de Medici depicts London's packed, closely crowded half-timbered houses.

From Country to Court

The urban boom brought a new dimension to British life—the mentality of the metropolis. By contrast, in Stratford-on-Avon, the rhythms of the rural world still held sway. Educated in the local grammar school, Shakespeare was taught to read and write by a schoolmaster called an "abecedarian", and as he grew older, he was introduced to logic, rhetoric, and Latin. Like most schoolboys of his time, he was familiar with Roman mythology and may have learned a little Greek, perhaps by translating passages of the New Testament. Thus while he never attended a university, Shakespeare could confidently refer in his plays to myths and legends that today we associate with the highly educated.

Beyond the classroom, however, he was immersed in the life of the countryside, and his writing all but revels in its flora and fauna, from the wounded deer of *As You Like It* to the herbs and flowers which Ophelia scatters in *Hamlet*. Pagan rituals abounded in the rural villages of Shakespeare's day, where residents danced around maypoles in spring, performed "mummers' plays" in winter, and recited rhymes year-round to ward off witches and fairies.

The custom most pertinent to Shakespeare's art was the medieval "mystery play," in which moral allegories were enacted in country homes and village squares by troupes of traveling actors. These strolling players—usually four men and two boys who played the women's roles—often lightened the moralizing with bawdy interludes in a mix of high and low feeling, which would become a defining feature of Shakespeare's art. Occasionally even a professional troupe, such as Lord Strange's Men, or the Queen's Men, would arrive in town, perhaps coming straight to Shakespeare's door (his father was the town's bailiff) for permission to perform.

Rarely, however, did such troupes stray far from their base in London, the nation's rapidly expanding capital and cultural center. The city itself had existed since the time of the Romans (who built the original London Bridge), but it was not until the Renaissance that its population spilled beyond its ancient walls and began to grow along (and across) the Thames, by whose banks the Tudors had built their glorious palaces. It was these two contradictory worlds—a modern metropolis cheek-by-jowl with a medieval court—that provided the two very different audiences who applauded Shakespeare's plays.

Londoners both high and low craved distraction. Elizabeth's court constantly celebrated her reign with dazzling pageants and performances that required a local pool of professional actors and musicians. Beyond the graceful landscape of the royal parks, however, the general populace was packed into little more than a square mile of cramped and crooked streets where theatrical entertainment was frowned upon as compromising public morals.

Just outside the jurisdiction of the city fathers, however, across the twenty arches of London Bridge on the south bank of the Thames, lay the wilder district of "Southwark." A grim reminder of royal power lay at the end of the bridge—the decapitated heads of traitors stared down from pikes at passersby. Once beyond their baleful gaze, people found the amusements they desired, and their growing numbers meant a market suddenly existed for daily entertainment. Bear-baiting and cockfighting flourished, along with taverns, brothels, and even the new institution of the theater.

Southwark, as depicted in Hollar's long view of London (1647). Blackfriars is on the top right and the labels of Bear-Baiting and The Globe were inadvertently reversed.

THE ADVENT OF THE THEATRE

The first building in England designed for the performance of plays—called, straightforwardly enough, "The Theatre"—was built in London when Shakespeare was still a boy. It was owned by James Burbage, father of Richard Burbage, who would become Shakespeare's lead actor in the acting company The Lord Chamberlain's Men. "The Theatre," consciously or unconsciously, resembled the yards in which traveling players had long plied their trade—it was an open-air polygon, with three tiers of galleries surrounding a canopied stage in a flat central yard, which was ideal for the athletic competitions the building also hosted. The innovative arena must have found an appreciative audience, for it was soon joined by the Curtain, and then the Rose, which was the first theater to rise in Southwark among the brothels, bars, and bear-baiting pits.

Even as these new venues were being built, a revolution in the drama itself was taking place. Just as Renaissance artists turned to classical models for inspiration, so English writers looked to Roman verse as a prototype for the new national drama. "Blank verse," or iambic pentameter (that is, a poetic line with five alternating stressed and unstressed syllables), was an adaptation of Latin forms, and first appeared in England in a translation of Virgil's *Aeneid*. Blank verse was first spoken on stage in 1561, in the now-forgotten *Gorboduc*, but it was not until the brilliant Christopher Marlowe (born the same year as Shakespeare) transformed it into the "mighty line" of such plays as *Tamburlaine* (1587) that the power and flexibility of the form made it the baseline of English drama.

Marlowe—who, unlike Shakespeare, had attended college—led the "university wits," a clique of hard-living free thinkers who in between all manner of exploits managed to define a new form of theater. The dates of Shakespeare's arrival in London are unknown—we have no record of him in Stratford after 1585—but by the early 1590s he had already absorbed the essence of Marlowe's invention, and begun producing astonishing innovations of his own.

While the "university wits" had worked with myth and fantasy, however, Shakespeare turned to a grand new theme, English history—penning the three-part saga of *Henry VI* in or around 1590. The trilogy was such a success that Shakespeare became the envy of his circle—one unhappy competitor, Robert Greene, even complained in 1592 of "an upstart crow…beautified with our feathers…[who is] in his own conceit the only Shake-scene in a country."

Such jibes perhaps only confirmed Shakespeare's estimation of himself, for he began to apply his mastery of blank verse in all directions, succeeding at tragedy (*Titus Andronicus*), farce (*The Comedy of Errors*), and romantic comedy (*The Two Gentlemen of Verona*). He drew his plots from everywhere: existing poems, romances, folk tales, even other plays. In fact a number of Shakespeare's dramas (*Hamlet* included) may be revisions of earlier texts owned by his troupe. Since copyright laws did not exist, acting companies usually kept their texts close to their chests, only allowing publication when a play was no longer popular, or, conversely, when a play was *so* popular (as with *Romeo and Juliet*) that unauthorized versions had already been printed.

Demand for new plays and performance venues steadily increased. Soon, new theaters (the Hope and the Swan) joined the Rose in Southwark, followed shortly by the legendary Globe, which opened in 1600. (After some trouble with their lease, Shakespeare's acting troupe, the Lord Chamberlain's Men, had disassembled "The Theatre" and transported its

> pendeſt on ſo meane a ſtay. Baſe minded men all thꝛee
> of you,if by my miſerie you be not warnd:foꝛ vnto none
> of you (like mee) ſought thoſe burres to cleaue : thoſe
> Puppets (I meane) that ſpake from our mouths, thoſe
> Anticks garniſht in our colours. Is it not ſtrange,that
> I,to whom they all haue beene beholding: is it not like
> that you,to whome they all haue beene beholding, ſhall
> (were pee in that caſe as I am now) bee both at once of
> them foꝛſaken? Yes truſt them not : foꝛ there is an vp-
> ſtart Crow, beautified with our feathers, that with his
> Tygers hart wrapt in a Players hyde, ſuppoſes he is as
> well able to bombaſt out a blanke verſe as the beſt of
> you : and beeing an abſolute Iohannes fac totum, is in
> his owne conceit the onely Shake-ſcene in a countrey.
> O that I might intreat your rare wits to be imploied in
> moꝛe pꝛofitable courſes : & let thoſe Apes imitate your
> paſt excellence, and neuer moꝛe acquaint them with
> your admired inuentions. I knowe the beſt huſband of

Greene's insult, lines 9–14

timbers across the Thames, using them as the structure for the Globe.) Shakespeare was a shareholder in this new venture, with its motto "All the world's a stage" and continued to write and perform for it as well. Full-length plays were now being presented every afternoon but Sunday, and the public appetite for new material seemed endless.

The only curb on the public's hunger for theater was its fear of the plague—for popular belief held the disease was easily spread in crowds. Even worse, the infection was completely beyond the powers of Elizabethan medicine, which held that health derived from four "humors" or internal fluids identified as bile, phlegm, blood, and choler. Such articles of faith, however, were utterly ineffective against a genuine health crisis, and in times of plague, the authorities' panicked response was to shut down any venue where large crowds might congregate. The theaters would be closed for lengthy periods in 1593, 1597, and 1603, during which times Shakespeare was forced to play at court, tour the provinces, or, as many scholars believe, write what would become his famous cycle of sonnets.

THE NEXT STAGE

Between these catastrophic closings, the theater thrived as the great medium of its day; it functioned as film, television, and radio combined as well as a venue for music and dance (all performances, even tragedies, ended with a dance). Moreover, the theater was the place to see and be seen; for a penny you could

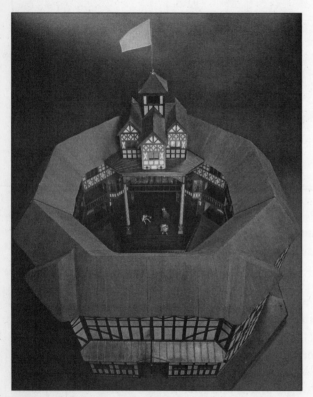

Famous scale model of The Globe completed by Dr. John Cranford Adams in 1954. Collectively, 25,000 pieces were used in constructing the replica. Dr. Adams used walnut to imitate the timber of the Globe, plaster was placed with a spoon and medicine dropper, and 6,500 "tiny" bricks measured by pencil eraser strips were individually placed on the model.

stand through a performance in the yard, a penny more bought you a seat in the galleries, while yet another purchased you a cushion. The wealthy, the poor, the royal, and the common all gathered at the Globe, and Shakespeare designed his plays—with their action, humor, and highly refined poetry—not only to satisfy their divergent tastes but also to respond to their differing points of view. In the crucible of Elizabethan theater, the various classes could briefly see themselves as others saw them, and drama could genuinely show "the age and body of the time his form and pressure," to quote Hamlet himself.

In order to accommodate his expanding art, the simplicity of the Elizabethan stage had developed a startling flexibility. The canopied platform of the Globe had a trap in its floor for sudden disappearances, while an alcove at the rear, between the pillars supporting its roof, allowed for "discoveries" and interior space. Above, a balcony made possible the love scene in *Romeo and Juliet*; while still higher, the thatched roof could double as a tower or rampart. And though the stage was largely free of scenery, the costumes were sumptuous—a theater troupe's clothing was its greatest asset. Patrons were used to drums in battle scenes, and real cannons firing overhead (in fact, a misfire would one day set the Globe aflame).

With the death of Elizabeth, and the accession of James I to the throne in 1603, Shakespeare only saw his power and influence grow. James, who considered himself an intellectual and something of a scholar, took over the patronage of the Lord Chamberlain's Men, renaming them the King's Men; the troupe even marched in his celebratory entrance to London. At this pinnacle of both artistic power and prestige, Shakespeare composed *Othello*, *King Lear*, and *Macbeth* in quick succession, and soon the King's Men acquired a new, indoor theater in London, which allowed the integration of more music and spectacle into his work. At this wildly popular venue, Shakespeare developed a new form of drama that scholars have dubbed "the romance," which combined elements of comedy and tragedy in a magnificent vision that would culminate in the playwright's last masterpiece, *The Tempest*. Not long after this final innovation, Shakespeare retired to Stratford a wealthy and prominent gentleman.

Beyond the Elizabethan Universe

This is how Shakespeare fit into his age. But how did he transcend it? The answer lies in the plays themselves. For even as we see in the surface of his drama the belief system of England in the sixteenth century, Shakespeare himself is always questioning his own culture, holding its ideas up to the light and shaking them, sometimes hard. In the case of the Elizabethan faith in astrology, Shakespeare had his villain Edmund sneer, "We make guilty of our disasters the sun, the moon, and stars; as if we were villains on necessity." When pondering the medieval code of chivalry, Falstaff decides, "The better part of valor is discretion." The divine right of kings is questioned in *Richard II*, and the inferior status of women—a belief that survived even the crowning of Elizabeth—appears ridiculous before the brilliant examples of Portia (*The Merchant of Venice*), and Rosalind (*As You Like It*). Perhaps it is through this constant shifting of perspective, this relentless sense of exploration, that the playwright somehow outlived the limits of his own period, and became, in the words of his rival Ben Jonson, "not just for an age, but for all time."

Acknowledgments

The series editors wish to give heartfelt thanks to the advisory editors on *Othello*, David Bevington, Barbara Gaines, and Peter Holland, whose brilliance, keen judgment, and timely advice were irreplaceable during the process of assembling this book.

We are incredibly grateful to the community of Shakespeare scholars for their generosity in sharing their talents, collections, and even their address books. We would not have been able to together such an august list of contributors without their help. Thank you to Tom Garvey, Doug Lanier, Lois Potter, Janet Suzman, and Andrew Wade for their marvelous essays. Extra appreciation goes to Doug Lanier for all his guidance and the use of his personal Shakespeare collection. Thanks also to the following professors for answering questions and discussing our ideas, no matter how unusual they may have sounded: Michael Best, Regina Buccola, Mark Burnett, Paul Cantor, Michael Cordner, Larry Friedlander, Suzanne Gosset, Katherine Maus, and David Nicol. We want to acknowledge the editors of our future editions who have already contributed much to the series: Terri Bourus, Rob Ormsby, and William Williams. We are especially grateful to William for his astute guidance and hand-holding on all issues textual.

We want to single out Tanya Gough, the proprietor of The Poor Yorick Shakespeare Catalog, for all her efforts on behalf of the series. She was an early supporter, providing encouragement from the very beginning and jumping in with whatever we needed. For her encyclopedic knowledge of Shakespeare on film and audio, for sharing her experience and collaborating on the explanatory notes, for introducing us into her estimable network, and for a myriad of other contributions too numerous to mention, we offer our deepest gratitude.

Our research was aided immensely by the wonderful staff at Shakespeare archives and libraries around the world: Jane Edmonds and Ellen Charendoff from the Stratford Festival Archives; David Way, Richard Fairman, and the Sound Archives group from the British Library; Susan Brock and the staff at The Shakespeare Birthplace Trust; Georgianna Ziegler, Richard Kuhta, Jeremy Erlich, and everyone at the Folger Shakespeare Library; Lynne Farrington from the Annenberg Rare Book & Manuscript Library at the University of Pennsylvania; and Gene Rinkel, Bruce Swann, Nuala Koetter, and Madeline Gibson, from the Rare Books and Special Collections Library at the University of Illinois. These individuals were instrumental in helping us gather audio: Justyn Baker, Janet Benson, Annie Hughes, William Housely, Linn Lancett-Miles, Janet Suzman, and Tamar Thomas. We appreciate all your help.

From the world of drama, the following shared their passion with us and helped us develop the series into a true partnership between between the artistic and academic communities. We are indebted to: Graham Abbey, Kate Buckley, Paul McCleary, Steve Pickering, Joseph Plummer, Bob Scogin, Julia Watson, Scott Wentworth, Marilyn Halperin and the team at Chicago Shakespeare Theater, Beth Emelson from The Folger Theatre, Beth Burns and the team at the Guthrie Theater, Michael Kahn, Catherine Weidner, Lauren Beyea, and the team at The Shakespeare Theatre, Steven Tabakin and The Public Theater, Jeffrey Horowitz from Theater for a New Audience, George Joseph, Cleo Haynes, the 2005 *Othello* cast of Actors From The London Stage, and Lucien Riviere from the RSC. Special thanks go to Nancy Becker of The Shakespeare Society.

With respect to the audio, we extend our heartfelt thanks to our narrating team: our director, John Tydeman, our esteemed narrator, Sir Derek Jacobi, and Daryl Chapman and RNIB Talking Book Studios. John has been a wonderful, generous resource to us and we look forward to future collaborations. We owe a debt of gratitude to Nicolas Soames for introducing us and for being unfailingly helpful.

Our personal thanks for their kindness and unstinting support go to: Charlie Athanas, Ray Bennett, Marie Bennett, Marissa Colgate, Josie Macaisa, Maribeth Macaisa, Sheila Madigan, Mary Ellen Zurko, and our families.

Finally, thanks to everyone at Sourcebooks who contributed their talents in realizing The Sourcebooks Shakespeare—in particular, Samantha Raue, Todd Stocke, Andrea Edl, Dan Williams, and Megan Dempster.

Audio Credits

In all cases, we have attempted to provide archival audio in its original form. While we have tried to achieve the best possible quality on the archival audio, some audio quality is the result of source limitations. Archival audio research by Marie Macaisa. Narration script by Marie Macaisa and Joseph Plummer. Audio editing by Marie Macaisa and RNIB. Narration recording, Audio engineering, and mastering by RNIB Talking Book Studios in London, UK. Recording for "Speaking Shakespeare" by Guthrie Theater.

Photo Credits

About The Contributors

SERIES EDITORS

Marie Macaisa is a lifelong Shakespeare fan who has seen at least one production of each of the plays in the canon. Her first career, lasting twenty years, was in high tech. She has a B.S. in Computer Science from the Massachusetts Institute of Technology and a M.S. in Artificial Intelligence from the University of Pennsylvania. Macaisa contributed the "Cast Speaks" essay for this book. She is currently working on the next books in the series.

Dominique Raccah is the founder, president and publisher of Sourcebooks. Born in Paris, France, she has a bachelor's degree in psychology and a master's in quantitative psychology from the University of Illinois. She also serves as series editor of *Poetry Speaks* and *Poetry Speaks to Children*.

ADVISORY BOARD

David Bevington is the Phyllis Fay Horton Distinguished Service Professor in the Humanities at the University of Chicago. A renowned text scholar, he has edited several Shakespeare editions including the *Bantam Shakespeare* in individual paperback volumes, *The Complete Works of Shakespeare*, (Longman, 2003), and *Troilus and Cressida* (Arden, 1998). He teaches courses in Shakespeare, Renaissance Drama, and Medieval Drama. He also contributed the essay "As Performed" to the Sourcebooks Shakespeare *Othello*.

Barbara Gaines is the founder and Artistic Director of Chicago Shakespeare Theater. She has directed over thirty productions at Chicago Shakespeare, and she serves on the artistic directorate of Shakespeare's Globe Theatre in London as well as on Northwestern University's Board of Trustees.

Peter Holland is the McMeel Family Chair in Shakespeare Studies at the University of Notre Dame. One of the central figures in performance-oriented Shakespeare criticism, he has also edited many Shakespeare plays, including *A Midsummer Night's Dream* for the Oxford Shakespeare series. He is also General Editor of Shakespeare Survey and co-General Editor (with Stanley Wells) of Oxford Shakespeare Topics. Currently he is completing a book about Shakespeare on film and editing *Coriolanus* for the Arden Third series.

Essayists

Thomas Garvey (In the Age of Shakespeare) has been acting, directing, or writing about Shakespeare for over two decades. A graduate of the Massachusetts Institute of Technology, he studied acting and directing with the MIT Shakespeare Ensemble, where he played Hamlet, Jacques, Iago, and other roles, and directed *All's Well That Ends Well* and *Twelfth Night*. He has since directed and designed several other Shakespearean productions, as well as works by Chekhov, Ibsen, Sophocles, Beckett, Moliere, and Shaw. Mr. Garvey currently writes on theatre for the Boston Globe and other publications.

Douglas Lanier (*Othello* and Pop Culture) is an Associate Professor of English at the University of New Hampshire. He has written many essays on Shakespeare in popular culture, including "Shakescorp Noir" in Shakespeare Quarterly and "Shakespeare on the Record" in *The Blackwell Companion to Shakespeare in Performance*. His book, *Shakespeare and Modern Popular Culture*, was published in 2002. He is currently working on a book-length study of cultural stratification in early modern British theater.

Lois Potter (In Production) is Ned B. Allen Professor of English at the University of Delaware. She has also taught in England, France, and Japan, attending and reviewing as many plays as possible. Her publications include the Arden edition of *The Two Noble Kinsmen* and *Othello* for the Manchester University Press's series Shakespeare in Performance.

Janet Suzman (As Performed) has twice won The Evening Standard Best Actress Award, and earned Academy Award and Golden Globe Nominations for *Nicholas and Alexandra*. Suzman's distinguished acting career includes playing many major roles at the RSC and in the West End of London. Other films include *The Draughtsman's Contract*, *The Singing Detective*, *A Dry White Season*, and Fellini's *E La Nave Va, Nuns on the Run*. Her *Hedda Gabler* was chosen as the BBC's 50th Anniversary Play of The Month repeat. In 1987 she directed *Othello* with John Kani in her native South Africa, and filmed it for Channel Four TV. She has written and directed her own response to Chekhov's *Cherry Orchard* set in post-democratic South Africa and renamed *The Free State*. She directed *Hamlet* in South Africa, again working with John Kani, in the summer of 2005.

Andrew Wade (A Voice Coach's Perspective) was Head of Voice for the Royal Shakespeare Company, 1990–2003 and Voice Assistant Director from 1987–1990. During this time he worked on 170 productions and with more than 80 directors. Along with Cicely Berry, Andrew recorded *Working Shakespeare*, the DVD series *Voice and Shakespeare*, and he was the verse consultant for the movie *Shakespeare In Love*. In 2000, he won a Bronze Award from the New York International Radio Festival for the series *Lifespan*, which he co-directed and devised. He works widely teaching, lecturing, and coaching throughout the world.